A Time For Love

A Time for Love

AN AUTOBIOGRAPHY

SHIRLEY ANNE FIELD

BANTAM PRESS

LONDON · NEW YORK · TORONTO · SYDNEY · AUCKLAND

TRANSWORLD PUBLISHERS LTD
61-63 Uxbridge Road, London W5 5SA

TRANSWORLD PUBLISHERS (AUSTRALIA) PTY LTD
15-23 Helles Avenue, Moorebank, NSW 2170

TRANSWORLD PUBLISHERS (NZ) LTD
Cnr Moselle and Waipareira Aves,
Henderson, Auckland

Published 1991 by Bantam Press
a division of Transworld Publishers Ltd
Copyright © Shirley Anne Field 1991

A catalogue record for this book is available from the British Library

ISBN 0 593 01161 9

Typeset in 11pt Garamond by
Chippendale Type Ltd, Otley, West Yorkshire.
Printed in Great Britain by
Mackays of Chatham, PLC, Chatham, Kent.

It seems such a long time since I began my journey. Another time, another world!

A third girl born into a working class family, who wanted a boy!
I live in a different world now.

Often I struggle trying to overcome the feelings of the little girl I was.

This book is about a search for love, a search for the other part of myself, a search for a soulmate, maybe my other half, but can I find that other half while the first half is so incomplete? The answer is yes.

I have found by being a mother myself that love is a birth right and not a gift given for favours received.

This book is for every child who grows up without love, and of course for my daughter, Nicola, who will always have mine.

A Time For Love

INTRODUCTION

About ten years ago on a warm, sunny day in Hampstead, London, the phone rang. I hoped the call might be a film offer, as I was in the middle of a professional lull. Though I was happy just being with my ten-year-old daughter, Nicola, I was at the same time panicked that I might never work again.

The voice on the other end asked for Shirley Broomfield. Whoever could that be, I thought. I hadn't been called that name for years.

'Hullo. This is Miss Gautry here.' Miss Gautry was my favourite after-care worker from my early years in the children's home at Edgeworth. She was one of those rare people who kept in touch with you long after you had been just a statistic in the children's home's files. Large, clumsy and nearly six feet tall with a sharp sense of humour, she was the only authoritarian figure there I had any rapport with.

'Hullo, Miss Gautry, how lovely to hear from you,' I said.

'I don't know if you'll think that when I'm through,' she replied. 'Better sit down. I have something to tell you.' Surely I couldn't have done something wrong at this stage of life, I thought. I sat down hurriedly.

'We have a woman here claiming to be your mother.' I must have screamed and dropped the phone.

'No! No! No!' I shouted. 'It's too late!' All through the bleak, loveless years at Edgeworth I had told myself that she had been killed at the end of the war. It was the only explanation I could give myself. I had last seen her when I was seven years old.

For much of my life I had simply wanted to be the same as everyone else. I wanted to be able to refer to my mother and father like most people I knew. But the years had passed and I had grown up. Now, in my mid-thirties, I had just begun to have some order in my life. My instinctive reaction was – why more complications? Why now?

Sunny, my older sister, had always thought our mother had left England with an American serviceman after our parents had separated. Tragically, though, Sunny had died at the age of thirty-three of cancer and was never to find out the truth.

It was this phone call that told me Sunny had been right and I had been wrong. I was at home looking after Nicola and her friend that day. They were jumping about and laughing in the kitchen as usual. At the sound of my voice Nicola rushed into the room. 'Momma, Momma, what's the matter?' I told her what the call was about. 'Oh, please, Momma, please, find out the details! Let's hear her story anyway. I would like to have a grandma.' It struck me that I had always wanted to know about my own grandmother, but never could. Now the daughter I had tried to bring up as normally as possible wanted to know about hers.

I looked at my daughter in her innocence and realized at last I had to find out what had happened and why, as much for her sake as for my own.

After I calmed down, I realized the woman claiming to be my mother was in fact not at hand, but living in Hemel Hempstead, not far from my home. I asked Miss Gautry how I could contact this person. She told me her name was Kathleen Lloyd.

The room spun. I knew this couldn't be right. I knew my mother's name had been Ivy! After ringing the woman all day I finally received a reply in the early evening.

'My name is Shirley Anne Field,' I said. 'The children's home tells me you are claiming to be my mother.'

'No,' she replied. 'I'm not your mother, but I'm overjoyed to hear from you.' Years of my own searching and many people coming forward to claim me had made me very wary. Two months earlier an Indian man in a theatre had told me he was my long-lost brother. Fortunately, he didn't know my original name or I might have travelled to India to be disappointed yet again.

Why was she so happy to hear from me, I asked. 'Because I know your mother, Ivy Collins, very well.' I still couldn't believe this wasn't a hoax. Ivy, yes. But Collins? I knew of only one other person by that name, and she was a beautiful English star.

The woman asked me about Sunny and my younger brother Ernie. I told her that Sunny was dead and Ernie now went by the name of Guy Field and was living in America. She was very upset to hear the news about Sunny.

'Oh, dear. How am I going to tell Ivy and Bill?'

'Who's Bill?' I asked.

'Your stepdaddy,' she replied. 'You'll like him and he loves you.' Not only did I not know this man, but until a minute before I didn't even know he existed. I decided then I had better meet with Kathleen and find out the truth.

The next day I left for Hemel Hempstead, leaving Nicola with a babysitter. The trip took one hour. One hour to find a mother I had not seen or heard of for over thirty years.

Sitting on the bus that day brought back a flood of memories. Almost as long as I could remember I had craved information about my start in life and the fate of my parents. I thought of how I had idealized my mother during all the years I grew up in that Victorian institution: slim, tallish, red-haired, smelling beautiful, always loving, promising she would come back for me. There were so many times that I had sat on the wall with my brother at Edgeworth after sneaking away from the other children, patiently explaining to him that she would come, and urging him to wear his orange knitted suit so that she would be

11

sure to see us as the same small single-decker bus came round the corner, the one that would hopefully be carrying her.

There were so many other memories as well: memories of my babyhood in London during the bombing raids, a little girl with her Minnie Mouse gas mask always at her side; of being sent to the baby home in Surrey with little Ernie and taken away from my mother; and of my father, lorry driver Ernest Broomfield, who was hardly at home in the first few years after I was born and seemed to disappear from my life when I was three. He came to visit me when I was thirteen and I was so thrilled that he was alive, and that at least I had one parent. And what's more my dad told me he loved me and wanted me to be part of his life. I was overjoyed.

My father was very much like Jimmy Porter, John Osborne's protagonist in his play *Look Back in Anger*. He was the one who gave me the insight to understand the character of the working-class heroes that I was to play opposite. If I hadn't met him when I was thirteen and known him for those few short years I would never have been able to recognize my own working-class roots. On my visits to his home, with his second wife and her daughter in the East End of London, I had seen at first hand how English working-class families behaved with each other.

These visits became a strange eye-opener for me. I saw the awkward way the family behaved with each other, and with me, and felt the currents of emotion and long-held silences that always accompanied my visits. Yet I saw in my father a different man as soon as we were outside. He was quiet at home, but became extrovert in public. Five or six years later I would be starring in movies like *The Entertainer*, and *Saturday Night and Sunday Morning* with Albert Finney's portrayal of Arthur Seaton being a younger version of my dad's type, the working-class man who does what he has to to get by. Hopefully, I could put my roots up on screen because I had observed them.

In the early sixties, I jumped at the chance to play Daphne in *The War Lover* opposite Steve McQueen and Robert Wagner, when I was offered it, not because of the starring role, but because I could create on screen in the character of Daphne the person I hoped my mother had been. I created the character from my few childhood memories of her and from my father's anecdotes told over a glass of beer in the local pub. But it would be many years before I would not have to use my imagination to discover what my mother was really like.

All these images flashed through my mind that day on the bus. I was frightened as well as excited to know that I was soon to find out the story of my family, the story that I had sought for so long.

The ride lasted for what seemed like a lifetime, but I finally arrived in Hemel Hempstead. I nervously called Kathleen from a local phone box and she sent her daughter to pick me up.

It was a surprise to me when her daughter Jennifer arrived, recognized me immediately and introduced herself. I asked her how she had known who I was and she told me she spotted the resemblance to my mother straight away. As I found out shortly afterwards, Jennifer had known my mother all her life. She was raised in the same small American town in Georgia where my mother had settled.

Jennifer told me that Kathleen had, on her own initiative, traced me when she came back to England to live after her husband died. It was painful for me to meet someone younger than me who had known my own mother far better than I ever had. But never mind. The important thing was that at last the mystery was going to unfold.

After a brief drive we arrived at the apartment. The door was opened by a lovely looking woman with a welcoming smile. It was Kathleen. The apartment was a charming, spotlessly clean place. It was full of flowers, and Kathleen made me feel at home immediately. The resentment and hostility I had encountered before with close friends and relatives of my family were absent. What a relief to finally meet someone who spoke not only with kindness, but with joy about my mother!

Kathleen told me not only of my mother, but of my mother's husband, and their daughters! Strange names came tumbling out – Virginia, Jackie, Rebecca. It was overwhelming. These were my younger sisters I had no knowledge of until then. Kathleen must have seen that I was reeling from all this information because she suddenly asked me if I would like to speak with my mother on the phone.

'I've already told her I've found you,' she said. She dialled a longish number, and spoke to someone by the name of Becky. She asked for Ivy, and the next minute I heard a frail but unmistakable

English sound on the other end of the phone. I recognized her soft London voice as if I had heard it an hour before.

'Shirley, is that really you? Do you remember me?'

'Yes, I do, Mummy,' I said. I had not been able to say that word for thirty years. My feelings had been so strong I had even encouraged Nicola to use the word 'momma' instead of 'mummy' throughout her life.

Now the words came falling out, as all the years I had been without a mother seemed to vanish. For a few moments, time raced backwards and I felt again as if I was a four-year-old child.

CHAPTER ONE

'Hitler don't eat all the jam, do he?' I grumbled to Sunny after she refused to give me any more. Sunny, the grown-up six year old, told me in no uncertain terms:

'Don't you know there's a war on?' I was about three at the time. The Blitz was in full swing. Even bread with hot milk and sugar was a great delicacy, or at least my mother seemed to think so.

At night my sisters and I would often sleep under the kitchen table in case there was an air raid. In the day I would walk up and down my street with a saucepan on my head, the handle pointing toward the back. With the intention of making everybody rush to the shelters, I would yell out 'air morning!!' It made me cross that no-one would obey me and I wondered why they were laughing. No-one told me that I was getting the words wrong.

Until I was three my family lived in the East End, close to the docks that were a prime target for German planes. Bombs would shake the house, and ours was hit on a few occasions but never destroyed. We were away in the shelters at the time. At night, usually around nine o'clock, we would hear the sirens blare, and Mummy would get us out of bed and tell us to put our coats over our nightclothes. Then we would walk to our shelter.

I longed to go to the public shelters. It was much more fun than being on our own. There we learned songs and danced and saw all sorts of people dressed in funny clothes. Many would arrive dressed in layer upon layer of clothing in case tragedy struck. Some of the women appeared wearing long evening dresses with furs round their shoulders, their hair full of curlers and topped by a turban tied at the front in the latest wartime fashion.

The sounds of guns firing overhead were like a giant tapdance in the clouds. On the horizon purple and pink hues lit up the sky forming a rainbow of colour. I remember the waiting in the air-raid shelter, waiting to get out so my family and I could see what was happening to our neighbourhood. Was it still standing? I would hear the neighbours calling out to my mother, asking if her girls were all right.

It was normal for my father to be absent from the house. In my early childhood he would either be away on his long distance lorry rides or collaborating with my uncle on schemes to make a few quick pounds any way they could. Pretending to be cleaning men, they once walked into a local cinema and lifted a sixty-foot carpet, then carried it out in broad daylight. Our family was divided in its opinion on the incident. Half of them felt that any way we could get by was OK; the others were afraid of the policeman's knock on the door. The real difficulty came later when my dad tried to unload it and found, to his chagrin, the words 'Odeon Cinema' woven indelibly into the middle of the carpet. However, my Aunt Lily was more than happy to hide the motif under her sofa.

I know he wasn't at home the night my brother Ernie was born. At the age of two I sat on the stairs outside my mother's bedroom and listened as she went into labour. I remember hearing her cries through the door. I couldn't bear to hear my mother crying. I rushed in to comfort her and climbed into bed and got as close to her as I could. Two adults I didn't recognize tried to get me out, but I cried so much my mother told them I could stay. I clung to her side and tried to love her pain away.

Then, all of a sudden, there was this little baby boy! I thought he was so beautiful. My father came back to see his Ernest Jr and he was overjoyed. From then on Ernie became very special to me. I came to feel as though he was my own little boy.

About the time Ernie was born we moved to two small rooms above a chemist's shop. One very cold winter night my eldest sister Joy began to cry with painful chilblains. Our family had very little money, even for necessities. But Joy had to have medicine, and so my mother decided I should be the one to go downstairs and pinch the chilblain ointment. She knew that if I were caught, the owners would make less of a fuss, since I was only three. This did not console me in the least. However, I didn't have a choice. I demanded that Sunny go with me. Dressed only in our nighties, we crept down the stairs to the back door of the shop.

Sunny was to stay and keep watch while I was inside. With the blackout on, all was dark in the shop, save for a few diffused beams of light from the moon. All I knew is that I was supposed to get something that came in a round white and blue tin. I searched as quietly as I could and then, just as I came upon it in the dark, I accidentally trod on the chemist's cat prowling silently at my feet. The cat squealed and I almost screamed, and nearly tipped everything off the shelf. Then, without warning, the man who owned the shop appeared at the till, his eyes shining from the reflection of the torch he held in his hand. Very quietly he spoke out into the darkness.

'Whoever's there, you'd better come out before I call a policeman.' I sat very still and small for what must have been half an hour before the chemist finally returned to his flat.

I dashed for the door. Sunny was waiting on the landing and, in tears, I punched her on the arm as soon as I saw her. Why hadn't she warned me? She said she had not seen the owner until it was too late to do anything but hide. My mother and Joy were relieved to see that I had returned safely. Then I pulled out not only one, but six tins of chilblain ointment from my pockets.

17

I didn't know it, but these innocent episodes with my sisters were not to last. The reality was that London was not considered a safe place for a child to live, and this was one of the last winters we would all spend together. At Christmas time, before my sisters were evacuated – five was the youngest allowed age – my mother made the three of us beautiful dolls. She had to make a few sacrifices to be able to afford these gifts. The problem was only two of them had hair and, because I was the youngest, I ended up with the bald one. This didn't seem fair to me. So to make things even, one day I borrowed their dolls, went behind the sofa and cut all their hair off.

With bombs falling every night on the city, many of the children were evacuated to safer areas. I remember the trip I took with my mother to the train station to see my sisters off. It was jammed with all the other children and their parents. Each child had an identity label tagged to his coat. I asked to be labelled, too, and go with my sisters on what seemed a glorious adventure, but I was not old enough.

Sunny and Joy carried cardboard boxes with their dearest possessions stored inside. We sat on the floor of the station and Sunny opened her box and tried to give me her colouring book. I knew whatever was going to happen was serious, because Sunny was always very protective with her possessions.

Joy held the baby, and Sunny and I sat locked together, both of us crying great silent tears. We stopped crying when we saw Mummy. She was even sadder than we were. Sunny made her laugh by saying, 'Cockneys don't cry, do we,' and we sat in a circle repeating this phrase.

The laughter made our goodbyes easier, but in my chest I felt a big weight and a feeling of despair. I knew my whole world was changing.

We returned to our house that night. How large and empty it seemed without Sunny and Joy there.

Mummy decided to take me to the cinema to cheer me up. This was a real grown-up treat. She let me hold the torch as long as I minded to keep it face down to the ground so the light could not be seen from above.

Having my mother all to myself was like being wrapped in a silky blanket of love. Now I wasn't the youngest girl anymore. I was my mother's oldest helper and confidante. I bathed my tiny brother for her when she was tired and needed to rest. I felt so important and necessary that I nearly forgot about everyone else, even my sisters. Sometimes I would think about them on their unknown train journey and feel sad. I was very careful not to let my mother know what I was thinking. I didn't want her to be upset again. I wanted the wonderful moments to go on and on. It compensated for losing my sisters.

My brief time alone with my mother and brother was not to last. Without Joy and Sunny to take care of Ernie and me and no income to support us, my mother was forced to make alternative arrangements. Within a few weeks she took Ernie and myself to a baby home in Godalming, Surrey, just outside London. The local nursery had been evacuated to a so-called 'safe' spot there.

From that time on, our family was always split up. The year or two of shelters and gas masks, bombs and rubble, were to be the only time we would all spend together.

My mother worked at the baby home for a short time, but had to leave when the superiors decided that she had been favouring Ernie over the other infants. When she left, I was put to bed in a little cot. I was so furious at my predicament that I began to pull tufts of the stuffing out of it. By the time they came to wake me after the rest period, the whole mattress had been destroyed.

One day when I hid away to cry I was soothed by Nurse Eva who sat me on her lap and tried to comfort me. She assured me my mother would come back for me. Eva told me that she had had to leave behind in Germany not only her mother and father, but aunts and uncles, and a brother and sister as well, all of whom would never come back. When I asked her why she said, 'Because I am a Jew.' I didn't understand. I thought she was German.

At Godalming, as soon as you reached the age of five, your parents were notified that they could come and pick you up. My fifth birthday arrived and no-one came for me. A woman named Doctor Anne, one of the staff at the baby home, volunteered to look after me until I was either claimed or was found a more permanent place to live. She was a sweet woman with no children of her own.

Ernie was barely three and had to stay at Godalming while I went off to the doctor's house to live. I missed my baby brother terribly. My fifth day there I smeared raspberry jam all over the doctor's luxurious Victorian furniture. Then I climbed a six-feet garden wall, intent on getting back to Godalming to see Ernie. Unfortunately, I got lost within the first hundred yards.

The good doctor, busy enough with her own life, could see by now that my stay with her was not going to work out. I think she wanted to adopt me, despite my behaviour, but couldn't obtain legal permission without the consent of my mother or father. It seemed my parents felt unable to care for me, but still wanted to keep their options open in case their situation changed.

Too old for the baby home, too badly behaved for a private residence, I was found a place by the matron in a children's home at Edgeworth, north of London by about 300 miles. I had no idea why I was being sent away again. Was I being punished for being a naughty girl?

The train ride to the north of England was an eleven-hour journey, one that it seemed to me would never end. What an exciting sight it was to see through my window the long lines of soldiers in uniform, boarding or getting off at each stop. Was my father there, I wondered? Or perhaps one of my uncles? I already missed Ernie, but I was consoled by my belief that Sunny and Joy and my mother would be at Edgeworth to meet me. Then we would all be together once more.

The guard on the train told me to sit in the guard's compartment. He warned me not to speak to anyone, especially not the jolly soldiers who smiled and waved at me as they passed by.

As the train moved north and night started to fall on the English countryside, I started to feel afraid. With no-one to keep me company, the darkness became very frightening and I started to cry. But it was no use since I could not be seen or heard.

The guard came in and told me firmly to stop being a baby. He offered to share his sandwich, but only if I promised to be a good girl. He complimented me on my smart green kilt with the pin in it and asked if it was the proper Scottish kind that really opened. I started to get uncomfortable and asked him if I could go to the lavatory. He offered to take me, but when I got there and went inside, he warned me against locking the door. But I promptly did lock it, which seemed to make him furious. I wanted to be private. I was mortified to find out in my haste that I had wet my knickers. I spent a long time tidying myself up, and wished that someone could be there to help me. When I tried to unlock the door, I found to my horror it would not open. I screamed and banged with my fists but no-one came. I carried on until I'd worn myself out, then sat on the floor and cried. Just as I began to fall asleep I heard a loud woman's voice telling the guard that the lavatory door was jammed. It opened, finally, and a very large lady appeared, wanting to know how long I had been there. I told her.

Hearing this commotion, the guard came back and scolded me for causing so much trouble. He tried to get me to return to the guard car with him so he could keep an eye on me. Thank God the large lady intervened and suggested that I sit with her until we arrived at our destination. The guard told her he was responsible for me, but she insisted. A few hours later we arrived in Bolton.

I sat in the station office waiting for someone to come and collect me, expecting it would be my mother and sisters. By now I had really had enough of the war. I wanted Hitler to stop the bombing so I could go home again.

A small woman with white hair and a Navy blue dress appeared. She told me not to worry, that I was going to be a part of a big family now, and be in a safe place where there wouldn't be bombs any more. We piled into a dilapidated truck, driven by a small man with a limp by the name of Mr Etheridge. He was the 'clogger' at the children's home. Clogger was an old-fashioned Lancashire word for shoe mender. The workers in the cotton mills had worn clogs for years and the name had stuck.

Edgeworth was just outside Bolton, a nineteenth-century mill town. It was deep in the Lancashire countryside, with towering bleak moors on one side, endless stretching fields on the other. Edgeworth was six miles farther north, and was even more remote than Bolton. Situated on a small hill two miles above Edgeworth was the National Children's Home and Orphanage. It seemed to be completely cut off from the rest of the world. As we drove up the hill I saw a large horseshoe of houses, bathed in a grey mist of fog and cold. It was a community in itself with twelve residential houses, a school, hospital, chapel and governor's house.

The third house on the right was called Eric House. This was to be my new home. I was taken to the front door where I was

21

greeted by the head of the house, a tiny older woman named Sister Nancy. The children's home was founded by Methodists and all the women who were employed there were called Sisters. She led me into a large, brightly-lit room full of girls talking all at once. There was a lot of confusion and someone parked me on top of the sofa as thirty girls surrounded me, their ages ranging from roughly my own to what seemed like giants of fifteen or sixteen. There was great excitement at this new arrival from London. Whenever I opened my mouth to speak they hooted with laughter. They couldn't understand my way of talking any more than I could understand theirs.

When I had left Godalming, they made sure I was dressed smartly in the new outfit my mother had sent to the baby home especially for my new school: the green Scots kilt with a matching soft angora jumper, and black patent 'Shirley Temple' shoes with white socks. My long shiny hair was tied with pretty white ribbons.

I looked around at the other girls. No wonder I looked different. They wore grey socks with brown sandals, and jumpers so old and faded that you couldn't tell what the original colour was. Every girl had her hair cropped short in a pudding basin style with a fringe. I could hardly tell one from the other! No wonder they stroked my long curly hair.

I was becoming quite enchanted with all the attention until a very large girl grabbed me from the back of the sofa and plonked me down roughly on the floor. 'Can't you see she's spoiled enough already. There won't be any dealing with her if she isn't put in her place right from the beginning. Besides, she won't look so good tomorrow when she gets her haircut!' The attention quickly faded away and I found myself sitting on the floor alone, dreading the next day's appointment with the scissors.

Eric House was built for half the thirty girls it housed, but with the war raging there was a shortage of space. Inside the young girls' dormitory were two rows of about ten beds, each one covered with a pink and white counterpane. Myself and the other youngest girls went to bed by seven at the latest, while the older girls followed in half-hour intervals, according to their age. By nine o'clock everyone was in bed with the lights out. At quarter to seven in the morning we were loudly awoken by the Sisters. It became a mad scramble to see who could make their beds first. The strict rule on bedmaking was that the beds had to be made with hospital corners and be completely free of wrinkles. After being shown the proper way to do it on the first day, we were left on our own.

Morning chores included dusting and polishing the stairs and dormitory, and emptying the chamber pots. After breakfast we had to 'strip wash' in the communal bathroom. Wearing our knickers, we washed ourselves and then stood while one of the Sisters made an 'inspection'. A competition ran between the Sisters to see whose house could have the best behaved, most well-mannered and finely scrubbed children. It felt like being in the army for a small girl!

Twice a week, before we went to school in the morning, there would be a brief chapel service. On Sundays, attendance was compulsory on three separate occasions.

If you misbehaved, there was a choice of punishments given. You could either do a chore, such as cardinalling the bathroom floor with a sticky red polish – which often stuck more to you than to the floor – or you could be locked in the cold cellar for an hour. But that was for the first offence only. A second infraction and you got the slipper on your behind. The third time and Sister Nancy went for the cane. I never found out why, but for some reason, she kept the cane stored up inside the chimney.

Despite her firm discipline, Sister Nancy was basically a humane woman, but at the age of about sixty five, she was probably too old to be looking after thirty big, hearty girls. The home couldn't retire her, as they were short of staff. It was considered a vocation, not a profession, and the Sisters were not paid, but given two pounds a month for expenses. Sister Nancy had a small private income from her father, and would generously make sure that all her girls had something to spend if our relatives hadn't sent us any pocket money.

Every day after school we would have teatime, which was a drink and thick slices of bread and margarine. A loud bell rang and we would all rush to our assigned places at the large scrubbed pine tables. The seating was done entirely by rotation and age. On my first day I was put on the end of the little girls' table, ruled with a rod of iron by a small girl named Elsie. She wielded considerable power over her table of eight. Not only was she Sister Nancy's undisputed favourite, Elsie had an older sister named Pauline who would not hesitate to administer discipline if you so much as crossed her younger sister. Just what we need, I moaned to myself, a nine-year-old Hitler.

It was a strange place for me, with strange faces. I began to cry. As soon as I was heard, a deathly silence came over the entire room. Crying, as all the girls knew, was not the done thing. But try as I may, I couldn't stop. Sister Nancy came whooshing down the aisle like a great blue bird, a flurry of navy silk topped by her starched white collar. She firmly took my hand and led me to the Sister's private sitting room. I was sure my mother and sisters would be here, I told her. Why hadn't they come for me? Sister Nancy smiled and stroked my hand and assured me in a gentle voice, 'Now, Shirley Broomfield, you've got to realize that we are your family now. You don't have a mother and two sisters here.' This only made me cry more.

Finally she was able to calm me down. She took me upstairs to the dormitory and showed me my bed, then made some hot milk and put me to bed with half an aspirin. I pulled the covers high over my head and sobbed myself to sleep. I dreamt of when my family would all be together again. I hoped that my real mother and family, wherever they were, would be thinking about me as I was them.

It was during these first few weeks at Edgeworth that I went through my 'head banging' phase. Nobody would believe me when I said I had a family of my own: I got so frustrated at this that I would bang my head against the wall or a table until someone physically stopped me. They accomplished this by picking me up and dropping me, fully dressed, into a bath of cold water until I calmed down. Usually I was left in the bath for at least half an hour.

I used to envy Mavis, one of the girls about my age. She could cry and keep it going for hour after hour. It seemed to me that because she was able to cry for so long, the Sisters were always nicer to her. Tantrums would get boring after half an hour or so for me, not to mention exhausting.

For some girls wetting the bed became a problem. It was a humiliating experience to make this mistake. Not only did it make you late for the morning routine, but the punishment imposed on you was, to say the least, unusual. Thankfully, I wasn't a bedwetter (not often, that is) but whenever I got excited, usually at Christmas or on my birthday, I would occasionally have an accident. It would then be my turn to stand on the hall landing with the sheet over my head, remaining there until it dried. We called the punishment playing 'ghosts', and all day long the other children would be encouraged to ridicule and laugh at you. If one house had more bedwetters than the others, it soon became public knowledge through the older girls who worked in the laundry.

Luckily for myself and two of the other youngest girls, Elaine and Jessie, this form of discipline was dying out in Eric House. Several of the younger Sisters had convinced Sister Nancy that the practice was unfair to the children. It was almost as if she had inherited one of the old ritualistic punishments from Victorian times. Still, it did continue to flourish in some of the other houses.

But there were good times, too. To me the most wonderful thing would be a parcel that would come in the post from my mother, reassuring me that I was not dreaming in vain. There would be a letter with love from Joy and Sunny, little children's books, a packet of boiled sweets and a tin of biscuits from Woolworth's. She would also send me dresses that had belonged to my sisters.

As the first Christmas approached, the excitement was all around me. Most of the children had received presents from their families by post, but no parcels had arrived for me. I wondered how my mother could forget me. I felt sad and alone.

We all polished and scrubbed Eric House to make it sparkle for the Christmas holiday. Even though I missed my family, I was beginning to feel something. Christmas Eve came and Father Christmas arrived all in red, with a long white beard and a sack filled with gifts. After we younger children were put to bed, he came round to each child in turn. He told me to dip in to his sack and take out a present. I felt so happy when I pulled out the most beautiful black baby doll. What's more, it even opened and closed its eyes! I couldn't speak or move, and sat on the bed as if I was frozen. Father Christmas spoke to me but I couldn't answer him. I tried to say something, but no sound would come.

Sister Nancy sat down on the bed and put her arms round me. 'It's all right, Shirley. You can cry now.' At last I could feel something besides the anger I felt at having been parted from my family. I cried for a long time.

My mother's first visit didn't come until I had been at Edgeworth for about a year. That was such a glorious day. She came with an American man whose name I think was Johnny. He picked me up off the ground and said, 'How would you like to go to a big country one day and have all the things a little girl should have?' We took a trip into Bolton by bus, and she bought half a pound of broken biscuits and some sweets.

I sadly said goodbye to my mother and Johnny and stored all my precious treasures in my locker, watched by my little friend Elaine and by Mavis. The three of us were the youngest girls. Elaine was the prettiest, a tiny girl with black hair and blue eyes, and a few days younger than me.

Mavis had her eye on my biscuits. She was always eating when she wasn't whimpering. We were always stuck with Mavis. Most of the time we didn't mind. She was plump with fair, lank, very sparse hair on a rather sad-looking enlarged head. The sisters said she had something wrong with her and she was always slow to respond, if she responded at all. Usually this didn't bother me, but now I wanted some privacy to share my treasures with my special friends, Elaine and Morwyn. I wanted to show them my most precious possession, a small black-and-white picture of Sunny and Joy standing in a garden wearing Wellington boots. I loved this picture my mother had given me, I carried it everywhere. I had to let Mavis see the photograph as well, but she became furious when I wouldn't share my biscuits with her. Broken biscuits were a treat. They were a quarter of the price of whole ones in packets but were just as delicious.

Mavis reported me to Sister Lisa, who at teatime announced very loudly that there was one selfish girl present, and would she please go to her locker, get her biscuits and share them with *everyone*! There was no way of hiding and I slowly got my biscuits and took the box round, and reluctantly allowed each girl to take some. When I got back to my place, there were none left.

Months went by and I gradually settled into the routine. Then a wonderful thing happened. A parcel of twenty seven of the most beautiful dresses I had ever seen arrived from my mother – all different sizes, for all different ages. There was one for every stage of my life! I didn't know whether to laugh or cry. I was delirious

26

with joy that these lovely clothes were all mine. But seeing dresses that I knew I couldn't fit into for almost ten years intimidated me. With my Aunt Lily, my mother had sewn all the dresses by hand. Some had belonged to Sunny and Joy, which made them even more precious. I later found out my mother was planning to leave England for good, and she was trying to see that I had enough clothes for the rest of my childhood. I think it was her way of saying goodbye.

Sister Nancy didn't see it this way. She told me I had to share the dresses with everyone else and that I was allowed to keep only one for myself. It infuriated me to see my mother's beautiful hand-sewn clothes on the other girls, knowing that the dresses would be old before I could wear them. By the time they got to me, they were smelly and worn out and full of holes. I never really got over it. I had to see other girls walking around wearing my dresses for many years to come.

To my great delight, my mother did visit again but, this time, with someone else. As she was getting ready to leave, I ran to her, only to hear Sister call out to me, 'Come back, Shirley. This is your home now. Besides, your mother is pregnant by an American now.' Those two words stuck in my head, 'pregnant' and 'American'. I didn't know quite what they meant. I knew America was a country, but what was 'pregnant'?

She left. As she got smaller and smaller in the distance, still waving and still crying, I felt more empty and alone than ever. Sister Nancy tried to cuddle me, but I just stood there stiffly. I didn't want to be cuddled. I wanted to scream and shout and bang my head.

I didn't think my mother would be gone for ever at that time. I believed she would be back. It wasn't until I was in my teens that I formed the idea she had been killed.

After Ernie turned five and was too old for the baby home, he was sent to join me at Edgeworth. We had a glorious re-union. He was a beautiful little boy with bright, shiny blonde hair, like a field of corn. We sat together for two hours and I stroked and cuddled him. He had brought me a gift from the matron of the baby home, a wonderfully detailed, colourful book on all kinds of birds. This book became a great treasure to me.

At the end of our visit, Ernie was taken to Beckett House, which was on the other side of the half-circle from me, about a mile and a half away. I hated to be separated from him and so I would walk around the semicircle to visit. This was against the rules, but I missed him so much. Sometimes, to take a short cut, I would cross the field in the middle of the semicircle of houses, where the cows were grazing, or whatever. I would have preferred to have been dodging double-decker buses any day or night rather than these silly cows. After dark, this was a frightening journey. The cows were hard to see, if I had bumped into one and fallen, there would have been no-one to pick me up.

Seeing Ernie, it was clear to me that he was as unhappy as I was when I first arrived. It took him a long time to settle down.

On Sundays, after breakfast, we walked three miles, there and back, to church in Edgeworth Village, all dressed up in our Sunday best. It was worth it to come back to the one really enjoyable meal of the week – home-cooked Sunday lunch, prepared by the Sisters themselves. In the afternoon we were released and trusted to go to Sunday School, unsupervised. This was a big plus, because I could be with my brother.

One afternoon I was called unexpectedly by Sister Helen, the Sister in charge of Ernie's house, to go and be with him. He had fallen into a near coma and no-one knew exactly what was wrong with him. Around his bed they had placed curtains on stands to give him some privacy. I sat with him and was told to keep cold flannels on his head. He was so hot that he would flinch when the cloth touched his forehead.

Each time I came to see him, I had to come over to the boys' side of the horseshoe. I sat with him as the evening went into the night, the night into early morning. It terrified me to be alone there with the bigger boys all around me. At night they came home and I would sit quietly in my chair behind the curtain while they got ready for bed. The next morning, I would wait for them to go to school before I dared to go and spend a penny.

I felt so helpless in my effort to get some response from Ernie. But, about two weeks after he became ill, when I was ready to give up, something happened. I was resting my head on his bed, completely exhausted, when suddenly his hand touched mine. At that moment I knew he would be all right. I sat very quietly holding his hand, afraid to move for what seemed like hours.

Then he coughed, opened his eyes and asked me for a glass of water. My little brother was back! And the next few days were some of the best in my life. Nobody ever said what had been wrong with him.

Sister Helen told me that I had been a great help. She let me bathe in her bathroom, gave me clean clothes to wear and even let me use her talcum powder. Then I was sent up a celebration lunch that she cooked herself. It was delicious: cold ham with mashed potatoes and jelly and custard to follow, a real treat in return for the long days I had spent with my brother.

I stayed with Ernie for another few days, but, at night, I would go back to Eric House to sleep. The days I spent while Ernie recovered were peaceful and quiet. Soon the school work I had missed was sent over for me to catch up with. Ernie could be difficult when I was studying, but I was so glad he was getting better that I let him do whatever he wanted.

Then, a few nights later, after I had gone back to Eric House, I was shaken awake by Sister Nancy in the middle of the night. 'Come quickly. Don't dress. Put your coat over your nightie, Ernie is ill again.' I knew it must have been very serious because Mr Brooks, the Governor, was there to drive me in his car to Beckett House. I prayed all the way, please let my brother live. *Please!*

We arrived at Beckett House to see all the lights blazing away inside. Boys of all sizes were standing about, staring and gaping. I pushed everyone out of my way and rushed to my brother. He was lying on his bed with his eyes closed, his body rigid as a board, rasping and choking for breath. I pulled him into a sitting position to cuddle him. It turned out to be the right thing to do. He was violently sick all over me and everywhere else. Then he opened his eyes and slowly began to breathe properly. He kept repeating my name over and over again.

It took him two or three months after this to get better. When the authorities were sure he was back to normal, they decided to separate us and made plans to send me off to a different children's home. They thought we were too dependent on each other.

At least they were right about one thing.

CHAPTER TWO

When I was about ten I was moved to a new place, away from Ernie and all my friends I had grown attached to. It was never clear to me whether they moved me because of my behaviour or whether they simply wished to separate Ernie and myself. No explanation was given.

In their wisdom, the authorities decided to try an experiment. There were to be sixteen children in all: half of them bright, hyper kids who were considered 'difficult', and the other half rather 'slow' children. All of them were to be placed together in a large country house in a small industrial town called Blackburn, fifty miles from Edgeworth, which could have been another planet as far as I was concerned. On our first night in Blackburn, Sister

Edith sat us in a semicircle, split into two groups. She told us that the more 'fortunate' ones would be required to look after the less fortunate ones. I was placed on Sister Edith's 'fortunate' list. I was told it was my job to look after Eileen or, if she wasn't around, Margaret. I couldn't see why they needed looking after in the first place. They were less adept at school but that was all. Compared to my friend Mavis who was left behind at Edgeworth, most of them were potential members of the Brains Trust!

Blackburn was like starting all over again, as we were separated from our own 'adopted' families. I missed my two closest friends, Morwyn and Elaine. One compensation was that two new little boys arrived, aged three and five, who I loved: Rupert and Godfrey. For some reason, though, there were no boys of our own age. It was strange that there were no contemporary male figures in the house, though perhaps that's not so surprising when you think of the strong church influence.

Sister Edith was Head Sister and Matron, in charge of the house at Blackburn. Sister Edith was a warm, big-bosomed woman of about sixty who could be rather formidable to confront. Her assistant, Sister Betty, who looked like the Walt Disney character Goofy, was very skinny, wore glasses and her hair scraped back in a tight bun. The two of them together made quite a pair.

They said they found me to be quite a handful. Sister Edith didn't know quite what to do. I was a rebel, but I never meant to be. I missed Sister Nancy and my old home and, most of all, Ernie, who nobody would give me any news of, and I made the mistake of saying how I felt. I felt lonely without them and showed it and, as a result, ended up disappointing Sister Edith constantly.

I misbehaved, but it wasn't so much that I was deliberately difficult, more that I was angry and excited all at the same time. I had gone from my mother who was completely loving, when she was *around*, to Sister Nancy, who was firm and preached love and kindness but who never got too close to any of her girls, to Sister Edith, who, with the benefit of hindsight, was more balanced than most of them. But, at the age of ten, my loyalties were very much with Sister Nancy as I had spent more of my life in her care than I had with anyone else.

Although Sister Edith and myself were often at loggerheads at least she didn't have favourites, and I still felt she cared about me despite my behaviour; but I couldn't seem to help disappointing her and that was the worst feeling of all.

She did allow myself and the other girls to change our hair and grow it if we wished. It was a huge relief not to have to wear that ugly pudding basin haircut any more. But she might have had a motive for doing so, for whenever I misbehaved she would cut my hair as a punishment. Sister Edith may well have been a very clever child psychologist.

Now that we were out of the completely contained community of Edgeworth, we had to go to school in the nearby town with the local children. I was designated to go to the Blakely Moor School for Girls, and found that I was the only girl there from a children's home. We had to wear uniform which, for once, I was pleased about because I looked just the same as the girls from private homes: navy blue gymslip, white blouse, school tie, long grey socks in the winter and lace-up shoes. We also had to tie our hair back with a navy blue ribbon. The uniform cost a lot of money, which Sister Edith didn't mind, but the ribbon she thought was just too much. She said an elastic band would do just as well. One day in Maths class, the teacher noticed I wasn't wearing any ribbons. She hauled me out in front of the class by one of my bunches. It was such a small detail. It would have been so easy to have bought the ribbon but now, because of this ridiculous economy, the secret of my coming from a children's home was exposed to the class. I ended up feeling more of a waif and stray than I ever had at Edgeworth.

I suspect, in a begrudging way, Sister Edith was proud of me as a child, perhaps because I stood up for myself when many of the other children did not. Ironically, she may have given me the beginnings of some kind of shaky self-esteem. If she had to punish me, she would tell me something positive about myself, just to let me know I was worthwhile.

It wasn't until about two years later that I settled down and started to do well at school. Books became my new fascination. I would spend all day up in the attic of the house reading *David Copperfield* or *Little Women* or other classics that were given to us at Sunday School. We would also receive books left to the home in the wills of several local residents. Reading became my favourite way to pass the time. It made me realize, along with rounders and acrobats, how much there was to see and to do!

Singing and dancing were just beginning to interest me too. That's why it was such a happy surprise to be given the lead in the school play. I remember that the girl who was supposed to dance the lead twisted her ankle, and I was asked to take over. I didn't mind being the second choice, it was just such a joy to be chosen, especially as most of my classmates were having private dancing lessons. The music in the play was *Swan Lake* and whenever I hear Tchaikovsky, it brings back melancholy memories of the play and my unfortunate experience.

What happened was like a bombshell at my young age. I didn't know it, but Mr Milverton, the new Governor from Edgeworth, had visited Blackburn and formed an opinion of me as a responsible, nice girl. He had made plans for me and another girl of my age. He wanted to move us both back to Edgeworth. I had just found my feet in the play and, within the week, was to give the first performance when Sister Edith came to me with an unusually serious expression on her face.

'You won't be dancing in the concert, dear.'

I was stunned. 'Why not, Sister? I *must* dance in it. I've been picked for the lead.'

'I'm sorry. You're going to have your dream come true. You're going back to Edgeworth.'

That wasn't my dream. My dream was to dance in the school play. I couldn't understand it. I pleaded with her. 'Please may I go on Wednesday, because Tuesday is the performance?'

But she was firm. 'No, no, it's all arranged. Mr Milverton thinks you're a nice girl and feels you'll do better at Edgeworth.'

I was too proud and too hurt to cry. I felt broken. I had danced so hard and now it was coming to an end even before I had a chance to perform. I felt ashamed. In my mind, I was letting the whole school down. And there was nothing I could do about it.

With less than a day to spare before our performance, I was shipped back to Edgeworth.

The most difficult and frustrating thing was that not only were these decisions made for me, but usually they were never explained. There was a dreadful code of procedure that prevented us from knowing why these choices were made. It was simply for us 'not to know'. Or rather, it was the Sisters and the Governor who knew best.

I was twelve years old when I was yanked out of Blackburn. Two other girls of the same age were sent back with me. It now seems a strange coincidence that we were sent back to Edgeworth just before the onset of puberty. At Blackburn we couldn't be watched so closely as at Edgeworth. Perhaps the authorities felt nervous because we attended a local school in the town and associated with people in the 'real world', many of whom were of course the opposite sex.

Edgeworth had changed in the two years I had been away, and so had I. Sister Nancy had retired and Eric House was no longer the home of the girls I'd known. Ernie had been transferred to a sanatorium in Harpenden. I was put in Moscrop House where Sister Hilda was Head Sister with her junior, Sister Jessie. I could tell on my arrival there that Sister Hilda was not too pleased. She let me know it. 'In forty years of child care, I've only ever had boys, except for my four German girls, who are nearly as good as boys anyway.' My heart sank on hearing Sister Hilda's comments and, worst of all, I was now in a house with boys of all ages – but my brother was separated from me still, 300 miles away in Harpenden.

The four German refugees in Moscrop were rumoured to be daughters of SS officers. Of course, it wasn't the girls' fault any more than it was mine, but they were nasty girls all the same. I longed for my old friends.

One of the first things I saw after I arrived was a cruel punishment meted out by Sister Hilda. A little boy of about five had an accident and marked his pants. While the whole house was made to watch, she took a large brush used for cleaning floors and scrubbed his mouth with it. The boy screamed, but she went on scrubbing and scrubbing until his mouth was raw and bleeding. I watched with disgust, not strong enough to do anything about it. Of all that I had experienced, I had never seen this kind of behaviour before. I was disgusted. I was determined not to come under Sister Hilda's influence.

This early adolescent phase of my life would turn out to be my worst. I went from Blackburn, where I was one of the most responsible, oldest girls, to Edgeworth where, as a twelve-year-old living in a house of fifteen and sixteen-year-old boys, I was embarrassed the whole time. I felt overpowered living so closely with these large boys who were virtual strangers to me.

We were made to 'strip wash' with the boys. I was shy and didn't want to take my vest off. Iloa and Annekine, two of the German girls, couldn't care less. They stood there without any clothes on. But the boys were used to them.

Sister Hilda watched as we went through our 'Soap on, Sister, soap off' routine, holding our arms out in front of us for inspection. She got to me and noticed that I still wore my vest. 'Take it off,' she shouted. I said I didn't want to. All at once she struck at me and knocked me to the ground and what followed was a knock-down, drag-out fight all around the bathroom, with all the other children watching. Sister Hilda had me pinned in the corner and was banging my head against the skirting boards so hard that she cut my head open. I couldn't move. Sister Hilda had more on her mind than discipline. She had shouted that I was a 'cocky little madam' and needed 'to be brought down a peg or two'.

Most of the other children watched in horror and fear. One of the smaller boys was rooting for me. He didn't know any better, poor love. Every time I landed a punch I'd look up and see his smiling, encouraging little face. Eventually, Eric, one of the oldest boys, pulled her off me. He was the only long-term boy not completely cowed by her. After ten minutes, we were finally separated. Blood from the back of my head left a puddle on the floor. If I sit under a hot dryer even today, the scar I got then becomes tender. It makes me sure that I remember Sister Hilda.

Sister Hilda was aware that she had a teenage girl in her care who didn't think her way was right. Most of her charges had been with her since they were toddlers. They had no idea how the other Sisters or their families lived. They thought fear was natural and were used to her as a total disciplinarian. But, after this incident, luckily for me, Sister Hilda was planning to get rid of me. I was 'sent to Coventry' and lived for the next two weeks in deadly silence. Eric was punished severely for coming to my rescue. And then, in one swift move, Sister Hilda got her way.

Within two weeks I was sent to Stephenson House, the house where most of my old friends from Eric House now lived. It had the reputation of being a house for hardened troublemakers, but most of them were merely high-spirited. I was given the punishment of washing huge, greasy cooking pans twice a day in the central kitchen by Mr Milverton, the Governor, who because of my behaviour at Moscrop, came to see me sadly on my first day in Stephenson.

'What happened to that nice little girl I met at Blackburn who was one of the brightest lights of the house and who sparkled whenever I saw her? What happened to you, Shirley Broomfield? You've only been back two months and you were always telling Sister Edith that you preferred Edgeworth. Now you're back and you can't get along with anybody. You were such a lovely little girl. What happened?' He looked at me in amazement when I tried to explain to him. When I showed him the cut on my head, he just looked nonplussed.

I was both relieved and ashamed to be sent to Stephenson House, three doors away from Moscrop. Just after I arrived there something dramatic happened. Sister Julie, one of the younger Sisters, ran away. When she had gone, there was a scandal because our pocket money was missing. As she was only paid two pounds a month, she may have used the money for her fare back home. Two months later she sent it back, with no return address. I was sad that I couldn't tell her how much I liked her for the short time I knew her.

My new house parents, Sister Annie and her assistant, Sister Winifred, were both kind women who truly cared about their girls. They certainly had a difficult job in raising so many teenagers who were considered to be troublemakers, but you never felt that they pitied you or that they had given up on you. Sister Annie had been a sergeant-major in the Army, but we all knew her bark was worse than her bite.

It was hard for her to deal with us. She was used to being in charge of women of her own age. Teenage girls confused her. Whenever we didn't do our chores correctly she would get very upset and her neck would flush bright red. We used to try to make her mad just to see her neck change to vivid scarlet.

There was a special person at this time who made a deep impression on me: Mr Barron was our English teacher and was one of the best influences of my childhood. He was in his middle years, healthy, with reddish hair, and he had been a professional football player. He made the lessons exciting and inspiring for us. To him, learning was achieved by taking an individual interest in his students. He could see my inclination towards theatre and the arts and would encourage me all the time.

One of Mr Barron's gifts was that he could look at each of us and see our personalities without bias. He taught us that there were more important things in life than being the best games player or the most popular girl in the house. He searched for the raw material in each person. The choices he made in the school plays, for instance, were based on the ability of each of us. I was not used to such fairness. With some of the Sisters it was your position on their list of favourites which determined your luck. He produced a play called *The Monkey's Paw* and I played the lead in it. It was a wonderful experience for me.

The choir at the Home was a quite different thing. Even though you could sing well, you still had to be in good favour with Sister Grace to be in it. On high days and holidays we would perform for visitors. I used to sing a hymn called 'Count Your Blessings', that once or twice got a great response from the congregation. In 1988 I sang the hymn at a benefit for the NCH and found it had the same effect on the audience.

Sister Grace would play the piano for Keep Fit, as our exercise class was called. But she had a mean streak. If I had displeased her at choir practice she would miss a piano beat and I would look stupid during my acrobatic routine.

At this time I was going through a strange period physically. After wanting for so long to be like the older girls, now I was becoming a woman and it frightened me. I felt uncomfortable for days at a time.

My feelings about boys were changing as well. Just a year ago I had been competitive with them. On the playing field, I was even one of the games captains, but now I felt uncomfortable. It made me act silly in one of the school plays because I was embarrassed. I had suddenly become self-conscious with boys of my own age watching me. I wouldn't allow myself to play the character, preferring instead to be silly, missing a line or a cue. In fact, being awkward generally.

Our school had been built for the first children in the NCH in 1869. Only children in care had ever attended. That's why the village children were horrified when the government, insisting that we had better facilities, decided to integrate them into our school. When the village children first arrived at Edgeworth there was a great animosity between them and us. They were afraid of us – they looked on us as the 'orphan kids at the top of the hill'. The only time we had ever seen each other before was at the Methodist church on Sundays.

Thirty years later, I was reminded of an incident I had completely forgotten, when a woman who had been one of those village children related this story to me. Apparently it was I who broke the ice on that first day. She told me I walked across the floor and spoke to the village children. 'We'd better all start talking to each other if we're going to be in the same school.' The woman said when she saw me do this she knew I would succeed at something later on. It's funny because I have no recollection of it. It may be because I had been at Blackburn – 'out in the world' a little – that I was able to make peace between the two sides.

Now we had friends in the 'outside world' beyond the Home and it was wonderful. Life was much less claustrophobic than it had been before. Occasionally Sister Annie would let us go to the village social where there were boys, many of whom were friends from school. It was an exciting time. Two boys in particular I liked. Melvin was thin and studious looking, and the brightest person in our class. Brian was, even at the age of fourteen, a big, tall, handsome boy. They were my first teenage crushes.

One of the occasions I remember was a fancy dress competition. I went as Mrs Mop, with my hair piled up in a bun, wearing a long skirt and boots and carrying a bucket and mop. I put them down to dance and became so excited that my hair fell down. Then the announcements came and, to my surprise, I ended up winning the competition, but not as Mrs Mop: with my hair hanging to my shoulders and free of my mop and bucket, they thought I had come as *Alice in Wonderland*. The clothes I was wearing were Victorian taken from our dressing-up box, donated by the church – who knows which elderly Methodist lady had helped me win this competition.

When you reached the age of fifteen at Edgeworth, a decision had to be made about your future. They would try to return you to where you originally came from. Ten years before, I had left London on an eventful train ride and now I was to return. My friend, Marion, and I were kitted out with our 'outfit': a dress, a coat, underwear and shoes. Every child who left the NCH was given an 'outfit' to equip them for the 'outside world' and the beginning of their adult life. It was like a demob suit in the armed forces – clothing for the start of our 'civilian' life! No doubt intending to allow for growth, Mrs Milverton had given me a dress that was too long and hung beneath my coat. My shoes were also a size too big.

As soon as we got on the train, we dived straight for the Ladies' Room and put on the makeup we had collected: red lipstick, bought at Woolworth's, peachy powder, pinched from Sister's dressing table, and high-heeled shoes, given to me by one of my village girlfriends, probably 'borrowed' from her mother. Our destination was a hostel in North London run by the NCH. We felt happy and free.

At the station in London we waited on the platform for the after-care Sister who was to meet us, feeling like 'women of the world' in our fancy new get-ups. Then, high above, coming towards us on a railway bridge, we spied a little dumpy woman in uniform with a pouter-pidgeon top and a very determined expression on her rosy face. In a flash Marion and I simultaneously pulled off our shoes, stuffed them into our pockets, and wiped the makeup off our faces, putting back on our conservative, flat shoes. We greeted her with nervous smiles. 'Hullo, Sister. I'm Shirley and this is Marion.'

Without preamble, Sister May took us off to the hostel. 'My job is to look after teenage girls and I've had them all my life, so you'd better behave yourselves before you start!' she announced on our arrival at the hostel. With Sister May, you were assumed to be trouble unless you proved yourself otherwise. She said she had had enough of teenage girls like us to last her for more than one lifetime.

Our bus and tube ride took us to a large, imposing building in the Highbury section of North London. It was rather forbidding but we shared our bedroom with just one other girl. Luckily I moved into Stephenson House (named after the founder) and immediately made friends with the oldest girl, Sylvia. Her sharp-tongued wit was great fun. We formed a friendship that still lasts.

Half the day I attended the Polytechnic; the other half I worked in the mail office of the NCH. The house had anywhere from twelve to twenty girls, all being prepared for their future. I was the Post Girl. It was my job to go around the offices and deliver the mail to the employees twice a day. I was a perky fifteen-year-old, eager to talk and received quite a few wide-eyed glances from the Methodist ministers, charity workers and health care people who inhabited these offices. They seemed amazed at this teenager who would bounce into their office with a friendly greeting, ask them about their families and then move on to the next office, asking questions all the time. I was full of life – London seemed a glorious adventure to me.

Sylvia and I went out one day with some other girls who knew their way around locally and we went to Finsbury Park where there was a lake and rowing boats to rent. In the middle of the lake was a tiny little island and I decided to try and get on it. I slipped, and with my feet in the boat, grabbed hold of a post. With my hands holding the post, my feet still in the boat, and the boat drifting further away from the island, the front of my new outfit was getting wet through, as I slipped further into the water, and eventually I was completely soaked. I was horrified, these were my best clothes, but luck was with me. When I got my coat and dress back from the dry cleaners, wonder of wonders, they now fitted me properly!

My excess energy continued to get me into hot water. Molly Coleman, a woman who was a psychologist for the NCH, would occasionally read out a list of my mistakes, but I was happy and I didn't mind. Often I would leave the hostel and have lunch with friends.

One of the first things I did after settling in was to try and find where my father lived. It had been two years since I had seen him and, in that time, I had grown up quite a lot. When I arrived at his address I was met by Gypsy, his second wife. She had coal black eyes, vivid red hair that was cut quite short, and an intense expression on her face. Gypsy had only seen me before in my conservative school uniform with white socks and pigtails, now I was in a flowery, summer dress with my hair long and loose.

'Good Lord, look who's 'ere. Where'd you turn up from?' she greeted me with. 'Gave you that dress, did they? Pity they didn't give you any underwear to go with it.' She opened the door and called to her daughter, Patsy. 'Call Ern, tell 'im the girl's 'ere, not Sunny, the other one!'

We sat in awkward silence in the sitting room, waiting for my father to arrive.

'You look different from how you used to,' Patsy said. I felt as if something was wrong. I didn't know what to do. I had taken a lot of trouble to look neat because I wanted to make a good impression. I wanted Gypsy's approval and was upset that the person I met two years earlier who had promised me a family, now seemed to resent me. I went to visit, happily expecting that I would be welcome.

When Gypsy had visited me at Edgeworth with my father and Patsy two years earlier she was friendly and had seemed pleased to meet me. Now it was as though she couldn't bear me and I didn't know why. What was it I had done?

My father came home and he at least seemed delighted and pleased to see me. He suggested we all go out and celebrate. To my surprise, Gypsy said she didn't want to be seen with me. She was afraid of the neighbours talking. When we got outside my father could see that I was near to tears.

'Don't take any notice, love. She'll get over it.'

On my visits to their house, my father would often take me to the local pub, sometimes he'd tell me about my mother, how lovely she had been and how I was beginning to resemble her. But he hardly ever asked me about my life or my plans for the future. He said he was thinking of leaving Gypsy and asked what did I think of taking care of his house and looking after him as well.

His way of being affectionate would often frighten me. He would see me to the Tube station and hug and kiss me goodbye. If I broke away he'd only hold me tighter in a bearhug and say, 'C'mon, girl, give us a real cuddle.' On the train I would wonder why I didn't feel happy about cuddling my father. Sometimes I'd wish he wouldn't take me to the station.

When Sunny walked into the entrance hall at Highbury I felt so delighted to see her and I could tell she felt the same way. I hadn't seen her since her last visit to Blackburn three years before. I thought she looked stunning, from the tip of her cropped, platinum hair to her five-inch spiked high heels. The years we had been separated dropped away and we stood locked in each other's arms, rocking to and fro, while we cried and laughed all

41

at the same time. Finally, we broke apart when Sister Mabel came into the room.

'Haven't you two got anything else to do than just stand there cuddling one another?'

Sunny stepped back and took a long look at me. She laughed at my outfit. But it didn't matter, she said, because I'd turned out to be nice looking and she could put the old-fashioned, frumpy clothes right in a day. Of course I didn't think they were frumpy but I didn't say anything. Sunny's remark was the first time in my life anybody had ever told me they liked the way I looked.

The next morning I was allowed to visit her where she lived, which was in Grosvenor Square, about six miles from the hostel. What a difference a few miles made. Gracious, Georgian houses surrounding a green, leafy square. The American Embassy was on the other side of the square.

Sunny and many of her friends dated mostly young Americans. They were stationed in London as part of the Western Alliance peacekeeping force. They all seemed to have lots of money and were mostly the same age as the young girls they dated. Romances thrived and blossomed in post-war London and the girls often lived with their American boyfriends. It was considered quite immoral and fast then.

It was a marvellous sight to see these tanned, young men spilling out of the Embassy on to the pavements in Grosvenor Square in their smart uniforms. They spoke with accents that were different from ours and came from a country we only knew through movies and records.

Sunny had told me to take the Tube directly to Green Park and then take a taxi to her address. This was the first time I had ever ridden in a taxi cab. I was terrified she wouldn't be there to meet me or that I wouldn't have enough money to pay the bill: one and sixpence ... two shillings ... three and sixpence! Whew! Four shillings ... four and six ... five bob! My God! Four times as much as I'd ever spent on the Tube.

We arrived and I ran to the door to ring the bell. The cab driver waited with the engine running and watched me suspiciously. A top window opened at least three storeys up and a handsome, but definitely sleepy head, popped out of the window.

'Hi,' said the head. 'I'm Larry. Are you Shirley? Here's a fiver! Pay the driver.' A crumpled shirt came tumbling down with a whole fiver in the pocket. I asked the driver how much it was and paid him. Larry called out of the window, 'Don't forget the tip!' I asked the driver what would be a proper amount. He said:

'Half a dollar will do, kid, and don't go getting mixed up with any of these bleeding Yanks.' I nearly replied a 'bleeding Yank' was paying his cab fare and telling me to tip him, too!

In the house I was met by the owner of the dark, sleepy head. Larry was tall and about nineteen. He wore trousers, no shirt and bare feet. In a soft, American accent, he told me to follow him, and then he raced up three flights of stairs to a top floor flat. Sunny was at the top of the stairs, dressed in a long man's shirt. She looked much younger than the day before. She told Larry to make some tea and took me to a bedroom where there was a bed piled high with clothes. They were all for me, she said. I couldn't think how Sunny had organized all this. She had only left me the night before.

'Easy,' she said. 'I telephoned round all my friends, told them I'd found my baby sister, and asked them to drop something in for you.'

A lot of the clothes were not quite right but there was one beautiful blue coat with a plaid collar which used to be Sunny's that I loved immediately. I also picked off the bed a black and white checked jacket, one dark skirt and two pretty white blouses. The shoes she had were slightly big and a bit high for me to wear, so Sunny and Larry decided they would buy me two pairs of shoes that would fit, of any kind I liked. I never felt so excited in my life! They were as happy as I was. We made plans to go out to lunch at a place Sunny knew, then we would do our shopping and finally we would go to a movie and a show.

We had our tea and toast and I dressed in my new clothes for lunch. I felt like a million dollars going out with my sister and her boyfriend, Larry. Sunny's delight made me feel loved, especially after feeling so hurt when Gypsy had made it clear she didn't want to be seen with me. I told Sunny about a visit to my father's house. How he had asked Gypsy to 'give me a hair-do'. As the fashion then was to have curly hair, the way Gypsy had hers, my father felt I should have the same. As she worked on my hair her hands slipped and she'd burnt my neck with the curling tongs. Sunny was furious when she heard this. When she saw the mark she said that it was no accident.

Sunny lived her life at a fast gallop and, a loud decibel level. But now she spoke gently and seriously, telling me I didn't have to take any flak from Gypsy or Dad. 'Shirley Pops, all you need are clothes that fit you and don't drown you. Besides, that old boiler would love your hair. Take no notice of her.' Her irreverent attitude delighted me.

Off we went for lunch to Piccadilly Circus to a pub called *The White Bear*. As we walked down the stairs, we could see the place teeming with handsome young servicemen and fabulous looking girls. Strangely, except for the bartender, there wasn't an Englishman in sight. The place suddenly became deadly quiet and everybody's eyes swivelled to the top of the stairs as we walked down them in what seemed to be complete silence.

'Is this your baby sister??!' the crowd yelled at Sunny. The place erupted as we got to the bottom of the stairs. We found ourselves surrounded by people, all shouting and wolf-whistling. 'Some baby!' shouted a tall sailor who picked me up and sat me on a high barstool. I didn't know what to order, so Sunny ordered for me: a gin and orange. But I didn't need the drink. The atmosphere of the crowd was intoxicating enough as I watched the party swirl around me.

I was just fifteen and really too young to have a serious romance, but nevertheless I was a great hit with this crowd. Sunny was protective. She tried her best to steer my eyes away from the more adult liaisons that were being made.

It was such a good feeling just being with my sister. It was as if I had my whole family back again. I sat on my barstool and felt a tightness inside. This was the best day of my life and I didn't want it to end. Larry said something quietly to Sunny and we left in a quick flurry of goodbyes just before afternoon closing time.

We went by taxi to Leicester Square, where we saw a film and a live show with chorus girls. Had I been told that six years later my name would be blazing in lights in front of the very same cinema I would never have believed it.

When they took me back to the hostel, Sunny gave me a five pound note and we stood hugging and rocking together as we had the night before. Then Sister Mabel came to the door and called me in.

When I was twelve, Sunny had introduced me to an older American man. He was quite different from anyone I have ever known. I think I was a fairly normal twelve-year-old, although I hadn't had a conventional family. Living without parents became a way of life; I knew it was different from some other children but that was the way it was. Though I had no idea at the time, this man, forty-odd years older than myself, was to play an important role in my future. Victor was a retired American Marines general, a much decorated hero of two world wars, now on 'inactive duty', as he liked to call it.

I was first introduced to Victor by Sunny on one of my weekend passes granted so I could visit my brother in the sanatorium. Sunny had known Victor for some time as a sort of father figure and benefactor. He didn't pay much attention to me the first time I met him. He was my sister's friend.

Three years later, when I next met Victor, his reaction to me was quite different. I was in London living in a National Children's Home hostel training as a shorthand typist and going to school part-time. Victor was very attentive now and would talk at length on any topic I wanted to discuss. He would compliment me as well – something I wasn't used to. During my lunch breaks I would take the bus to his flat at Marble Arch for coffee and a sandwich.

It was a completely new experience to be with someone who gave me their undivided attention. Sunny would try to be there at lunch times but, if I was invited there in the evenings, she would make absolutely certain she was. If we were asked to stay the night, she insisted we slept in Victor's very comfortable bedroom whilst he was assigned his rather more spartan sitting room.

When I first began visiting Victor he was in his mid-fifties. He was slim with a disciplined manner and a charming and appealing personality. Going to his flat was like entering a new and different world. He had magazines like *Nineteen*, *Silver Screen*, *Motion Picture Stars*, *Seventeen* and *Ebony*. I loved reading them because many of them were American and spoke of a world that seemed rich and glamorous. He would make his visitors instant coffee with Carnation milk – not ordinary milk. There was a feeling of specialness, it was like a sanctuary from the outside world. Victor would give advice, only when asked, on the problems of everyday life. We could take our time, bathe as often as we liked, try out new makeup, change our clothes and just generally relax and do nothing but enjoy ourselves. He was genuinely interested in all his young friends. After going through two world wars and having seen brutality and violence at its worst, I think he probably wanted to be surrounded by just the opposite of what had been his life.

'I've seen enough of man to last me a lifetime,' he would often say. He was kind and generous with his time, there was always a welcome, good food, freedom to just be and he would give modest pocket money, 'mad money' was his name for it. No wonder he was so popular!

About once a month he would give smart dinner parties for some of his fellow officers. There would be chilli con carne and other good food, and they were a lot of fun. His collection of waifs and strays would be mixed with these correct military men and their wives, and the effect was rather like combining oil and water. It was fun to be around these adults and see their reactions. With our clicking high heels, lace transparent blouses, hooped skirts and working-class accents, we were nothing like the other guests. This was a very attractive up-to-date fashion for us but to many of the guests it obviously wasn't. The more Victor became enchanted with his teenage friends, the more his contemporaries began to drift away.

Most of Victor's friends were sweet kids. One was Suzanne Steele, who was training to be an opera singer and later received an OBE. To make money for her tuition she'd clean restaurants. If she had a boyfriend she wouldn't go and see Victor. But, if she hadn't, she would spend time there. Suzanne was just one of many.

Conventional moralists would not have approved of Victor. To the parents and guardians of the young girls who knew him, most of whom were from poor backgrounds, he was a dashing figure, a man of style, rank and money. In fact, he was all of these things and more. But I wonder what they would have thought if they had known the real extent of Victor's friendships. He adored teenage girls and wanted to instruct them in the ways of the world – which he most certainly did!

One of the first things he said to me at the tender age of fifteen was, 'Honey, I've got a piece of advice for you: re-member, all men are bastards. Now what did I say?' And he would make me repeat this. 'Don't smoke, don't drink, and remember, all men are bastards.' Victor enjoyed the role of mentor and teacher to most of the young friends who came into his life.

He lived in a block of flats called Park West, near Marble Arch. It had eight separate entrances and exits and sometimes I would see another girl leaving by one door as I arrived at another. By our adolescent standards, it was a very comfortable flat. There was a kitchen, bathroom, a bedroom with large twin beds and a sitting room. It was what would now be called a 'service apartment' with maid service every day. The maid was Winnie, a homely-looking middle-aged woman who was probably rather astounded, but nevertheless tolerant, of all these young girls coming and going. She affectionately called Victor the General.

Victor was an outrageous success with most of us. But he never demanded favours. You were not obliged to share his bed though he would make it easy for you to do so. He would run a hot scented bath for you, then give you a robe and let you take an afternoon nap in his bedroom. Later, he'd awaken you and say, in a comforting way, 'Feel like a little loving, honey?' Some people might consider Victor a licentious old man; however, he was sensitive and he never resorted to coercion if he thought you too immature or fragile; he would still offer you a refuge but leave you alone.

Eventually, though, Victor became more and more addicted to his way of life. He gave the maid, Winnie, a 'leave of absence' because he said she interfered with his love life. He had begun to suspect that she was turning away his girlfriends. As a result his flat became shabbier and shabbier. Vacuuming became a second thought at best, as Victor would point out, just like Quentin Crisp observed some years later, after four years the dust couldn't get any worse. Newspapers and magazines would be piled high on the dining room table. When we sat down to eat, he would put a spotlessly clean white tablecloth over the mounds of paper. Then, when the plates were placed on top, they would all be at different levels as we ate our meal.

As time went on Victor started to become increasingly eccentric. His clothing was casual in the extreme. He wore what looked like large 'Baby-Gros' with large safety pins in them in place of buttons. It was really the strangest sight to see this retired American general walking around in what looked like outsize baby clothes. He occasionally wore transparent pale blue shorts around his flat. I remember pointing out at the time how inadequate they were, but Victor would say, 'Honey, I've got to be comfortable at home.'

Despite his unusual lifestyle, Victor could be serious about life. He had a superb financial mind and, at one stage, was running a small stock market investment company in America. He made me save money with him as well as investing it for me. He was also extremely thrifty with his money. For doorstops he used cans of peaches or Campbell's tomato soup. When he wasn't entertaining, he always seemed to be doing his income tax. The funny thing about him was that he wouldn't go out and pay for a good dinner at a plush restaurant but would spend any amount of money to buy a beautiful dress for a special occasion. He really enjoyed this, especially if it would help me in my work.

Once a week he would take me to the American Embassy. He refused to eat in the officers' mess because he couldn't bear the time that was spent on the rituals of separate courses and wine service. What he loved was standing in the basement of the Embassy among the non-ranking servicemen with a tray and eating this quite dreadful food for around two pounds – that, to Victor, was time well spent and the modest price with no frills delighted him.

As the years went on his eccentricity became more and more exaggerated. Twenty years later I took a boyfriend with my daughter to visit Victor's flat. He was stunned because the place was filled halfway up to the ceiling with old papers. His collection of newspapers and publications was accumulating rapidly and he literally threw nothing away. It was impossible to walk in a straight line from one end of the room to the other.

At the time I had a Swedish au pair to help me with Nicola. Victor fell for the girl, who was about seventeen. She was not impressed by him but he still bought her gifts and paid for a trip to Sweden, so she could visit her family. Of course, I was afraid of losing her but Victor was so enchanted by her that he paid no attention to my concern.

One day I walked into Nicola's room to find that she had built a miniature village out of cardboard boxes and spread it across her bedroom floor. She was about four at the time and Victor would often invite her to visit for the day. When I asked her what she was doing she replied, 'I'm doing the same as Victor,

Mummy, with his newspapers and income tax.' I couldn't get into her room either for a year!

About once a month, Victor would take Nicola out for the day to give me a rest. He was well into his seventies by this time. I would drop her off at his flat and he would take her to the Embassy for lunch and then on to Marks & Spencer's. On her birthday and at Christmas and Easter he would give her an allowance of twenty pounds and let her buy things for herself, as long as she stayed within the limit. Whatever she had left over he would invest for her.

Victor was a kind and magnanimous man. I never had an objective perception of him because I met him when I was very young. To me, he was very much like the father you love and don't come to question until you are an adult. But even after I matured, I could still see that this man, for all his unconventional attitudes, had a real sense of dignity and strength. He never hurt anyone although he'd been a professional warrior all his working life.

In his last few years, Victor's lifestyle began to change. He was still entertaining into his eighties but his friends became somewhat different. I remember one girl had her front teeth missing, another had tattoos all up her arms. He was also becoming sloppy and forgetful. He'd put the electric kettle on the gas stove and practically burn the house down. The landlords of his apartment building were trying to harass him out of his home because they felt he was a nuisance. The flat directly above Victor became empty so the landlord would flood water into Victor's flat. The ceiling was leaking badly but Victor would just move a couple of piles of newspapers, put some buckets under the leak and calmly get on with his life. He guessed he was being got at but he didn't let it worry him.

As the situation in Victor's flat grew worse, myself and Peggy, another friend of his, became concerned about what was going to happen to him. His family was thousands of miles away in America and not able to help him from such a long distance. Peggy suggested I should give him a room in my flat, but I was very apprehensive, knowing the way Victor was, and how very reluctant he'd be to leave his home of thirty years. However, in the end, he had no choice, his landlord foreclosed on him so I asked him to move in with my daughter and myself. He really had nowhere else to go unless he went back to America, which he didn't want to do. Still a very proud man in his mid-eighties, his immediate reply was, 'It's too far away. My friends won't be able to come and see me so much.' We finally persuaded him and he moved in shortly afterwards. Soon his end of the house looked exactly like what he had left behind in Park West – complete chaos! The floor was covered with old vegetable boxes containing all his possessions.

To my surprise, he was resentful about being a house guest. He had never lived with anyone in his adult life and now he had to share someone else's home. This was a real blow to him. To Nicola, now twelve, he grumbled that his girlfriends wouldn't visit him any more because he no longer lived alone.

His appearance now began to resemble a tramp more than the well-groomed officer of years ago, but he was still fiercely independent. He now wore his 'Baby-gros' morning and night, the red set for a week or two, then the blue. He'd wear them on his daily walks, throwing his old First World War great coat over the top with his black Homburg hat topping it off. On a rainy day he'd come back wet and retire directly to his bed, letting his damp clothes dry on him as he slept.

Victor could sense that I was getting frustrated with him. He patiently tried to explain to me more than once that he couldn't help it. His lifestyle and his young girlfriends were a part of his life now. It was much too late to change.

On his long walks, Victor would often get stopped by the police because he couldn't remember how to get back to my house and would be wandering around the neighbourhood, lost. The policeman would ask him where he lived.

'I live with Shirley Anne Field.'

'Oh yeah? I bet you bloody do!' they'd reply. Then they would escort him back to my house, ring the doorbell and I would come down the stairs to get him.

Victor lived at my flat for the last four years of his life, but it wasn't until his final year that he really became de-lightful and joyful again as he had been when I first knew him. He started to bathe and dress in the mornings then he'd enjoy sitting back and talking about his long colourful life. He told me many of his old war stories, most of which were truly amazing.

'Honey, I don't need television. It's all here in my head,' he'd say. He also began to help out around the house.

This lovely period was not to last long. Three months before he died, Victor became seriously ill with leukaemia. This was humiliating for him. Here was a proud military hero who had always been independent. Now he was frail and sometimes incontinent.

When I'd first met Victor I'd depended on him in many ways. Now the situation was reversed. I was taking care of him and it became difficult for me. At the hospital they gave him vitamin shots and told me privately that he could recover if he wanted to. But, at ninety-ish, they added, he didn't seem to have the will to fight another battle. Victor resented the fact that I had taken him to the hospital at all, so I brought him back home for the last month of his life.

He would use the bathroom in the middle of the night, lose his balance and fall over. In the morning he'd have bruises everywhere and wouldn't say how he had got them. One night I heard an awful bang from down the hall but no call for help. I went to find out if he was all right. He had banged his head as he fell and was unconscious. I cleaned his head and got him back to bed.

In this last month of his life his family called often to find out about his condition. They knew of his seriously failing health but were also concerned about his financial arrangements and whether he had completed his income tax. When they arrived shortly after his death, they were most concerned that if he had failed to pay his tax, most of his money would be going to the Inland Revenue Service. The situation was sad. I think some of his family were afraid Peggy and myself were gold-diggers. His relatives did send money after his death to pay for his expenses when they'd seen for themselves how Victor's last years were spent.

In his final days, Victor's mental state kept changing. Sometimes he was perfectly lucid; at other times he was obviously off somewhere else. One minute he was telling one of his heroic war stories, the next he would be talking about his tax refund that year. In a sudden burst of activity he decided he wanted to give everything he had to Nicola and myself. But his head was too cloudy to make any rational decisions and thereby change his Will. To my knowledge, anyway, all he had were his possessions stored in the thirty eight vegetable boxes in his room. A friend removed the boxes for me to put them in storage and Victor reacted as though the crown jewels were in them. As we found out after his death, at the bottom of the very last box was his Will, which he had agonized over in the early seventies and which remained intact until his death in 1984.

The day he had fallen so badly, I took him to hospital to have his cut head looked at and that was the last straw for Victor. Three days later he died. It was a relief for Victor but, for me, it was my greatest loss.

As I sadly said goodbye to Victor, along with his cousin Mike, memories came flooding back. Sitting in that small, dark hospital room I remembered how when I met him I'd been the one who needed help and care, not him. I had been one of the first generation of the atomic age. We had made up our own code of behaviour on the spot. Living for the moment. Although we had codes of behaviour romantically, which might be considered coy now, later the restraints we practised would all be swept away by the discovery of one tiny pill! My own life was doubly confusing – living at the religious hostel during the week and visiting my sister at the weekends, whenever I was allowed.

On other weekends, when I stayed at the hostel, Sylvia and I would sneak out. The rules were to be in by ten-thirty and allowed to talk until midnight. A few nights we managed to climb down the drainpipe and go back to the dance hall we had just left. We stuffed our beds with pillows, hoping it would look like we were still there. You never knew when you could bend the rules. We had relief Sisters at the hostel who were filling in between their other appointments. Some were stricter than others. There were nights you would get into hot water for just missing the curfew by ten or fifteen minutes. Other times you could stay out all night and not even be missed. Unfortunately, the one time they did miss me they rang the police and I was picked up by two policewomen. I was taken to the police station where I spent most of the night. It was an awful experience being put into a cold cell by these two policewomen who searched me roughly and tipped out my handbag. I felt frightened and, to make matters worse, I thought I now had a record. Sadly for me, Sylvia wasn't with me that night. I had been invited out by a girl called Ricky who worked at the Children's Home during the day. She told me she'd show me the bright lights and said she knew all about them because she was training to be a burglar!

Sylvia and I loved going to dances most. It was expensive for us, seven and sixpence entrance fee, so we could only afford to go every two or three weeks. My favourite outfit was an off-the-shoulder white blouse with puffed sleeves and a black taffeta skirt. The Lyceum and the Hammersmith Palais were great big places where you could meet and dance until midnight. The men at these dances used to divide into groups of three. One group would be made up of American servicemen stationed in England, another would be well-dressed boys who were great dancers and a third group would be your everyday Englishman. What was interesting about the second group was that hardly any of them were there on Fridays. It was a long time before I found out why. I asked one of the boys I was dancing with where he and his friends were on Fridays. He told me he was Jewish. It was the first time I'd met anyone of a different faith, except Nurse Eva at the baby home.

A big silver globe in the middle of the dance hall would spin around when they dimmed the lights and make rainbows and coloured shadows on us. As we danced, Oscar Rabin and his band, Joe Loss and his orchestra would play Big Band music. It was a magical time.

At one of these dances I met Tex, a young, handsome American about two years older than I was. As our romance progressed, I hoped that Tex would be my first real relationship. By now, I was desperate to find out about romance. What was it that everybody kept banging on about? Our good-night kisses became longer and longer, but I still held back. I had been taught rigid codes of behaviour, as had most girls, which would dictate how far you could let a boy go. Of course, I didn't know how I would feel myself. My feelings amazed me. Until I met Tex, it had not been hard to stop whenever I wanted to. With him it wasn't so easy.

Two Americans we met at the Lyceum one night told Sylvia and me they were looking for the servicemen's Coronation Queen of Great Britain. One bloke called Ed submitted my picture and arranged for me to go to their base outside London for the competition.

A couple of weeks later we went. We arrived late and I had to put my evening dress on in the ladies' room. We saw about twenty girls already in the parade, walking round in a circle. Ed pinned on my corsage, Sylvia grabbed my number, stuck it on and Ed shoved me into the parade. All of us got a terrific reception. The panel of judges told us to relax and enjoy ourselves – they would give us the results in a little while.

Ed and I started to jive, and Sylvia and her boyfriend joined us. Just before supper they said they would announce the winners. They began with the third-place winner. Sadly, it wasn't me. Second winner, a girl from Surrey. First prize, the huge sum of £250, plus free travel to any American air force base in Great Britain . . . the name was read out – it was mine! Sylvia, Ed, Joe and myself all hugged each other. It was the most money I'd ever had in my whole life. The judges asked me what I was going to do with it. I told them I was going to pay to go to drama school, and this pleased them immensely.

As the American servicemen's Coronation Queen, I was invited to all the American bases in England to visit whenever there was a dance or a special occasion. It was a great privilege, not to mention a lot of fun to get so much attention and be presented to the servicemen. Only certain people had passes to the bases, which, in their own way, were like small American towns to me. This glamorous world was far away from anything I had ever known.

It was a wonderful year for me. They were the most generous, hospitable people, and I made many friends. The money became my nest egg, and I put most of it in the post office, except for £50 Sylvia and I shared.

Naturally I didn't tell any of the authorities at the hostel what I was doing. If I was travelling to an American Air Force base, it was always at the weekends. I'd already been granted permission to stay at Victor's flat two weekends a month – my after-care officers trusted him because he was a General. Later, when Sunny and Larry moved to a house in Maida Vale, I met two older women who lived on the top floor of their house. When Sunny and Larry went out on a Saturday night, these two women would look after me.

Maggie and Frances were much older than Sunny. Most evenings they would leave the house dressed up to the nines and wearing full stage makeup. Maggie had raven-black hair and wore a low-cut white blouse and tight black skirt which made her look like Margaret Lockwood. Frances, with her long chestnut hair and fair skin, could have been pretty except for her missing front teeth. How great, I thought, to be able to go out most nights all dressed up in full party clothes!

One day Maggie sat me down and told me she was 'on the game'. She said she hated her life and had been trying to change it for years. She said she wasn't young enough for the Americans, like Sunny.

'Do you mean Sunny and her friends are doing the same?' I asked.

'No, it's very different for them,' she said. 'They have boy-friends they like who take care of them. Frances and I aren't that lucky. We've been at this for a long time. It's not like the war when everybody was stationed here and had money to burn. That's how I got into this game. Now I want to get out.'

Frances was different. She was older than Maggie, perhaps around forty. She wasn't so ambitious and I think she had children she'd left behind in Ireland. Her aim was to get away from London and go back to live a straight life. She attended Mass every Sunday. The rest of the time she was out looking for friendly providers.

I was fascinated by the two of them. Sunny didn't know I was finding out about their lives. If she had, she would have been furious. She had given me the impression that they both worked in a bar or pub, working the late evening shift. They were both protective of me. Maggie would stay at home if Sunny went out with Larry without me. Sometimes I'd go upstairs and listen to Maggie's radio with her and we would sit and watch her old black-and-white telly. It was cosy and comfortable, much better than being downstairs on my own. Maggie would get sozzled on gin and tonic and tell me all about herself and how she intended to give up her fast life. Her dream was to have a pub of her own in the country, and I told her I would help her when I made some money. She was the first person I told of my dream to become a film actress, apart from Sylvia.

Sylvia was about a year and a half older than myself, and was more self-assured. Though she lived in the hostel, she had spent more of her childhood with her own family. I think she was better adjusted and had more confidence than most of us, since she hadn't grown up in a Home. In the beginning, she was the one who spurred me on towards presenting myself professionally.

We used to read all the fluffy magazines like *Reveille*, *Blighty* or *Weekend Mail*. There would be articles about girls not much older than us who were highly paid models. It looked to us like a very glamorous and well-paid life. What caught our eye was an ad by a photographer. 'Would you like to be a model like the girls in this magazine?' I answered the advertisement and arranged a meeting with the photographer.

CHAPTER THREE

It was marvellous to have the first photograph of me to be published bring such good fortune. It was like my dreams coming true when my Uncle George came forward and offered me a home with his family. He had traced me after seeing my picture in the newspaper. What a joy it was to meet my Uncle!

It was the first time I had met him, and he had only seen me as a baby. I was delighted when he asked me to Bournemouth to live with him and his family. Mr Powell, one of the Methodist ministers from the office, had already asked me if I would like to live with *his* family. They were good people, and kind, but I was afraid of not living up to their high standards. But, now with Uncle George appearing, I could tactfully say No to Mr and Mrs Powell's kind invitation. Even though they had two small boys who I really loved, I felt I couldn't face any more restrictions. I was longing for my freedom. I think Mr and Mrs Powell must have been hurt by my decision, but Uncle George's offer was too good an opportunity to miss to find out about my own family. Maybe now I'd have a chance to understand what had really happened.

I hadn't learned much about my early years from my father or Gypsy on my few visits to their home. He couldn't tell me about my mother or why she had left. Gypsy, on the other hand, seemed guarded. I mostly felt in the way. So my father and I would go to the local pub. After a few drinks he would play the piano, sing all the old songs, then ask me how would I like to be his housekeeper. I knew it was only a dream, as his second family would never have allowed it, and I had dreams too which had nothing to do with housekeeping just yet. With Uncle George it was different. He offered me a real home. It was hard to resist.

I went to join my uncle's family, my Auntie Lily, my cousin Alan and my aunt's niece Rita, in Bournemouth, but it wasn't as I'd imagined it would be. I wasn't used to living in a small, intimate family and at first I felt like an intruder. My uncle adored his wife, Lily. She ran the house on her own since his job as a long-distance coach driver kept him away quite a lot. Auntie Lily had grown up in the East End and worked hard to make a new start for her own family. I tried hard to please her and make myself helpful: I'd hoover the flat, dust and polish where I could, and peel the potatoes to be ready for dinner when the family came back from work. Auntie Lily worked too; she was fair but firm that if I stayed in her home I must be employed. I think, if she accepted me, she wanted a young woman who could earn her living rather than a teenager she would have to take care of.

Having trained for office work, I found a job in town in a small company owned by an oldish man named Mr Berry. He made it clear that he was personally giving me a chance. He was about sixty, walked with a limp and had a strange manner. His wife and daughter worked there as well but whenever they weren't around, he would casually brush against me. I'd move sideways to avoid this. Somehow, wherever I'd move, he'd be there.

'Now look, we know you've been in care,' he'd say innocently, brushing his hand across my shoulders. I used to think I had imagined it. I was too young to know if he was showing me real affection or if he was merely being familiar, but I did notice that he kept his distance when his wife or daughter were in the room.

Mrs Berry was a nervous woman who put me on edge. I can't claim I was a brilliant shorthand typist, but I was hopeless with her breathing down my neck and watching my every mistake.

The situation at home was not going well either. I kept trying to fit in, but I still didn't feel right. Communicating with Rita was difficult, and it didn't make it any easier sleeping in the same room and never getting away from each other. My uncle was marvellous, but I wasn't sure if Auntie Lily really liked me. Now, with Mrs Berry complaining about my work, life in Bournemouth was proving difficult. The more Mrs Berry fussed, the worse I got.

Things came to a head very quickly and, after a month, they decided to get rid of me. It was a relief in one sense, as I knew I wouldn't have to avoid Mr Berry any more. But I needed the money. Out of the two pounds five shillings I earned weekly, I gave one pound ten shillings to my aunt. What was I going to do now? Later that day Mr Berry came to me.

'I feel very badly about your leaving. You're not a bad kid and the reason you're being sacked is because my wife knows I have a soft spot for you. But, as you know, I'm not an ogre.' If I hadn't been so tearful I might have told him what I really thought. What followed took me by surprise. 'If you'll meet me privately, I'll give you two months' money so you will have something to live on and I won't feel so badly about you getting the sack?' This was an enormous amount of money to me.

On Monday morning I left for work as if nothing had changed. I was ashamed that I had lost my job and couldn't tell my aunt or uncle. I went into Bournemouth and wandered about the town feeling terrible. Then, when I knew everybody was sure to be out, I went back to the house.

A couple of days later, after a phone call from Mr Berry, I went to meet him. It was late afternoon as I ran down the back alley to his office. At the top of the stairs, a thin, gnarled arm came out and grabbed me. I was so frightened by this that I was almost relieved to find that it was only Mr Berry. He looked different from when I had last seen him. His face was red and mottled and his thin, grey hair stuck to his head. It looked like he had been perspiring and I could smell drink on his breath. He moved close and made to embrace me. I stepped back, feeling sick, and ran as fast as I could down the alleyway to hear his voice screaming after me, 'If you don't come back here straight away I'm going to tell everybody what a slut you are!' I didn't know what he meant, but by now I was halfway down the alleyway. I raced towards the bus.

I didn't sleep at all that night. I wanted to be alone, but the loo was the one place I could go to cry which made Auntie Lily think I was ill. I didn't know what to do. Mr Berry *hadn't* given me the money he had promised me and sooner or later I would have to tell the truth. It would have to be later, I decided. I had been crying most of the night, keeping Rita awake with my tossing and turning. It was an awful feeling when I went back into Bournemouth the next day, again pretending I was going to work. I hoped no-one would recognize me who knew my aunt and uncle.

I wasn't home more than an hour when Mr Berry telephoned. He said he was sorry for his behaviour the previous night and would give me the money he had promised if I would come and meet him again. I needed the money, because I didn't think Auntie Lily would let me stay unless I could pay my way. Reluctantly, I agreed to meet him.

I ran back through the alleyway and up the stairs once more. He was waiting at the door. I wondered how he knew it was me.

'I recognized you by the sound of your footsteps,' he said as he walked back into the office and offered me a sherry. I took the drink, but only sipped it. He must have seen my nervousness. As he spoke he moved very close and I could see the gleam in his eye again. I was horrified when he tried to kiss me. I turned to one side but he managed to kiss my neck. Before I could catch my breath he did something that caught me off guard. He moved very close to me and started to hug me tightly. This only made me feel sick again. He started fiddling with the belt of his trousers, then all at once he gripped me very tightly and whispered hoarsely in my ear. As suddenly as he started, he was calm again. I couldn't believe it. As if nothing had happened, he poured another sherry and said how much he'd like to take me out to dinner, but that it was impossible since he and his wife were both so well known in the town. A few minutes later he went to his desk and pulled out an envelope. It contained thirty pounds – a fortune! I took the envelope and prepared to leave. Mr Berry put his hand on my shoulder and said:

'Why don't you sit down quietly, child.' I was just dying to get out of there. The last thing I wanted was him fumbling with me again and breathing in that horrid way. Though the sick feeling persisted, I managed to sit down and be reasonably polite to him.

'You know, Mr Berry, you shouldn't be out too late because your wife will wonder where you are. I don't think you should worry her like that.'

For some reason, this thrilled him. 'What a charming little girl you are. Thank you for being so considerate.' He gave me an extra fiver saying, 'This is nothing to do with your wages, this is a present from me. Even though you think Mrs Berry is a bad fairy, we both agreed on this thirty pounds for you.' I wondered if she could have guessed the way he was to give it to me.

At that age, the only men I had really known had been older authoritative figures. So, I assumed everything they said was right. With Mr Berry, I felt pushed into a situation I couldn't control. I'd never dealt with someone like him before. I hoped I never would again. It's almost funny, but sad too, to think how helpless I felt.

That evening Uncle George was at home and I was faced with several problems. Where could I hide the thirty pounds? It was burning a big hole in my handbag. Was there a place I could put it without Rita finding it? And how was I going to tell Uncle George about the money? I had a lot of respect for him and I didn't want to lie. As the evening ticked on, he seemed to be staring at me. He could see I was in some kind of distress. I hoped he wouldn't ask about the job.

'Is there anything you want to tell me?' he asked quietly.

I said, no, but that sometimes I just felt different from every-body else.

'It's not that you're so different, it's just that you're not used to us all. It's going to be all right.'

I slept a bit better that night and the next day a wonderful new guest arrived at the house, Rita's mother. My Auntie Olive had been considered the rebel of her family. She was easy to talk to and I liked her immediately. She was warm and friendly and the whole house seemed to relax the moment she arrived. Auntie Lily's sense of humour surfaced. I hadn't realized how witty she could be. It was nice to see Rita relaxing too. That evening, the atmosphere was funny and happy.

Later, Olive came into the bedroom and sat down beside me. 'You're not happy here are you, Shirley?' she asked. I told her it wasn't that. It was just that jobs were hard to get. I blurted out the story of my predicament with Mr Berry, skirting around the more awful details. After taking his money, I felt obligated to keep quiet about him. My aunt might think badly of me if I told her what had really happened.

After the weekend Olive surprised me by offering to take me back to London. With all that had been going on I felt a sense of relief. I knew Uncle George wanted me to stay. Auntie Lily amazed me by making me a lovely dress in just two days so I'd have something smart to wear for job hunting in London. My uncle quietly gave me five pounds.

I hadn't been able to find out much about my mother after all. My aunt and uncle had made only slight references to a 'fun person who had a romance with an American'. This only made me more curious to find out the truth. But I was heading back to London and, after retrieving the thirty pounds from under the wardrobe, I was off.

London didn't seem so overwhelming now. Maybe I had matured in the few months I had been away. Sylvia was the first to hear from me. We found two furnished rooms in Maida Vale. My share of the rent turned out to be the same amount I had paid Auntie Lily. For a few pounds we shared one large bedroom, a kitchen-cum-sitting-room and had the use of a communal bathroom along the hall with a bath that required a shilling each time we used it. Sparse accommodation, but it was ours.

One afternoon we went to Battersea funfair, a place full of amusement arcades and side shows. We saw a sign hanging up that read 'Attractive Girl Wanted. Mustn't be too large or too tall. Good wages for the right girl'. So I knocked on the door. The magician inside wore a yellow satin waistcoat with a combination of brown flowers and stains on the front and combed his hair forward from a parting far back on his head. He said he wanted an assistant and gave me a horrid looking, filthy costume to try on. If it fitted, I could have the job.

For two weeks I was his assistant and wore the awful costume and climbed into a coffin-shaped cupboard three times a day before being made to 'disappear' – Now you see her ... and now you don't! I squeezed in at the back, behind a little shelf so the audience wouldn't see me. He'd spin it around for the onlookers, which made me feel sick and dizzy. On top of that, I started to feel claustrophobic and, after about six days, I'd had enough. In the middle of the performance I banged on the lid and screamed for him to open up. He was furious and sacked me on the spot. I never saw the twenty-five pounds' salary he had promised either.

In tears, I went next door to what was called the 'small people's tent'. Their troupe had about thirty people in it, all very small. As they sat in dimly-lit little alcoves wearing period costumes, people trooped through to watch them on the other side of a partition. I think they were playing *Snow White* that week. I sat there sobbing my heart out while several sympathetic small people comforted me. Just then the man who ran their show stormed in and said, 'Who's that big, bloody girl in there?' He was just about to chuck me out when he noticed several tourists watching us.

'Isn't that sweet, that's Alice in Wonderland sitting talking to the dwarves,' they remarked. 'She must have tumbled through the looking glass.'

Suddenly I was no longer an intruder: I could be a viable money-spinner. He said he would pay me to play Alice! Our stage was set up as a tea party, one small person played the Mad Hatter, another was the White Rabbit and I, feeling big and clumsy, was Alice. I had several lovely weeks there and made some good friends.

But I still needed a steady income. Ironically, Mr and Mrs Berry had written a glowing reference and soon I got a job as a shorthand typist with the Gas Council. Sylvia had a similar job and was pleased that I was able to find work so quickly.

My ambition was still to be an actress, but I knew I needed some tuition, so I found the Aida Foster Theatrical School in Golders Green and joined the dancing class. It wasn't an experience I enjoyed because I felt like a fool. Most of the girls there could already tap dance and would sit or stand around in the cloakroom before or after the class, talking about their various possessions, gossiping about their boyfriends or showing each other their wonderful new clothes. Some of them had long, red finger nails and I was a very bad nail biter. I'd spend most of the class trying to hide my hands which doesn't help when you're dancing – you're constantly off balance.

A few girls came with at least three costumes to each class. Some of them had special shoes and tights, and little twinkly jackets that looked like they were straight out of a film. I felt awkward and shabby with my one pair of keep-fit shoes, but when I enrolled that's what I was told was required. Most of them were a little older than me. It didn't feel like a beginner's class at all and, from being one of the best dancers at the Lyceum, now I just felt a complete novice.

When it got too much, I'd skip out with a girl I liked called Marianne. She was gentle and pretty and we'd go to the cinema instead. She's still somebody I like today. She also only had a few clothes. She was modest compared to some of the others, but actually worked more than any of us – even then, she had jobs in commercials and films. I got the impression she used her earnings to subsidize her family.

The principal, Mrs Foster, and her daughter were nice, but eventually I left because I was losing confidence. The teachers weren't helpful either. They didn't want a beginner aged fifteen when most of their pupils had been dancing from the age of four.

I had begun to spend time with boys whilst in Bournemouth, but didn't have my first steady boyfriend until I had returned to London. Two years before, at the hostel, I had met an outgoing young man named Jamie. He was a radio operator and we had been friends for some time. The only rather different aspect of our relationship was the age difference, his thirty to my seventeen. Sylvia wasn't faring any better. She was dating a boy who worked as a fairground attendant, so most of the time he was travelling!

After a few months at the Gas Council in Knightsbridge, someone in the office asked if I would pose for an advertisement for the company. It was an easy job in a photographer's studio sitting on the top of one of the company's gas cookers. They certainly weren't very glamorous pictures but, on the strength of them, it was suggested I make the rounds of photographers. Perhaps someone had suffered too much from my typing mistakes. Hoping to make a good impression, I dressed accordingly. The attention I got on my walk-arounds came as a pleasant shock. Sometimes lorry drivers would hoot their horns and shout compliments at me through the traffic. It was great to have approval. I had lived without praise until now, in fact had come not to expect any. It was an entirely new and pleasant feeling.

Through photographers I met on my 'go-sees', as visiting photographers was called, I heard about the Lucie Clayton School and Model Agency and went to see them. I met the director, Mr Leslie Kark, and his assistants, who told me they held a course for trainee models. If we finished the course, and got good marks, we could be taken on their books as models. The course cost something like £280 for six weeks. When I told Mr Kark I couldn't possibly afford that, he offered to let me take the course and pay them back as soon as I got my first job. I was delighted with that. It made me feel they believed in me. The only thing I needed now was a guardian's signature.

I thought of asking my father to sign but, at that time, he wasn't speaking to me. Whilst I was in Bournemouth I had sent him a letter adding as a PS to also give my love to Gypsy, 'if you wish'. She had read the letter and apparently been furious at being included only in a PS. A week later I received a nasty reply calling me everything from a 'cocky little brat' to the unprintable. Had I known it would poison the relationship with my dad for years to come, I would have avoided those three words. But it was done. The signature would have to come from the children's home and that would mean the modelling school knowing about my childhood.

Strangely, I was no longer the responsibility of the NCH. They had so many children in care that, once you left, it seemed the guardianship stopped. I was sad. Now I was really on my own. I missed them all and I hoped they missed me. As I faced the world, it felt very daunting. I wished Edgeworth was near so I could go back and see Sisters Annie and Winifred and some of the girls I had grown up with. Lancashire was a long way from London. Even the way they spoke was different. I wasn't sure where I belonged. I worked on sounding vaguely Cockney so I wouldn't feel the odd one out.

Mr Jacka was the principal after-care officer whose job it was to help young people from the NCH back into everyday society. He had already noted me as a troublemaker due to an incident that happened when I was fifteen. My boyfriend, Jamie, his friend Don and myself were playing around in the hostel grounds. I was wearing a pencil-slim, all-in-one wrap-around skirt with one button fastening at the top and when Don pulled the button, the whole skirt unwrapped, leaving me standing there embarrassed with my stocking tops and underwear showing. When it was reported to Mr Jacka, he told me in no uncertain terms that it was my fault for leading the boys on and for being provocative. I don't think he even reprimanded them. Still, there was always clumsy, loving Miss Gautry. She was only too happy to sign for me for Lucie Clayton's and stayed in touch with me for many years after.

My first day at Lucie Clayton's I met a completely different kind of person. Most of the girls wore fashionable clothes and shoes. They had designer named handbags, tastefully expensive watches and were the kind of girls who are very much at home in Knightsbridge. I felt odd with my inexpensive clothes and funny accent – and not paying for my tuition either. Luckily, one other girl and I hit it off. Just after the first roll call she came up and introduced herself. This funny, pretty girl was called Shirley too. She was warm and generous. She told me she was the daughter of a dry cleaner, neglecting to tell me her family owned the whole chain.

The school was a money-making enterprise training young women to become working models. It was proud of having trained Fiona Campbell-Walters, a very successful model who was also, so they informed us, connected with society. She was the most famous graduate of the school. There were thirty five girls taking the course with me. They or their parents seemed to regard it more as a fill-in or as a finishing school than a work preparation. We were taught social skills, makeup, keep-fit, how to give a dinner party and the proper way for a girl to get in and out of a car without showing her knickers. Mr Kark used to instruct us how not to get sweaty if one became hot. 'Low perspiration can be exciting sexually, but only in the right place,' he'd say, much to our amusement and amazement.

Now I found I could move in two different worlds – one with friends from my childhood and another with friends from elsewhere. I felt at home with both. It sometimes used to disappoint me that my closest friends didn't seem to get on with each other. Sylvia thought the idea of my working as a model was a silly, impractical thing to do. I wanted her to understand that I thought it was just a stepping stone to being an actress.

Before the end of the course, I was offered a job modelling English Rose bras. I was excited by this, now I could pay Mr Kark and his agency back. In a month's time I would see my photograph up and down the walls of the escalator in the tube stations. I'd had my picture taken for the Gas Council but this was different: I could see the results and I was pleased. Being the first one to get professional work gave me a good standing in the class. At an Edgeworth reunion two months later, it surprised me when I was ignored by some of my older friends who had seen my photograph on the escalators. They said it was wrong for me to do this kind of work.

As our course came to its end, there was a special 'passing out' parade, with an audience of sorts. We walked up and down a modelling catwalk in our best clothes, demonstrating what we'd learned in our two months of training. Shirley and I found that we both had the lowest marks!

Shirley went on to success after success. Besides creating new inroads in journalism with the most important newspapers, she wrote at least two bestsellers, *Superwoman* and *Lace*. She married Terence Conran and, when they had their first son, Sebastian, she asked me to take Terence out to dinner and keep him calm while she was at the hospital in labour. We had a great evening, but I'm sure if it had been today we'd both have been at the hospital looking after her.

Despite my low marks, I was more confident now about tackling the photographic world. I felt good because I had a diploma from a bona fide modelling school which also represented me as an agent. I went round the photographer's studios once again. Just as I was getting very nervous that I might never find work, the phone rang. It was a photographer called Russell Gay.

'What size are you? What are your measurements?' I described myself and he asked me to come to his studio which was in Brixton, a fairly long bus ride away. When I got there, I found out the pictures were 'cheesecake' photos printed in magazines like *Spic and Span*. Lucie Clayton told me that this was not really their kind of work, but I could have their blessing if it would help me. It was rather like being a 'page three' girl today. But, of course, we were covered. Russell Gay paid cash at the end of every day which was a great incentive – two pounds an hour. It was very helpful to be paid straight away and not have to endure the usual six weeks for which most of the other photographers kept you waiting. Often I went home with ten pounds in my purse for the day's work. Over a week, that was three times as much as I made at the Gas Council!

Most of the 'cheesecake' photographers in England and Europe were copying the American photographers of that time. They would pose us in shorts and a halter top or a bra. The storylines featured in the magazines were unimaginative to say the least: two young girls on a picnic or out horse riding; a day's adventure at the fairground; an afternoon on the beach. They were average pictures at best, and not particularly flattering. I'd hoped my pictures would appear in magazines like *Vogue* or *Harpers*. Oh well, it was a start of a sort.

One or two of the photographers also ran a club for amateur photographers who would pay to photograph us. We would get our usual fee of two pounds an hour while the photographer was making at least three pounds each from everybody who came in to photograph us. One of the girls I met at this time was called Sabrina, who later became famous on television with Arthur Askey. There was a similar club in Soho Square called the Visual Arts, a kind of bohemian place where we were also paid to be photographed. Some of the photographers were genuinely interested in photography, and some were only interested in the girls.

It was in Soho that I first went to Le Grande. This little café was run by two wonderful French women who had kept their restaurant going all through the war. Isabelle and Jeanne would tell us what it had been like, how they would close the café when the bombs fell, sitting under the tables and singing songs in French and English with their customers until the raid was over. It sounded great to me but, of course, like most of my generation, we were living through great times of our own.

Le Grande was a meeting place where would-be actors, models, stunt men, special girls, extras, and others starting out in the entertainment business would gather, make plans or just make friends. So many of us who would be established a decade later went there. Sean Connery was one of the customers, as were many more. Later, Sean became a dear friend. He would drop by before his evening's work in the chorus of *South Pacific*. You could sit all day for the price of a coffee and Isabelle or Jeanne would slip you the odd Danish pastry if you were hungry and couldn't afford to eat. It was our place in London. I wonder how many they fed over the years. Most of us who did have some success later went back and hopefully took them a present as a thank you for help in tougher times. They were wonderful.

Among the many young and hopeful people I met there were Tony Newley and Harry Fowler, and a lovely young man called Johnny Charlesworth. They were all a few years older than me and, except for Johnny, seemed sophisticated. Tony was attractive and funny, with engaging eyes and curly hair. He had already gained respect for his performance as the Artful Dodger in David Lean's film of *Oliver Twist*. Harry was a great Cockney charmer, a flirt who talked non-stop and made one laugh all the time. They could have been a double act, as they complemented each other perfectly. Johnny wasn't tall, but was shapely in a masculine sort of way. He had red-gold hair and a pale, handsome, sensitive face. I found him very appealing. His quietness compared to the rest of the group made me always want to cuddle him. Often with them was their close friend Steve, a man who strangely enough had no aspirations towards the film industry. He earned his living as a blouse salesman.

After a few months of meeting for coffee, we all got into the habit of going back to Harry's house at teatime where he and his wife Joan would make us thick slices of toast. I thought Joan was wonderful. I'd seen her in *Room at the Inn* and was impressed with her acting, as were many others. She was tiny, blonde and pretty in a fragile kind of way. I liked her very much and think she felt the same.

Eventually our group consisted of about eight regular friends. One of the girls was called Ann Lynn, who I would later work with in a stage musical. She was Tony's close girlfriend at the time. Sometimes, if we stayed later, Harry would dash round to the local fish shop for fish and chips and bring it back in newspapers. We'd all sit around in a circle and eat ravenously. Once or twice we'd play 'truth' games that would lead into other things. The atmosphere could become quite sensuous. We were mostly young and curious to find out how the adult world really operated. As a rule it was fairly even, about four men and four girls. Harry often got outrageous and made jokes about short men being the best equipped. Without much encouragement, he would try and show us what he meant. This only made us laugh, and it certainly got the party going and got rid of a lot of our inhibitions. Sometimes we would sit around in various states of undress just to look at each other. For all the heady atmosphere, it was still relatively innocent.

Sitting around eating our fish and chips, laughing with my friends at Harry's antics, would have seemed unthinkable just two years before. It was great having all this attention and sweetness from the others. It made me feel wanted. But underneath my bravado, I didn't feel good about myself. I loved the compliments but, if they stopped, I found I still lacked confidence. I didn't know it then, but I really had poor self-esteem. Why would I have any? I hadn't been taught it. Most people had automatically learned it from their families. My picture occasionally appeared in the newspapers, sometimes on the covers, and people had started to recognize me. This boosted my morale, but it never lasted. I was still Shirley Broomfield underneath.

As we talked I learned that Tony, and probably Johnny, had a background just as chaotic as my own. I think Tony only had a mother at that time, and I remember thinking I understood some of his feelings. I knew what it felt like. Sometimes I thought Johnny and Tony understood me as well. They seemed to know I was frightened of anything that went too far, and managed to keep the evenings from getting too out of hand. If we had a quiet moment at these get-togethers Tony would say gently, 'What's a matter, Shirl, don't you like us all then?' I assured him that I did. 'Oh, I know then, you're frightened of men.' It was true I wasn't very used to them. I'd only met three men while I was growing up in the Home: the Governor, the choir master and the cobbler. Tony was another waif and stray, so maybe that's why he could identify. He had a wonderful way of helping one's confidence along. Several years later, he was starring in a television show produced by Lew Grade and he suggested I appear in it with him. He encouraged me to dance and sing in one number.

'Oh, you've won that, love,' he said after the show. I didn't see it as a competition, but that was Tony's way of saying I was all right.

Work continued on and off with various photographers until a movie director named Val Guest noticed a pin-up photo of me in *Reveille* and rang up Bill Watts. Bill had been a small part player and now he ran his own agency called the Bill Watts Agency for Special Young Ladies. When a production needed a pretty girl for a scene, he would get a call and send one or two of his girls along. Bill Watts was a nice person and so was his wife, Cherry, who helped him run the office in Dover Street. They cared very much about their 'Special Young Ladies' and made us all feel like one big, happy family. Although I often barely made ends meet, at least I now had a legitimate theatre and film agent.

Moving into films was a break for me. I got out of photographic modelling at the right time. Usually I was asked to do more 'cheesecake' than anything else, which was the 'page three' girl equivalent of today. There was nowhere to go from there, except to do more 'cheesecake'. The pictures did help me to get work as a 'special' girl. A 'special' girl was a real misnomer. It meant that you were photogenic (and usually sat next to the star), wore next-to-nothing and were given one or two lines of dialogue, which I was so nervous about I often got wrong. I was one of the youngsters of the agency and, though the pay was low, got more than my share of work. Jackie and Mara Lane, Jill Ireland and Jackie Collins were with Bill Watts, as was Joan Collins, though she had just got a contract with 20th Century Fox when I started at the agency. There was little encouragement to refine our acting skills. In addition to the required glamour photo, a voice lesson might be suggested to get the correct 'pukka' accent that was so important in films in the fifties in England.

On my first day as a special girl, I got out of bed at four-thirty in the morning to catch the workman's bus to Pinewood Studios, a long way from where I lived, to arrive on the set for my first assignment and be in a line with twenty five other girls. The producer asked each of us to step forward and pull our dresses up to our thighs so he could check our legs. I froze when he came to me. My friend Jackie noticed my awkwardness and assured him my legs were OK, and he moved on down the line. There was this kind of camaraderie among the special girls. We knew we could be easily exploited and that gave us a stronger bond.

Ironically, in the picture I was picked for my legs weren't even seen. In the film, a comedy called *All for Mary*, I sat on a plane behind a copy of *Vogue* and lowered the magazine in order to wink at David Tomlinson. There were other small roles over the next few years; in *Dry Rot* I played a Cockney barmaid; in *Yield to the Night* I was leaning over a sofa to give an actor a kiss on the neck; in *Zarak* I sat at Anita Ekberg's feet and mouthed the lines to her to try and be of help. Michael Wilding starred in the film and one day it was very thrilling to see Elizabeth Taylor, his wife, arrive on the set in a full-length sable coat. That, it seemed to me, was true Hollywood glamour.

Seven Thunders was a forgettable film. I felt more like a movable set decoration than a budding actress. It was filmed at Shepperton Studios and, on the next sound stage, Richard Burton was filming *Sea Wife* with Joan Collins. He introduced himself to me and often asked me to the pub for lunch. Instead of the usual leading questions, all horribly familiar, Richard would ask me about my plans and acting ambitions. Sometimes he would quote Shakespeare or Dylan Thomas. His voice was beautiful and it sounded as though he were caressing one when he spoke. In other ways, he could also be macho and irreverent. I'd never met anyone like him before. After lunch one afternoon, Richard suggested I enrol in acting classes to develop my skills, and offered to pay for them. I only knew of the Royal Academy of Dramatic Art which I'd won a scholarship to attend three years earlier. Unfortunately, Mr Jacka from the NCH had informed me that another girl was 'more suitable for a theatrical life' than I was and the only other drama school I knew of was the Actor's Studio. I thought I'd missed my chance at acting school and here was Richard offering me another one.

Talking to Richard Burton probably did me more good than all those lessons. The school was a pale imitation of the Strasberg

School in New York, and full of rather limited types who had phoney American accents. Many of them had been sent for safety to America in the war and they'd returned with a way of speaking that was neither British nor American. I think some of them felt neither one thing nor the other.

In the film *The Silken Affair*, starring David Niven, I played a French maid. I was still getting up at dawn to catch the bus to work and returning at six in the evening, if I was lucky. It was a long day and, when the window rolled down on a passing Rolls Royce and the distinguished looking man inside offered me a lift, it was hard to say no. Mr Niven laughed when I said I was worried people might talk.

'I'm sorry, my dear, wouldn't dream of besmirching your reputation,' he said. Later that week, when it was pouring with rain, the Rolls Royce pulled up again. 'How do you feel about besmirching your reputation tonight, my dear?' Well it *was* raining, so I laughed and got in.

I continued to get lifts from him most days after that. A few weeks later a parcel with my name on it arrived on the set. Inside was a beautiful lace blouse with a card from David Niven:

'I hope this won't ruin your reputation any further,' it read.

I went to him and thanked him and, as I walked away, he said, 'One night, when you haven't an early call, would you care for a well-behaved dinner with me?'

A few nights later I went to dinner with him at Les Ambassadeurs, a very expensive, exclusive club. The membership was made up mostly of show business stars or society people. Now I knew why he had been so sweet and given me the blouse. Everybody was beautifully dressed and it was the only thing I possessed that was right. I felt a little shy among so many older, successful people, but David made me feel very comfortable. Halfway through the meal, an older man came over to the table. David introduced me to this old roommate, none other than Errol Flynn! He had been drinking rather a lot, his face was a little red, but he remained incredibly handsome and had impeccable manners. Unfortunately, it seemed he was going through a tough time and hadn't been getting much work.

Errol Flynn began to flirt with me, but David politely stopped him. 'Miss Field hasn't got time to waste. She has to be up early tomorrow for work. She's going great places.' It wasn't the last I saw of Errol Flynn, but I could never guess how we would meet again.

Two of my men friends at this time were Ronnie and Horace. Ronnie had been a help to me. He wrote a popular sitcom, and was a short, generous little man, who made it his business to befriend many of the special girls. He had found me a flat of my own in Hammersmith, as well as a job answering fan mail for a couple of famous entertainers called Jewel & Warris to supplement my income. Horace, a red-headed orthodox Jewish man, became a boyfriend, much to Ronnie's annoyance. I knew Ronnie wanted to be a boyfriend, too, but I only wanted friendship with him. Later, after he offered me an entire floor of his Mayfair house to live in he then sent Horace an anonymous letter telling him that I was 'living with another man'. It was an unhappy time for me. I felt miserable that Horace had been hurt as I cared about him a great deal. With these half-affairs and friendships, budding romances or unrequited loves, it felt like there was a whirlwind always around me.

A lot of my social life revolved around coffee houses like Le Grande. There was a flourishing coffee-house community in the late-fifties, probably a copy of the Greenwich Village cafés, and it was an ideal meeting place. You didn't have to drink, it was inexpensive, and the atmosphere was safe – a non-aggressive place to meet people. All of them had their own personalities. The Two Eyes in Soho was one place where the skiffle music trend began. Tommy Steele, who may have still been in the Merchant Navy, played there, as did Lonnie Donegan. It was in a coffee house in Park Lane, similar to Le Grande but more plush and grand, that I met Stephen Ward. I was sitting with a girlfriend when this charming gentleman came to our table and introduced himself.

'My name is Dr Stephen Ward and I would dearly love to paint you.' I was intrigued. He was of medium height, with light brownish hair, fine featured, handsome in a rather English way, and could have been anywhere from thirty to forty years old. I was busy playing hard-to-get, so he didn't make much headway, although I was utterly charmed. He asked casually if we had heard of Maureen Swanson. Of course we had. She was a small, slight girl who had a featured part in a Rank film called *Ill Met By Moonlight*. She was already working at what we were wanting to, so naturally we were curious. Stephen not only knew her, he said she was staying at his flat. He arranged to meet us in the coffee house the next day. In view of our budding careers, he told us that he would make sure we met the right kind of people. He said his love, Maureen, had just met Billy Edman through him. Stephen told us Billy would one day inherit a title. If Maureen could 'capture' him it would be a great help. I said I didn't see how this could help anybody's film career!

'Oh, sweet little thing,' Stephen replied. 'Influential friends can always help.'

The next evening we met him again and he took me to his house in Devonshire Mews for the first sitting to be painted. It was a medium-sized second-storey apartment in the fashionable medical district, somewhat shabby but very comfortable. He sat me in a window bay and began to draw. His patients kept ringing to make appointments. A girl dashed into the room wearing an evening gown, looking very excited, saying she was on her way out to dinner and a nightclub with Billy. He introduced her.

'This is my lovely Maureen,' he said. She and Stephen kissed passionately, then a car horn sounded and she was gone. Stephen told me how much he loved her, and that they'd been together two years. I felt sad for him.

I went on sitting for Stephen two or three afternoons a week, and we became good friends. Sometimes he would offer me a poached egg on toast instead of taking me out to dinner and the money he saved he gave me to buy a pair of stockings or perhaps sometimes new shoes. He never tried to take advantage, but he was affectionate and often asked me to stay the night. I wondered what Maureen, who was older and more sophisticated than I was, would say, to which Stephen would reply, 'She won't mind, my love. The more the merrier.' I was now growing very fond of him. I knew Stephen was one of the few men I could flirt with who wouldn't become cross if I didn't want it to go any further.

Sometime later he invited me to his cottage in the country at Cliveden. One weekend there I met up with a friend I already knew from the film studios. She was called Jeanne Baldwin, a dark-haired, attractive girl and a publicist with the Rank Organisation. She was Maureen's great friend and was staying at the cottage that weekend as well. It was in the grounds of a vast estate, which looked like Buckingham Palace to my eyes. One bedroom was for girls, but some mornings Stephen would tuck us all up in his own large bed, and bring us up breakfast on a tray.

Stephen's great dream was to launch all of us into society and land us a rich husband to boot. Another of his occasional visitors was Margaret Brown, a stunning red-haired model who later married Jule Styne.

Sometime during the weekend, Stephen took his whole house party over to the main house where we were invited for a formal dinner. There were a group of his friends at the house, most of whom dressed formally and talked as if they had plums in their mouths. No-one was anywhere near my age, nor were they interested in my work. They seemed to think I was marking time until something better turned up. Stephen could see I was bored and told me to pay attention and make an effort. He said it was no good showing I was bored if I was to be a success. I told him it was not my ambition to be part of this world, much to his amazement.

After dinner we swam in the pool wearing bikinis, while the other women guests from the main house wore swimsuits which looked more like one piece school suits. Afterwards, most of us went back to Stephen's little cottage and I noticed our own party seemed to have acquired a few extra people. One of them was a tall foppish man, called Billy, who said he was in shipping. He wanted to play 'nursery' games, his favourite being a version of Blind Man's Buff. It would involve tying him to a chair and shouting at him for being a naughty boy. I thought it was a silly game, and so did Jeanne, but Billy said he found it very exciting, especially when we turned out all the lights and left him sitting there! When I asked Stephen about his friend's funny ways he'd say:

'Well, little one, he's had too many nannies!' Fortunately, Billy was funny and charming, otherwise he would have really been foolish.

About this time I also met Anthony Crosland, who was a Member of Parliament. I was invited by a woman I met to a dinner party at her lovely house in Knightsbridge where she lived with her wealthy American husband. I was asked to be Anthony's dinner companion. I remember one of the other guests was Dr Eustace Chesser, who I think had just written *Love Without*

Fear, an early sex manual. The dinner conversation was about the book he'd recently finished.

Anthony and I formed a friendship that was to last several years. He was in the middle of a divorce. I was drawn to him, not only because he was witty and confident, but because he was committed politically. He told me of all the policies he wanted to instigate and, on some occasions, I went with him to his constituency in Grimsby. I didn't know the political world he came from and it fascinated me. Although I was very young and naive politically, he was never patronizing. One of the things we discussed was his desire to reform the British educational system from top to bottom. Anthony felt strongly that higher education shouldn't only be the right of people who could afford private schooling.

In the time I spent with Anthony, I realized that some politicians have, like other successful people, an extra edge of energy with more drive. He was passionate about everything, not just his political beliefs. It's no wonder some politicians are in the headlines for private reasons as well as public ones.

It was quite difficult to meet and keep the romantic part of our relationship going. My work schedule was frantic and Anthony's was twice as much. When he wasn't at the House of Commons, he'd be working at his 'political surgery' as he called it, looking after the needs of his constituents. Sometimes at dinner he'd be called back to Parliament to vote on an important issue.

Many years later I heard from Anthony, he was to marry again. His bride was Susan, the same person who had first introduced us.

My first long relationship was with a BBC announcer named John Fitchen, a man who came up to me at a first night saying, 'Oh, I have always thought you were lovely, but you look so tired tonight and I don't know if I want to ask you out.' Despite a tactless approach, which may have been a line, he proved to be a charming man and we had a romance on and off for about two years.

John had the right demeanour and that voice enabled him to fit in wherever he went. Physically, he was about the most exciting man I'd known until then. More importantly, he helped me overcome my fear of men. He had quite an influence on me. John seemed connected to everyone – not only film producers, but bankers and financiers, society people and foreign industrialists. Though he didn't have much money himself – later, after he lost his job with the BBC, he was to rely on me to pay many of the bills – John knew his way around people. He would take me to Les Ambassadeurs on the chance that well-heeled friends would be there to pay for the meal. One night we walked in and I noticed that everybody had put down their knives and forks to stare at us. As their silence carried us to our seats, I wondered what was wrong; had the heel of my shoes come off, was there a hole in my skirt? I knew I was younger than most people in the room, but I hadn't thought it mattered till then. We were escorted to our table by John Mills, the owner of the restaurant and, no sooner were we seated, than a television announcer called MacDonald Hobley came to the table and asked John who I was. On hearing my northern accent, he said he was surprised to find out that I wasn't an Italian princess!

John could be a debonair man but there was another side to him, one I hadn't realized and definitely not expected. The casual sexual get-togethers with Harry and Tony of a year earlier were really just a few kids fooling around. John's acquaintances were altogether more sophisticated. There was a circle of people John knew who referred to themselves as 'swingers'. They were a group of people from mostly moneyed backgrounds who wanted to have sexual parties. The open house Sunday lunch was usually the occasion that brought together these people – often young, beautiful girls with older, wealthier upper crust men. This was in the mid-fifties and would come to an abrupt end after the court case with Stephen Ward, Christine Keeler and Mandy Rice-Davies, which helped bring about the fall of the Conservative government in 1963. Stephen was not alive very long after that.

Some time earlier, when I had still been sharing the flat with Sylvia, something really awful had happened. I hadn't been feeling well and went to visit the local doctor in his surgery, a seedy office in West London. He asked several embarrassing questions until finally he asked, 'Could you possibly be pregnant?' I said I didn't know. I felt like running away and he sensed this.

'You'd better stay here, young lady, because if you are in trouble, I might be one of the only people able to help you.'

Then he examined me in a way that was both uncomfortable and painful. He said the procedure was necessary, all the while dropping cigarette ash over me and making personal remarks about my shape. 'Luckily for you, young lady, you're not in trouble this time. You're just putting on weight and outgrowing your strength.' I was relieved to hear that. But I still felt sick every day. I couldn't bear the smell of alcohol and, if there was any cigarette smoke around, I felt faint. For three weeks now I hadn't had a meal without vomiting. I was frightened to go back to the doctor because of the way he had been. I didn't know what to do or who I could go to for help.

In desperation I phoned my doctor friend, David, who was immediately helpful.

'Stop worrying and come and see me as soon as you can.'

When I saw him, the difference between the two doctors was like night and day. He was kind and gentle and didn't hurt me at all. Then he told me what I feared most. Not only was I pregnant, but I could be almost three months. He thought it was too late for a medical termination but said he'd do what he could to help. The first step was to take the pills he pre-scribed me, but they only gave me horrible cramps. I went back to him and this time he gave me a different treatment. I felt nothing for two or three hours and thought it wasn't going to work. Little did I know what I was in for. Suddenly I was in terrible pain that came in awful spasms, which went on and on. I crouched by the bed, stuffing the edge of the pillow in my mouth. This continued for two and a half days. I started praying that I would die and it would all be over. Would Sylvia ever get home?

I heard a loud banging at the door, and realized I must have passed out. 'Are you all right?' a voice called. It was Mr Baker from downstairs. If he knew what was happening, he might call the police. I could be put in jail, along with David. I cried out it was all right, I just had the 'flu. It seemed he stayed outside the door for ever. Another spasm came. Oh, God, please help me, I begged. All I had to help the pain was a bottle of aspirin and they were mostly gone. Finally Mr Baker went away and I made my way down the hall to the loo. I was retching, crying and having spasms all at the same time. I kept pulling the chain so no-one could hear me. Finally, I crawled into the kitchen to call Sylvia. 'Please, please come back with the pills David had prescribed,' I begged.

When I heard footsteps on the stairs I was still in the loo, afraid to open the door. Then I realized it was Sylvia. She was shocked and scared by the way I looked, but I was in such agony I didn't care. I took the painkillers she brought. Still the waves of nausea and bleeding continued. Sylvia turned up the radio so the Bakers wouldn't hear my moaning. Finally, when I couldn't bear it any more, she called David for me. He wasn't keen on coming, as he knew it could be dangerous. We were breaking the law. Four hours later, a nurse arrived who gave me stronger painkillers for the pain. It would be better, she told me, if I could have done without the pills, it would be over quicker if I kept moving. She made me pace about the room and, for the first time, I started to cry.

'That won't do any good,' she reprimanded. 'You're all alike, you young trollops.'

Sylvia said the nurse sounded just like the Sisters in the children's home, and that made me laugh so much I became hysterical. The nurse became a little worried, but thankfully the pains were slowing subsiding.

Mr Baker banged on the ceiling, and Sylvia screamed down that we were having a party! I thought I was beginning to feel a little better, then all of a sudden it started, worse than ever, waves of pain coming and going, coming and going. I crouched by the bed and sobbed. I became oblivious to anyone or anything. Sylvia and the nurse were so scared they were going to call an ambulance. I pleaded with them not to.

It wasn't until the next morning that the pains stopped. I was worn out, and cried with relief. The next week I spent in bed. At last I could rest! The spectre of prison wasn't looming any more and, more important to me, I wouldn't have to have a baby that wouldn't be wanted. I knew only too well what that was like.

At this stage, life seemed to be either black or white. One week would be horrendous, the next would be filled with friends and laughter, bright lights and parties.

Brian Peters was a dear friend of mine. He was tall and dark, with one side of his family having come from Armenia. In some ways he resembled Omar Sharif. He was not involved in

80

show business, though I met him at an opening night. He was escorting a young woman named Corinne, who was besotted with him. Though he asked me out, I refused because I thought he was having a relationship with her. He told me she was just a friend.

Once, when I was quite ill in hospital, Brian came to visit me, unlike a lot of my glossier friends, and that meant a great deal to me. That's when he found out I didn't have a family. From that moment we forged a close link. He practically adopted me. Brian had come from a family that was not anything like my own. They were warm and close, and came from an exotic world. As part of the British Raj in India, they had also been quite wealthy. Even though his parents had separated, Brian's family had a stability about them that attracted me. Brian's own father was no longer alive, but his mother, sister and brother were all very close and loving to each other. It wasn't until after I broke up with John Fitchen, whose social manners were impeccable but whose domestic ones left a lot to be desired, that we began a serious relationship. We formed a friendship that lasted for many years, throughout our relationship and long after it.

Brian was pleased for me when I was recognized in the street. I really hadn't accomplished anything to merit the attention I received. There had been maybe half a dozen small roles in films but the publicity for the special girls was more intense than the film roles warranted. At the end of shooting a film I and other young actresses would be called in to pose for the pictures. Newspaper offices would then be flooded with them. Unfortunately, one couldn't get paid for modelling work because there were too many free pictures available, so in between films, it could be a little rough making ends meet. Whenever I wonder what happened to those pictures, twenty-odd years on, someone will approach me at a theatre and ask me to sign one. Usually they tell me they got them from the film collector's shop. I wonder who gets paid for them now?

With the first taste of fame came the requests to attend events. As a Bill Watts girl I was asked to make lots of appearances for various charities. They were great fun but I wonder if anyone knew I couldn't really afford the fare there, let alone a pair of new stockings. I'd cover my legs with an evil-smelling liquid, that was called of all things, Man Tan. It would turn them an orangey-brown overnight.

Gloria and Jackie, two close chums of mine, would often be with me. Gloria was a neat, pretty blonde who was staying with Elsa, Jackie and Joan Collins' mother. I'd envy Gloria that she had found a home. Jackie Curtis was slightly taller than me with dark hair, fair skin and a stunning figure. She had a terrific personality, as did Gloria. Together we felt like the Three Musketeers.

At some of the appearances we would be put up in holiday hotels for the weekend. Lots of older men vaguely connected with the movie industry were there, away from home looking for amorous adventures. It was like walking a tightrope trying to stay friendly and polite without getting involved. It wasn't easy! We didn't have the funds to stay anywhere else, so the first thing we did was make sure our rooms were as far away as possible from the other guests.

At one of these appearances I met a man called Dennis Hamilton. He was flashily attractive and never drew breath between his many words. He wore a pinky purplish shirt open to the waist, tight white trousers and bare feet in white loafer shoes that looked like they were made of suede. He certainly stood out. His wife was Diana Dors and he managed her career. She was away in Hollywood filming with Rod Steiger. The newspapers were filled with stories and rumours about them. When I told him I was working twelve hours a day on *The Good Companions* during the week, he said I was wasting my time and going about a film career the wrong way.

'Look at my missus,' he went on. 'She's filming in Hollywood. It's a horrible place, but we're being paid a packet. I couldn't stand it, so I've come home. What you need is a manager. Now *you* I could really make a star.'

One of the producers on *Good Companions* was Kenneth Harper, a very fair blond man between the ages of thirty and fifty, who looked exactly like Michael Heseltine. He had a dark-haired wife called Mercia and, later on, I would end up in the middle of a domestic row between them. Kenneth was a helpful man and didn't have the nasty habit of treating his smaller artistes like a bunch of schoolgirls. One night he asked if I'd like to have dinner at Les Ambassadeurs with him, Anita Ekberg and Otto Preminger. I felt shabby and tired, as I'd been up since five in the morning working that day. I certainly didn't look as smart as I wanted to, but I thought Anita Ekberg looked statuesque and beautiful.

Otto Preminger was already a famous producer/director at this stage. He didn't seem to notice that I wasn't feeling confident and was very attentive to me. He was looking for an actress to play *Saint Joan*. He listened when I talked about my ambitions for work and I told him I was attending the Actor's Studio. Like many people, myself included, he confused it with Lee Strasberg's acting school. During dinner, I was delighted when he said he'd like to help me guide my career. I met him several times after that, and sometimes we discussed a film contract. The great ambition at that time was for young actresses to secure a contract with a production company and gain a steady income. The company, on the other hand, would be making an investment in their talent for the future. Maybe, through Otto Preminger, I could become a contract player too!

Dennis Hamilton rang me one morning and I told him about my meetings with Otto Preminger. He said it was a good contact, and thought we should discuss it further. 'Let's have lunch and I'll tell you how to handle him.'

We met at Les A where, after a drink, Dennis suggested we go to a restaurant where we could talk more privately. After we got into his huge, silver Cadillac and drove to his special restaurant, I asked him why it was such a long way from London.

'Because it's in the country, away from all those nosey people,' he replied. We had a fun lunch. Dennis was a great charmer and seemed to be much more in his element now. I think he'd been uncomfortable at Les A. In fact he told me so.

While we were having lunch, a friend of his called Jimmy arrived and joined us. Apparently they were working on a number of projects together. We finished our meal and Dennis suggested he show me his house. It was only five minutes away, he said, and I could see how a film star should really live. Sure enough, it was a big house, enclosed in its own grounds and, as you entered through huge, white arches, there was a large, turquoise-coloured swimming pool that covered the whole of the ground floor. I asked if they both swam very much. He told me neither of them could swim and, what's more, he hated getting wet. But he thought the pool was the perfect image for his Diana.

'You can have all this as well, if you are managed correctly,' he told me. The idea was appealing. Dennis turned to Jimmy and said, 'You're looking at the next big star and the next Mrs Hamilton.' I was taken aback. Although I liked Dennis, it hadn't occurred to me that there was romance on his mind. 'I know,' said Dennis, 'let's throw a party especially for you. I'll ring all the newspapers, invite them here and tell them our plans.' I was young and impressionable but things were happening too fast for me. I didn't want to change my life, though I was flattered. I was quite happy the way things were. Also, I knew I had friends like Otto Preminger looking out for me. Why would I need Dennis as a manager? I had an agent, and I certainly wasn't looking for romance.

Dennis then suggested I stay for the weekend so we could take care of 'our plans'. I said I couldn't possibly stay, as I had no clothes, toothpaste, or makeup with me. He then showed me a walk-in wardrobe complete with a makeup table crammed top to bottom with everything I could ever need. Any of the clothes I liked were mine to keep, he said. It was like walking into Aladdin's cave. It was a strange feeling because I knew everything belonged to someone else – his wife.

'I bought them for her work,' he snapped. 'She's gone off with Steiger, so they're mine now, to do as I like with.'

I rang Bill Watts, my agent, and told him what was happening. Bill said he had no appointments for me that Friday, then suddenly Dennis interrupted. To my surprise, he was listening in on an extension. He told Bill he was going to give a party for me and invite all the press. Bill seemed to think that was a good idea and this pleased Dennis. Now he had my agent's approval.

'We'll have the party tomorrow evening, Saturday, so I can make all the arrangements perfectly.'

Dennis never gave me time to think. He steam-rollered me off my feet. When I said it was getting late, he took my hand and walked me around his garden. The garden was enchanting, but it was growing dark and I wanted to get back to London.

'What's the hurry?' he said. 'Why not stay here for dinner. Then I'll get you home for an earlyish night.' But, after dinner, it was another story. Friends and neighbours kept dropping in and it turned into a social evening, which was great fun. I forgot about the time and that I was at least thirty miles from London. When the last of the guests left, it was only eleven-thirty but it seemed much later in the country. It was dark and quiet everywhere. Dennis said he had drunk too much champagne to drive me home and offered me one of his guest rooms. No sooner had I settled into bed when a very large dog came bounding in to the room, scaring me witless. I screamed. Dennis came in and said the dog was there to protect me. If I had been nervous before, now I was bloody petrified. I was frightened of dogs I didn't know, especially ones as big as this. Dennis said he'd stay in my room so I wouldn't be afraid. I didn't know which was worse, him or his dog. When I got cross at this and said I wished I'd gone home, he backed down.

'OK, OK, I'll go to my room and leave you alone.' I asked would he please take his dog with him. As soon as he'd gone I got up and put a chest of drawers against the door.

The next day I woke up looking forward to the party that evening. It was a full day with guests arriving all the time. There was swimming, game playing and lots to eat and drink, but not one journalist appeared. Dennis said he couldn't get everybody at such short notice.

It was hard not to fall under Dennis's spell. He was around me all the time and made sure the champagne flowed non-stop. But what started off as a funny light-hearted weekend in the country, soon became very different. I was getting anxious as the weekend came to an end. I had very little money with me and I wasn't sure how to get back to London without a lift. It was a large house in an isolated area that I was unfamiliar with. It could have been the far side of the moon for all I knew. Now it seemed Dennis had no intention of taking me back. Every time I walked down the drive, either he or his dogs followed me, or his housekeeper was there. I also saw his temper when he smashed a priceless set of china after one of his phone calls to Diana.

Any romantic feelings that may possibly have developed towards Dennis were now squashed by the situation. For a start I never felt safe. While I was getting dressed in the morning, he'd rush around with a Polaroid camera trying to take revealing pictures. They would be useful later in my career, he told me. Also the bathroom door never quite locked and he was inclined to walk in unannounced. Under these circumstances, there was no way I could feel secure. I really wanted to get home and no amount of champagne could soften that feeling.

Two days later, Dennis seemed to have forgotten about the press party, but said a journalist was coming that afternoon for lunch. As soon as the man arrived I told him that I wanted to leave. After lunch, I asked him if he would give me a lift back to London. Dennis said he was now my manager and he would let me leave on the condition that the journalist brought me back the next day for the party. He said it was a good opportunity for me to pick up some of my things. I got in the reporter's car and told him what had happened. I had no intention of going back, I said, ever. I'd have thought the whole episode was a bad nightmare, if the same journalist hadn't met me fifteen years later at a television event and reminded me of how he'd rescued me.

There were repercussions, as Dennis Hamilton had said there would be if I didn't return. I was cited in his divorce from Diana Dors but, when I said I'd tell the truth about what had really happened, I was dropped from the case like a hot potato. What they wanted was publicity as a sexy, racy couple. But, if the truth were known, that image wouldn't have stood up. Dennis was keen on his reputation with women, and my story would have discredited that in no uncertain manner. When Otto Preminger read the publicity regarding this incident, he told me that he was disgusted by it and that he was dropping the idea of a film contract with me. Over dinner at his suite, he told me what he thought. But what was to happen that night was worse than anything that happened at Dennis's house.

After his assistants had left and there was just Otto and myself remaining, he got up to pour himself a brandy, then offered me one. He set the drinks down and passed slowly behind my chair, then, out of nowhere, he swung round and hit me smack across the mouth. I was shocked and stunned and cut from the ring he wore on his little finger.

'There's no way I could test you for *Saint Joan* now. You should be more careful who you mix with.'

I wanted to cry. My mouth hurt and now I was not to be allowed to make the screen test. I had been preparing for it and paying for expensive lessons for some time. I was trying not to cry, but Otto started shouting insulting things at me, most of which weren't true. I was very hurt by this, especially since I'd only had reason to trust and respect him before. It seemed the more I cried, the more aggressive he became. Then he tried to strike me again and I knew I had to do something.

Somehow, although I didn't want to, I felt guilty. As Otto pointed out, I had got involved in some sordid publicity with Dennis Hamilton. He made me feel that I'd let him down. I couldn't help crying and that made him worse. He kept trying to grab me as I ran across the room trying to get away from him. My kind mentor had disappeared and become a raging madman. With Otto becoming more and more frantic, I told myself I had to keep calm, when a chair came flying through the air, missing me by a few inches.

What I did next was purely instinct. I tried to placate him. I would've promised anything to get out of that suite of rooms. I told Otto there was nobody like him, that he was a most attractive man, and that I would make it up to him for being such a 'naughty girl'. Those were magic words. He stopped ranting and raving and smiled. I told him I was going to the bathroom to make myself ready for him, disgusted at what was happening.

When I got into the bathroom I looked at myself in the mirror. There was blood on the side of my mouth, my blouse was all torn and my stockings were a mess. If I'd once admired Otto, now I couldn't bear him. I straightened myself up as best I could and tried the door outside the bathroom that led into the corridor. It was locked. That meant I had to go through the bedroom into the sitting room to get out. As I dashed through, I saw Otto lying on his large, double bed sprawled almost naked in the most unseemly position. I threw my shoes at him as hard as I could and just kept running. He couldn't chase me into the corridor without his clothes on. He shouted threats after me. I didn't even look back. I ran like hell for the lift and after what seemed like ages, it came. Luckily, there was no-one in the lift but the attendant. He was a small, sympathetic man and, when he asked me what the matter was, I burst into tears. He took me down to the basement so I could recover, then called the hotel manager.

I sat there quietly, grateful for the help. The manager was kind and attentive, and asked me if I wanted to go to the police station, until he found out it was Otto Preminger I'd been visiting. I had never seen such a quick change in a man. All of a sudden he

87

couldn't wait to get me out of there. I think he would have put me in a laundry truck if there had been one handy.

Beginning the next day and continuing for a week, gifts arrived every day from Otto. It started with a large bouquet of flowers and an apologetic note, and finished with a very large colour television set, which was a great luxury then. I'd still rather have had the film test! When I had time to think about it, I was sad about Otto. I had formed a good friendship with him and had been looking forward to a film contract and the security it would have brought me, as well as a mentor to guide me in my career. In some ways, it was like losing a relative.

A week later life was more or less back to normal. I had lots of work and lots of friends, but I couldn't tell them what had happened. If I had had somebody to talk to who was older and wiser, maybe I could have stopped feeling so badly.

It was good to be working, even if sometimes the conditions were rough. *The Good Companions*, which starred Celia Johnson and Hugh Griffith and a host of other very talented British stars, was filmed at Elstree Studios, Boreham Wood. It was the worst studio to work at. Simply eating lunch was a problem for myself and the other 'special' girls. There was one restaurant for the stars, one for the crowd players and another for technicians. We didn't fit into any of these categories, and ended up eating sandwiches every day in our dressing room. At least at Pinewood there was one huge, lovely restaurant where everybody from stars to small-part players mixed.

While filming I got another job on a Sunday night game show called *Yackety Yack*. It was hosted by MacDonald Hobley and broadcast on a new network called ITV, the first network in competition against the BBC. Leslie Goldberg was the entrepreneur behind the show.

I had given an interview in *Picture Show* magazine proudly saying I was going to be in the show. Leslie thought this was too pushy and sacked me before the programme went on the air. It wasn't until the producer John Irwin read the article that I was reinstated. It caused quite a bit of tension with Leslie and proved to be one of my first experiences of show-business politics.

Yackety Yack may have been the height of chauvinist silliness. A panel of pretty young girls were given words to describe, like 'filibuster'. We then had to talk as quickly as possible until the gong sounded, saying what we thought the word meant. 'Oh, it's the man who breaks in female horses,' one would say for a laugh. We knew we often looked ridiculous, but that was par for the course at that stage. The ten pounds I was paid when I was on the show doubled my income, and I was glad of that.

Leslie Goldberg had assured us we would all become famous. Sure enough today the occasional taxi driver will remember me, not for my film roles, but for my brief time on that lightweight show. It just shows what a powerful medium television is.

Television may have made me well-known but it was more reassuring that the film roles were improving. I played a student in *Once More With Feeling*, a comedy directed by Stanley Donen. It starred Yul Brynner, who took wonderful photographs of me, many of which ended up on the covers of magazines. Needless to say, he was a very good photographer.

One night after filming, Stanley Donen invited the musical director and a party of other people working on the movie, to see a show in Montmartre and asked if I would like to come along. I didn't want to miss anything, I told Stanley.

'I don't think you will,' he said, 'when you see this show.'

When we got there we were ushered into a room with a bed at the other end and a small section curtained off in a red silky material.

Before we had time to sit down properly two girls and a young man came in. They bowed to us, and then went behind the curtain one at a time. There were some splashing noises, then the first girl reappeared with nothing on and lay down on the bed, to be followed by the young man and then the second girl. They started to fondle each other in a rather half hearted way. I noticed one of the girls still had her stockings rolled down round her ankles. The three of them looked so funny I got the giggles. This made the French girl furious and the young man became too embarrassed to proceed. They would have been fascinating to watch, the girl said crossly, if I hadn't been so rude as to laugh at their show, and she wasn't going to continue any more. The others moved off and I was left with the young man. He spoke to me very quietly and apologized for his performance.

'I'm sorry I wasn't at my best, mademoiselle, but it threw me when I saw you laughing. Please excuse me, I've been studying hard. I'm going to be a doctor.'

In one or two smaller films, I played the second lead, such as in *Horrors of the Black Museum* where I was the juvenile heroine. I felt I was making progress. However, I still had to convince everybody else. When I went to see about a decent part, I would first be asked where I had done my training and if I had been to drama school or to rep. It was a weak point for me. I had hardly done any of these things. What I didn't know was that I was getting the best training by actually working. One of my interviews was with a kindly gentleman called Dennis van Thal. I think he was the casting director for Alexander Korda at that stage. He was later to break away and form a school of talent with EMI/MGM, based loosely on the American contract system of looking out for young players while they were being trained.

I was the youngest player of the people Dennis put under contract, and we were paid various salaries. My own was ten pounds a week but there were perks. Voice lessons were paid for, acting coaching provided, and beautiful clothes were lent to me for opening nights. Some of the other players were Millie Martin, John Turner, Ann Firbank and Maggie Smith, whom I liked a lot. We were all different, and some of the others were already established. Dennis and his wife, Mary, would have parties occasionally where we'd all get together.

EMI/MGM's was an interesting group of people. They were unlike the other film studios, Rank and ABC, whose contract players mostly acted and sounded like bank clerks, nurses or teachers. I felt I was beginning to fit in. In their own way, everyone else in my group looked and sounded as different as I did. It was a delightful company to be part of.

Dennis suggested I join a repertory company and found one in the Isle of Wight. The company was called The Freddy Frinton Players. As the newest member, I was the one to do the chores, including cleaning the stage and ironing the clothes in the wardrobe: this part I was good at! The NCH training was useful here but, at the most important job, I was hopeless. It was called 'being on the book' and I had no idea what that meant.

The rehearsals were held in a big, empty schoolroom next to a pub. On my first day an actor asked me, 'Are you working the corner, dear?' I said I'd be glad to, which corner would he like? At that, he glared at me and said to the rest of the company, 'We've got a right one here. Seems to be too big for her boots.' I asked the assistant director what being 'on the book' meant.

'You'll just have to find out,' he replied.

The first week was painful and I think most of them thought I was stupid. I didn't know what 'OP' meant or where the damn 'corner' was they kept referring to. There were several hysterical rehearsals with actors shouting at me for their lines before I realized how to prompt them. In desperation I went home and learned the whole play. By the end of the first week, much to their astonishment, I could prompt them without looking at the book from any place in the rehearsal room – I still hadn't found the silly 'corner'.

As a result of my diligence, the director gave me the lead in the next play! It was a huge part for me. I may have been able to learn a play quickly, but I had no idea how to act on a stage in front of an audience. I was terrified, and I was terrible. I probably could have got away with this and gone on working with the company but, during the rehearsals for this, my picture had been all over the newspapers because of a dinner date I'd had.

'Oh, that's why you were so awful in your first big part,' they summarised. 'You've been rushing out to glamorous dinners instead of concentrating.' They'd quite forgotten that two weeks earlier I'd memorized the whole of the previous play. Even if they did remember, it didn't seem to count for much.

The infamous dinner date was with Frank Sinatra. The first week of rehearsals my phone rang and a voice said, 'Is that Shirley Anne? My name is Frank Sinatra. Bob O'Neil has a photograph of you and you look like a fun girl. Would you like to have dinner?'

'Yes, I would. But if you're Frank Sinatra I'm Marilyn Monroe,' I replied. After about five minutes, I realized he was genuine and that he *was* Frank Sinatra.

'Tomorrow evening. I'll get my people to call you. What would be a good time?' I told him, early in the evening as I had to be at rehearsals by nine in the morning. He seemed surprised that I was working.

His public relations man called me the next day to arrange a car to pick me up, and I told him I didn't think I had anything smart enough to wear. He told me not to worry and said he would send something with the driver. When I told some of the others at rehearsals that morning, I don't think they believed me. I'm sure they thought I was showing off. I was twenty years of age and all I could think of was what could I wear.

The car came to pick me up. It was a large limousine. It took me to Siggi's Club, a well known smart restaurant in Mayfair. The chauffeur opened the door and Frank Sinatra greeted me and kissed my hand. We walked through the restaurant to a long table with about thirty people seated round it. I noticed the conversation came to an abrupt halt as we made our way to our places.

Sammy Davis Jnr was there, as was Peter Lawford with his wife, Pat, and various others. Some very upper crust English types as well as several men with strong, New York accents I had difficulty understanding. Frank's dinner guests were very quiet whenever he spoke and sometimes laughed before he finished a sentence. As a dinner companion, he was friendly and considerate. When he asked me what I'd like to drink, I told him I didn't want anything strong. I didn't want to tell him that one of the actors had suggested a 'pep' pill to give me energy after a tiring rehearsal and I had taken half of it. 'In that case, have a little champagne,' Frank said.

The champagne was good and I didn't feel tired any more, just relaxed and happy. But as the evening continued my arms suddenly felt like lead. I put my drink down and it fell off the table, so I picked up the glass meaning to put it more in the middle. It fell to the other side, straight over Mrs Lawford's beautiful gown. I was mortified. She was charming and said it couldn't matter less. Two minutes' later I knocked another drink right over Mrs Lawford again. Frank Sinatra took the drink away and said sweetly, 'I think it's better if you stop now, don't you?'

After leaving the restaurant, we went to a nightclub called The Pigalle to see the show. Frank Sinatra was warm and attentive in the limousine and we talked more than we had all evening. He asked me about my work and told me about some of the horrible places he had worked in at the beginning of his career. At The Pigalle, as we watched the cabaret in the dark, he relaxed even more. We turned our chairs round so we could see the show more clearly and he put his arm around me. The mood was light and happy. Then suddenly flashing lights exploded all around us, in the shadows were at least six or seven press photographers snapping away. All I could think was to keep my head down, hoping that Frank would notice I was not anxious to spoil his private evening. It completely changed his mood and it wasn't long before we left to go back to a party at his hotel suite. On the ride back he hardly spoke a word.

Back at his suite at the Dorchester a party was in full swing, with most of the people we had been with at the club. Frank's records were playing and he would stop to discuss with Sammy Davis how they had made them. I was fascinated by this talk of work in the middle of the party. When it was nearly two in the morning, I told Frank I had to go because of rehearsals the next day.

'That's a shame,' he said. 'Stay a bit longer. The party's just beginning.' He asked how would I feel about going to the Derby with him next week, and perhaps Ascot later on. I said it was a lovely idea and stayed another hour.

Just as I was falling asleep in my chair, a PR man came up to me and asked me to follow him. I thought he was organizing a lift home. In fact he showed me into a stunning bedroom and said, 'Lie down here. Have a rest while I arrange your car.'

The next thing I remember, it was very early in the morning and he was shaking me awake. I got up quickly and walked through to the sitting room on my way out. There were one or two people still around, mostly asleep in large armchairs or sofas. The PR man asked me if I would leave the borrowed dress. I said no, I'd return it later. How did he think I was going to get home? As we got to the door, Frank appeared wearing a silk robe over his clothes and asked me if I was all right and had I enjoyed the evening. At the lift, he kissed me on the cheek.

'I'll be in touch, baby,' he said and told his PR man to tell the driver to take me wherever I wanted to go.

I went back to work in the morning, not realizing that in the following week I would be besieged with phone calls by people wanting to know about my dinner date with Frank Sinatra. The photos taken at the club had been all over the newspapers. I rang the Dorchester after rehearsals to let Frank Sinatra know that I was not going to talk to anyone who rang and especially not the press. But instead of Frank I got one of his aides who said brusquely, 'Frank was expecting your call this morning. Where were you?' I told him I was at work. 'In that case,' he said, 'make sure you ring Frank tomorrow and explain.' I rang the next day and got another aide, who again was very abrupt. My phone was still ringing non-stop.

Suddenly my life was not my own. People I didn't know came up and stared at me in the street and asked me personal questions. Meanwhile I still couldn't get Frank Sinatra on the phone to tell him what had happened and ask him what to do.

CHAPTER FOUR

Other than my little brother, Ernie, who wasn't little any more at nearly six feet four inches, I had hardly any contact with my family. The infamous letter was still keeping my father away at Gypsy's insistence. My sister Sunny had left for America. She'd married a GI sailor called David. I would hear from her every once in a while, but mostly when she was in trouble.

I saw more of Ernie than any of my other relatives. He was always welcome, but I felt more like his mother than his sister. He had left Edgeworth a few years earlier than me, after his illness, which had been diagnosed as tuberculosis. He was transferred to another home of the NCH at Harpenden where there was a sanatorium. After he got over it he stayed there and began his training as a printer. He had been through a lot of stress in the last few years and, when he came to visit, I felt I was the one who had to be strong.

Meanwhile, the film business was quiet back in London. I was still under contract to EMI/MGM and Bill Watts informed me that I couldn't do any more special girl roles without the studio allowing it. Even with the bona fide contract, I was often more hard up than before. It was a little disconcerting to attend an opening in a borrowed fur one day and be looking for a job the next. I was no longer in the market for paid photographic work either – the pictures taken of me were the property of the studio, and I wasn't paid for them.

Half-heartedly, I returned to the lessons I had begun before the rep. My voice teacher was Iris Warren, a magnificent woman: tall and stately with a sense of humour – an inspired teacher even if I was not the most attentive pupil. I'd arrive at her studio in Wigmore Street running a few minutes late and out of breath. One day as I recited the 'Once more unto the breach' speech from *Henry V*, a leg of my pyjamas slowly rolled down from under my skirt. I'd thrown my day clothes over my night clothes in my hurry to be on time for my lesson. It made Iris laugh.

Once, as I was charging up the stairs, a few minutes late as usual, I bumped into a man coming down. 'Don't worry, dear,' he said. 'Iris is waiting for you. She thinks you're a complete original and a deadly mimic.'

In the studio I asked Iris who the person was. 'Don't you recognize Sir Laurence Olivier, dear?'

Iris told me my voice would one day be an asset. She thought it was well-pitched and encouraged me not to change my accent. Until then, most people had told me how dreadful I sounded, so I'd compensate by trying to sound like everybody else. I couldn't put her help into practice immediately but one day it would be very valuable.

Just as I would get into a panic about money, something always turned up. Dennis van Thal's office called to tell me a photographer named Terence Donovan was shooting the young hopefuls of today as the stars of yesterday. Would I like to play Carole Lombard? I hadn't seen her films but American friends in the film business had told me I was like her.

At one interview I met a pretty girl called Beth Rogan. She was under contract to the Rank Organization but was different from the other contract players. Beth was very much her own person, a free spirit who wasn't even very interested in acting in films. She wanted to paint and travel. The Julie Christie film *Darling* was based on her lifestyle. She and Jeanne Baldwin had developed the idea, wrote the original draft of the script together and took it to Joe Janni, one of the resident producers at Pinewood. When the film was later made, I don't think they got any credit.

Beth had an apartment in the middle of Edwardes Square, a quiet, beautiful French tree-lined square – Napoleon had supposedly commissioned it to be built before the Battle of Waterloo. It was to be homes for his officers' wives and mistresses. Of course, being Napoleon, he presumed he'd win the battle. After his defeat, the square became crown property. It was a peaceful part of town, and I loved the fact that Beth lived there.

At that moment I was living in a small flat in Abbey Road. Brian Peters and I were together most of the time now and he would stay most nights with me. Soon, though, I realized that I was living above my income. After listening to my anxieties about the costs, Brian suggested I move in with him above his coffee shop in Kensington High Street. The move saved me getting into debt but, better still, I felt secure with Brian. He was from a close family and made me feel as if I were part of it.

Sadly, the EMI/MGM studio was closing. The tax concessions that the Americans had in England were coming to an end and they were pulling out of Britain completely. That meant the end for my group of players run by Dennis van Thal, as well. It was like going back to square one. Fortunately, I was still with Bill Watts, who found me a co-starring role in a film called *Beat Girl*. It was my largest part so far.

The salary was very low for such a big role. 'Oh, well,' said Bill, 'if we ask for too much money they won't give you the job.' That was the ironic thing about Bill. Much as he loved his stable of special girls, he really didn't have the confidence to get for us what we were worth. I was travelling long hours every day and spent half my salary on getting to some remote location, having to be there at five o'clock in the morning.

Beat Girl was to star a newcomer called Gillian Hills who modelled herself on Brigitte Bardot. Adam Faith, a young rock star-to-be, played her boyfriend in the film and Peter McEnery and I played the other leads. A lot of the scenes were shot in the Chislehurst caves, which meant a long bus ride twice a day. A nice, older man called Freddie who lived next door sometimes gave me a lift. At dawn he would come in and lean over Brian to wake me up.

The caves were cold and damp, but the days were fun because of the people I was working with. Adam Faith was beginning to be a teen idol at that time. With his striking face, which reminded me of how I thought Hamlet should look, I could see why. He could always make me laugh, and was a dreadful flirt. Peter McEnery was perhaps the most handsome man on the picture and was very serious about his acting, but was rather shy in comparison to the others. A couple of nights he stayed at my flat to save himself a long journey in the morning. I didn't get to know him as well as I would have liked. I wished we'd both been less shy.

John Barry wrote the score, including a song for me to sing called 'I'll Never Be Bad No More' that was released on the soundtrack. He had an intensity about him that was very attractive. John and Adam were great friends, but I felt there was a competitiveness between them. John often did sweet unexpected things like arriving on the set with a flower for me. As well as these two very attractive men there was the assistant director, Kip Gowan. He was slight, handsome and dark, unlike Adam and John who were both fairish. I'm happy I have stayed friends with these three. Six months ago I had dinner with Kip and his beautiful wife, Lee Remick. They've been happily married for about twenty five years.

During the filming I was shocked to find out that in fact some of the extras were being paid three times more than me! I didn't have much money to start with, and it really upset me. I couldn't make ends meet after playing the largest part I'd had so far. Bill was so glad to get you the job that he didn't negotiate enough for your salary. I heard the same story from some of the other girls. Many of them ended up leaving him because of this. Thank goodness, despite these difficulties, I made these marvellous friends and going to work with them every day was a joy.

I finished the film and realized I had been five years in the film industry and I was getting nowhere. I was no longer under contract and I missed the wonderful group of players I had been with who had all gone on to other things. I wondered what my next step should be. I wanted to be secure like other people, perhaps with a husband and children.

Just when I thought I would leave the film industry and settle down, Bill Watts phoned me. They were going to make a film of the John Osborne play *The Entertainer*, about a vaudeville comedian. It was to star Laurence Olivier. The play had been written for him, and was a big success at the Royal Court. But, in the stage play, the part of Tina, the beauty queen, was only referred to. This was the film role I went to see about.

I arrived at the audition in Piccadilly Circus, dressed in the standard outfit of the day – hooped skirt with petticoat, hair in a pony tail, and heavy doe-eyed makeup made popular at that time by the model Barbara Golan. There were about a hundred girls in the room. To my horror, I saw that we all looked alike! I don't know what made me do it, maybe an actor's instinct, but I went to the ladies' room and scrubbed most of the makeup off, brushed my hair down, took the hoop out of my petticoat and went back in. I knew I wasn't so striking now – or as fashionable – but it didn't matter; at least I didn't look like everybody else.

My name was called and I went into the office. The director, Tony Richardson, was there with his assistant director, Peter Yates. Tony spoke calmly and quietly.

'Can you speak in a northern accent?'

'Yes, I can,' I replied in a strong Lancashire voice. 'I've just spent two years learning not to.' Tony and Peter both laughed out loud.

'Where did you learn that?' Tony said.

'I was brought up in Lancashire,' I replied. 'They all talked like that!' Some years later, Peter told me that, on my way out of the room, they had seen that one of my shoes needed mending. They guessed that I was paying my own way without the help of a sponsor or well-off parents.

A shortlist was picked and this time about five girls and myself were asked to read on stage. We were told to be at a theatre on the following Friday afternoon. As soon as I got the pages of dialogue, I was overjoyed. The part was ideal for me, I thought. Not only was it wonderfully written, but also it reminded me of my earlier forays into the beauty contest jungles. I rang up Iris Warren to tell her the news and to ask for her help.

'Just go by your instincts, Shirley Anne, you know you can do most accents well. Just feel it!'

When I got to the theatre, the other girls were already there, all of them stunning. Usually this would have intimidated me. But for once it didn't matter. In the auditorium sat John Osborne, Tony Richardson, Oscar Lewenstein, the associate producer, Jocelyn Richards, the costume designer, and a couple of others I didn't know. Backstage I couldn't see them so it didn't throw me. Three others went first, then it was my turn. For once I felt at ease.

'The stage manager is going to read with you,' Tony told me.

I said, 'Fine, thank you, could he please sit to my right?'

'Would you like to begin?' I waited until they were all quiet. I hadn't learned the lines, but it didn't matter. It was as if they were coming from somewhere deep in my memory. I read quietly in my Lancashire accent, and afterwards there was a silence. Tony and John both came to the front of the stage.

'Thank you. We liked that very much. Would you like to come out for dinner tonight and get to know us all?'

I was so pleased they liked my reading. Then Tony made a suggestion.

'You don't need to wear beauty queen makeup any more. It makes you look at least thirty. We want to see what age you really are.' I was glad he asked me to do this, because, from then on, I had more confidence to let people see me as I really was.

Dinner at Tony's house was a lot of fun. He told me I had got the role. I spent the evening celebrating, laughing and joking with him and other members of his company. Woodfall was the name of the production company Tony had formed with John Osborne and a few others. Their first production had been *Look Back in Anger* a few years earlier with Richard Burton and Mary Ure. They were a group of rebels at that time, experimenting with something new and exciting in the film industry. I felt instantly at home with them. They were intellectuals, with egos to match, and they were also a sensitive and caring group of people.

Two weeks later I was on the train to Morecambe. Brian took me to the station at Euston. As soon as I was in my seat, I started to cry.

'What's the matter?' Tony asked me gently. I told him I always cried when things were about to change. I sensed I was taking a big step now and that things would never be quite the same *again*.

This was the first time I'd ever stayed on location in England. It was so comfortable and civilized, quite different from any of my other film jobs. Though my scenes were only five or so weeks' work, they were spread out over the three-month shooting schedule and so I stayed in Morecambe almost the whole time, except for the occasional weekend back in London. Sometimes the film crew would gather for a drink at the end of the day. I went sporadically – I was so excited by the work I couldn't think of anything else. I felt as if I were part of a big extended family. It was by far the best feeling I'd ever had workwise.

Alan Bates played one of Laurence Olivier's sons in *The Entertainer*. We became friends, though once when I'd asked him to the cinema on a wet afternoon when we both had the day off, he said 'No'. Perhaps he didn't want to see any other performances when he was creating one of his own. I see him now from time to time, and he's done great things in the cinema and theatre since, but he's still as unaffected and friendly as he was then.

Apart from our encounter on the stairs, I first met Laurence Olivier in a small theatre dressing room where we were all waiting to film a scene. In his Archie Rice get-up, he reminded me of my dad. It wasn't at all how I expected him to look. I was too young to realize how clever he was with his appearance. The man I saw was the opposite of the marvellous heroes he'd played. He was of medium height with his hair slicked back from a centre parting, and he wore a white silk scarf around his neck. I was doing a crossword with some others rather loudly and we were all shouting questions at each other about the clues. Sir Laurence sat quietly by himself in a corner. He seemed cool and aloof, and stayed that way for the first few days.

He was still married to Vivien Leigh at the time. I'd always admired her, and occasionally I would ask him about her. This must have been difficult for him and my questions seemed to make him sad. One thing he did tell me was that she had been ill for a long time. He said he'd tried to help her, but it hadn't worked. Later I found out he was now deeply in love with Joan Plowright, who was playing his daughter. She was a smallish girl with big brown eyes, a wide-open face, brown hair and a slight Yorkshire accent. She was warm and friendly to me. I assumed she and Sir Laurence had met three years earlier when they'd played *The Entertainer* together on stage at the Royal Court.

When he appeared in the public dining room, Sir Laurence was always with a group of people. I think it was his way of protecting himself against the gossip. We all know the press can be vicious about people's private lives and that may have been why he was stand-offish when we first met. I was in the papers so much in those days, he may have thought I was chummy with them. In fact the journalists I knew got quite put out with me because I wouldn't talk about the people I was now working with.

The beauty contest was my first scene. We used genuine beauty queens and shot it at the huge open air stadium in Morecambe. They were warm, generous girls, most of them a head taller than myself. When we did the walk-round, we had the public in and I think we convinced them it was a real contest! I was relieved to get a good response, what I remember most was how cold it was. Thank God one of the girls had lent me some of her fake tan which Jocelyn Richards had helped me put on or I'd have looked as blue as I felt.

The love scene between Tina and Archie Rice took place in a caravan. Those marvellous words that had first excited me when I'd read for the part were now mine. The scene seemed to play itself. First thing in the morning we rehearsed it for moves with the camera crew, while we were both in dressing gowns and I was still in my hair rollers. When we came to film the scene, I wore a short pink-and-white lace petticoat. A lot of the clothes I wore in the film were my own. This is where Jocelyn was so sensitive with her design. She let you pick or wear your own clothes so you were comfortable.

In between takes in the caravan, I told Sir Laurence the two actresses I admired most were Vivien Leigh and Marilyn Monroe. He told me how difficult Marilyn Monroe had been when he'd produced and directed her in *The Prince and the Showgirl*. He said her addiction to sleeping tablets had caused the film crew to wait all day because she was unable to function until the pills wore off. Apparently, doctors often had to be called in. I jumped out of bed, angry at his criticism. These women were my teenage idols and I didn't want to hear anything bad about them. It was only much later that I realized how expensive and frustrating it is to sit around all day for other actors who may or may not even show up.

After one take, Sir Laurence had an idea for the scene and quietly whispered to Tony. 'Tell her to do this,' he said, and showed Tony a movement which suggested that I was pulling up my underwear. Of course, this helped the scene and made it more real. He could have told me himself but he had the tact to know the director should be the one to instruct the other actors.

He was still distant with me but the next evening he asked if I were going to watch the rushes. I said I'd rather not – I didn't like seeing myself on the screen. In lots of my special girl roles, one had very little to say or do, and the photography was haphazard to say the least. One producer had told me I wasn't photogenic because my jaw was too big, another that I was too short. Consequently, I didn't have much confidence and I was afraid of losing what I did have if I became self-conscious by watching myself. I told Sir Laurence I thought I'd stay behind.

'Rubbish, young lady,' he said. 'This is the only medium where you can correct yourself as you go along. It's the greatest privilege. No, you come to the rushes, my dear. In fact, you come along with me.'

Roger Livesey, who played his father, came with us and we three sat together. As I watched, I knew that Sir Laurence was right. From the rushes I could see what was working and what could be improved. He taught me to look at my work objectively. We came out and I couldn't believe the difference. He linked his arm in mine, Roger Livesey took my other arm, and off the three of us went down the road, skipping and dancing!

'I'm glad you came, dear. Well done! I don't think you need to correct anything in that.' He was so warm and affectionate after that first day. From then on I was always young Shirley to him and he was gentle and caring Sir Larry to me.

The next morning I went back to continue shooting the caravan scene with Sir Larry. I was very excited and pleased. He was now different from before, telling me funny anecdotes about himself.

We were having a marvellous time, laughing and joking. Just before we shot the scene, he did something I remember well. He could see how over-excited I got and he put his hand gently on me to quieten me down. We sat together for at least five minutes without saying a word, and when we came to shoot it, my whole mind was concentrated and the scene just played along wonderfully.

Brenda de Banzie was wonderful as Archie Rice's wife. Off stage most of the cast found her tiresome. I liked her because she reminded me of the Sisters who'd brought me up: fussy and bossy, but nice underneath. One day she took Joan Plowright and myself out for tea, which sounded almost like a royal command, given Brenda's personality. When we got to the tea room, we asked for some toast but Brenda informed us very grandly that she'd asked us out for tea and cakes and that is what we'd have! As we finished, she called to the waitress and asked for the bill.

'Come along, dear,' she said. 'I'm Brenda de Banzie. I'm in the theatre. I'm on in half an hour!' The waitress said she was sorry, but there were other customers there going to the theatre too. 'Well, it's no use if I'm not there, is it? There won't be anyone to see!'

Tony Richardson produced as well as directed *The Entertainer*. He found some of the best people, like the marvellous cinematographer, Oswald Morris. During one of our rehearsals, Ozzie stopped me and said, 'It's very moving what you're saying, but we can't see your face, only the top of your head. Just keep your head up. However good you are, it won't work if the audience can't see you.' It was great advice that I still use and I haven't played a love scene since without thanking Ozzie silently.

In the evenings, after dinner, sometimes we'd all sit and play word games that even John Osborne, with his great gift, could get caught out on, or psychological truth games, which Tony instigated. They were a good insight into the workings of people's minds. He'd ask us all impossible questions, and there was no way you could escape without revealing too much of yourself. But the games never got too malicious, or at least not while I was around. Once or twice I did hear that they'd ended in tears.

As the film was coming to an end, Joan Plowright threw a party at her flat in Knightsbridge. We had a great time, but Sir

Laurence wasn't there. Not long after that time, they announced they were going to marry.

I continued to share Brian's flat and life seemed exactly as it was before. *The Entertainer* still hadn't come out. I missed being on location with the people from the film. My brother was a frequent visitor and Brian was always wonderful with him. At Christmas time he would help me prepare a great cardboard box full of gifts for Ernie and the boys at his house in Harpenden. Sometimes Ernie would arrive with six or seven other boys for a visit. He had a powerful personality and was always the leader of his group. He could be fragile as well. I think he needed both Brian and myself. We were his only family.

One day he and one of his friends went to visit our dad and Ernie came back dispirited. He said he'd sat in a corner and dad had hardly said a word to him. Gypsy had been in and out, and they never even turned the television off. He told me Gypsy had made critical remarks about me. Who did I think I was always being in the papers? Did Ernie know I'd once written a vicious letter to her? It was sad that the letter I'd written to my dad she now thought I'd written to her. The visit upset my brother a lot. He thought his dad didn't have much interest in him. What neither of us could know was that, in the East End, memories are long and people are very clannish. Apparently Gypsy didn't want any of her husband's children from a former marriage turning up on her doorstep, especially when she and my father lived in the same house that he had actually lived in with my mother.

There were a few other things that had put Ernie on edge. He'd had a big clash with Mr Shut, the Governor and Headmaster at Harpenden. Mr Shut had a reputation among the older girls for touching them, but no-one had ever reported it. When Ernie was training as a printer, Mr Shut (a Methodist Minister and an ex-Governor of Edgeworth) had recognized me in a few pictures in *Spic and Span* and showed them to Ernie. 'Look at that, there's your sister posing for rude photos!' he shouted.

Ernie thought he was sacked by Mr Shut because he had defended me. What really happened I don't know, but later my older sister, Joy, pointed out that Ernie would hardly have got the sack for something like that. Still, it remained a sensitive point between us for years and it was a long time before I stopped feeling guilty, thinking I'd spoilt my brother's chance of training.

I felt lucky to have Brian there to help me through these difficulties. He had a calming effect on my brother. I don't think I could have managed emotionally on my own.

Beth was still living in Edwardes Square. I met up with her again and found a house to buy in the same square. I didn't have much money, but the bank was willing to lend it to me on the strength of my potential career success. I had just enough money now for a down payment.

On one of my first nights in the house, before I had even completed the paperwork, three youngish men broke in through the skylight to try and burgle the house. I had no furniture yet, but I did have several pieces of jewellery in the house – they were the only valuable items I had. It was obvious they were three working-class lads and I remember arguing with them: 'Don't you realize my background is the same as yours?'

'Oh, very good, miss,' one said ripping the chain off my neck. 'I can see that.' If they needed it that much, I said, furious with them, they could have anything they wanted and I was so sorry my furniture hadn't been moved in. Perhaps they needed a sofa? At that, one of the boys got angry back and hit me round the ear. Then he tried to fondle and kiss me. The other two ran out of the front door and I was left alone with a young man who definitely had other things on his mind. I told him he was a fool and he didn't need to behave like this, that he could have a girl of his own. He was attractive enough, why did he need to try and have women this way? Luckily for me this approach worked. He stopped trying to fondle me, sat on the floor and burst into tears. I now felt sorry for him so I made him a cup of tea. Then I asked him would he please leave now because I was going to report the robbery. I struck a deal with him – because he hadn't carried on attacking me, I wouldn't report *his* behaviour to the police.

When he'd gone, I rang Brian immediately. He wasn't there, so I rang John Fitchen, who came straight away. I never returned to that house. Three days later I went into shock. It took me completely by surprise. I realized I couldn't be alone at night any more and needed someone with me.

I reported the robbery and they found the three boys. It became a police case and I was asked to be a prosecution witness. The police thought I was stupid when I said I wouldn't testify. I was so relieved that the boy who had tried to attack me had listened to me and left me alone. But the police didn't know of our deal, of course.

After this incident, I found I could not live in a house by myself. Beth helped me find a flat along the corridor from her and I moved in. I wanted to be able to knock on her door and have lots of friends around me, so I could feel safe. She often had tea gatherings between four and six in the afternoon: a very English tea; toast fingers with Marmite, Earl Grey tea and currant cake to finish. Beth made sure everyone knew each other. They were great fun.

We were all mostly in our twenties; some, like myself, just twenty, some nearly thirty. Beth's guests were an interesting mix of artistic and media people: a few who worked in Fleet Street, advertising types, photographers and maybe a dancer or two. Many came from privileged backgrounds, though they desperately pretended not to. Hugh Hudson was a regular visitor. I don't know what he did at the time, but he spoke with a very pukka English accent, counteracted entirely by his mop of curly blond hair and his mischievous stories. He later became a big success when he directed *Chariots of Fire*.

One day a smallish, boyish-looking man arrived. At first he sat quietly in the corner and seemed to be watching us all intently. Whenever I looked up from the conversation, he was looking at me. Usually I would have found this annoying, but it wasn't unfriendly. Beth told a story about Sammy Davis Jnr and asked him to show us what he was like. He got up immediately and launched into a very funny, accurate impression. We all laughed and cheered, and he sat down again quietly in the corner. As people started to leave, he came up to me.

'My name is Terry O'Neill. I've just got a job for the *Daily Sketch*. Can I take some pictures of you? I'll give you some for your work.' I'd heard this before, but Terry was sincere. Whilst we were talking, I noticed he was younger than I thought. In fact, he was a few months younger than I was, and spoke with a cockney accent, not unlike my dad's family.

The next day he called. 'Hullo, I'm Terry, the quiet one from yesterday.' He then proceeded to talk non-stop for a full hour, telling me all about himself and asking me lots of personal questions. I couldn't have known then I would speak to him at least twice a day for the next four or five years.

A day later Terry called at my flat carrying his camera. He was very quiet, not like he had been on the telephone. He took some photographs and left, and two hours later, he was back with the best pictures I'd ever seen of myself. I was delighted. I'd been given the impression I was difficult to photograph and told Terry so.

'Look at the pictures,' he said. 'They speak for themselves. I wasn't even trying. You can't lose!' He gave me such confidence in myself and had a way of making me feel beautiful.

We found we had a rapport. The pictures he'd taken pleased me and I told him so. He said he liked the photographs, but he'd rather have the real thing. He was cheeky and cheerful, and interested in everything about me. It made him irresistible.

Terry was covering a foreign news story when I first met him. He didn't have much interest in politics then, so I said why not concentrate on photographing women. He obviously liked the work, and if my results were anything to go by, he was bound to be a big success.

When I wasn't working, Terry would pop in for tea and Brian would drop by just as he was leaving. I tried to tell Brian that I was beginning to care for Terry. He'd shrug it off. I didn't break with Brian, but our relationship changed once Terry came into my life. I found out later that Terry thought I was married to Brian at this time.

I filmed *Peeping Tom* a month after I finished *The Entertainer*, although *Peeping Tom* was released first. It starred Carl Boehm and Anna Massey and I had a small role playing a film star. The larger role of the understudy was played by Moira Shearer, a beautiful woman who had starred in *The Red Shoes*. I enjoyed working with Michael Powell as a director, although he had a reputation for being hard on his actors. If this was the case, I didn't see it.

I was still with Bill Watts when I got the part in *Peeping Tom*, but now Dennis van Thal, the man who had first got me a contract with the film studio, had set up his own agency and asked me if I would like to join him. Just before this I heard about a job which I landed independently.

The Royal Court Theatre was producing a new play called *The Lily White Boys*. It was taken from a story written by Wolf Mankowitz and the script was written by a poet, Christopher Logue. On my way to the audition I found out it was to be a musical!

The Royal Court was a small theatre, but it was a breeding ground for new writers, many of who are heavyweights now, like John Osborne, Harold Pinter, Arnold Wesker and David Storey. They all wrote very different kinds of play and there was a little rivalry between them. It was a hotbed of talent with all of them working at what was in fact a fringe theatre. Tony Richardson, the artistic director, wasn't involved with this show, but he would pop in to see how things were going. The administration was run by George Devine. He was responsible for finding and putting together these marvellous new writers and plays.

I went on stage and sang for the director, Lindsay Anderson, the writer and the producer. It was a song called 'Mr Wonderful'.

'That's nice. What else can you do?' I told them most of the songs I knew were hymns. That's all I had learned in the choir at school. I sang again and they liked it. I didn't tell them I wasn't trained.

Lindsay Anderson was great to work with. He seemed to understand what I was trying to do before I did it. I think the rest of the cast felt the same way. We all came from fairly working-class backgrounds, but in his duffel coat and scarf and with his soft accentless voice, it was hard to tell what kind of background Lindsay had come from. People in the theatre said he was from a military family, but he neither confirmed nor denied this. However, when I needed advice for social occasions, Lindsay was the first person I would go to. He always knew what the code of behaviour would be and what the correct dress was.

He had unusual creative ideas. One scene I played high above the stage while behind me, on a big screen, he projected a scene we'd filmed at a New Year's Eve Ball. It was a comic moment where Ronnie Stevens, a marvellously funny actor playing a Boy Scout leader, asked my character, Efth, about her ambitions. 'Would you like to be an actress?'

'Oh no,' Efth would reply. 'I'd rather be a film star!' On opening night this scene got a rapturous reception.

The Lily White Boys was the story of three young teddy boys and girls who were rebels against society, but who find by the end of the play that you can only beat the system by becoming part of it. I should have taken the show's advice!

Albert Finney, Monty Landis and Philip Bond were the three teddy boys. The three girls were played by Georgia Brown, Ann Lynn and myself. Rumour had it that Albert was only free to take the part because he had missed playing the lead in *The Long, the Short and the Tall* through having to have his appendix out. Peter O'Toole starred in that play instead. Albert had left RADA with a dazzling future predicted for him. I was unaware of this, not having been to a conventional drama school myself.

As I have said, on opening night my scene high on the staircase stopped the audience in their tracks. They were standing up and clapping and cheering. I'd never experienced anything like it. It was the most amazing feeling. The next night it happened again, and on each night for three weeks after.

Then, a dreadful thing happened. I went to play the scene as usual, confident and happy, and there was no response. You could hear a pin drop. It was the most awful feeling standing there. I felt naked and alone. I couldn't understand what was wrong. The more I tried to get it right, the harder the wall of silence became. Somehow I got through the scene and came off stage, I wanted to cry. I didn't know what was wrong, nor why they had loved the scene for three weeks, and why it now didn't work. When I asked Ronnie what had gone wrong, he replied, 'Now you know you're funny, and you're playing it for laughs. Before, you played it from your heart.' It took me another painful three weeks to get back to the truth of that scene. It was one of the hardest lessons of my career.

The music wasn't easy either. Tony Kingsey was the musical director and a marvellous jazz drummer. The tunes were nothing like the hymns I'd sung as a choir girl in the chapel at Edgeworth. To complicate matters more, Sean Kenny, our brilliant set designer, knowing we were meant to look as if we were working in a factory, designed an egg testing machine that flew in from the ceiling just as the jazz number began with the three girls on stage. Our lines came exactly on the off-beat of the music while the eggs whirled through a spool arrangement on Sean's factory design. If one of us missed a line, it was difficult to find where to come in again. During one of the performances Ann Lynn, who was between Georgia Brown and myself, laughed so much she hardly sang a word. Georgia and I carried on, making very little sense of the storyline, but the audience hardly noticed. Perhaps they were fascinated by the complications of the *very* intricate egg machine.

Georgia was a little older and had worked more than I had. She'd sung in nightclubs and told me how tough it had made her. She could be quite difficult to be on stage with. I dreaded making a mistake. There was one scene where I was facing the audience and Georgia was down at the front with her back to them. If I didn't come in clearly on the right note, she would laugh at me, pulling a face, which did nothing for my voice. But I wouldn't give up.

At the dress rehearsal an odd thing had happened. The three girls were on different levels of the stage getting dressed in the scene. I was in white underwear and Georgia in black, which she had asked for. As we began to rehearse the scene Georgia suddenly insisted that she should have the white, and sure enough on opening night that's exactly what happened. I had to wear something else.

Halfway through the run, Albert became ill with pharyngitis, which affected his voice. Everybody suggested various cures: he went to the doctor; Georgia made him lemon and honey, and he tried other potions, but still he was croaky. I'd learned how to hypnotize people from a doctor friend of mine called Leonard Henry and offered to try it on Albert. He had nothing to lose – we had a matinee to do and he still hadn't recovered his voice. It worked. Albert sang well that afternoon, but as soon as he finished the performance, he started croaking again.

One performance Albert helped me. My boyfriend in the show was played by Monty Landis. He had to tap me on my behind in one of the scenes. Unfortunately, Monty's taps got more and more enthusiastic. What had started as a gentle pat ended up as a hard thump which propelled me across the stage. Albert saw Monty's slaps getting harder each day, and one day he grabbed Monty in the wings. 'We're ******* actors, remember. You don't have to sock her for real. If you do it again, you'll deal with me.'

Lindsay had two assistants, Tony Page and Stephen Frears. Both of their subsequent creative records speak for themselves.

Tony directs here and on Broadway and works in television in both countries. I worked with Stephen recently in *My Beautiful Laundrette*, and recently he won international acclaim with *Les Liaisons Dangereuses*, a beautiful film. He still looks as he did then: attractive, with black hair and blue eyes, just a shade more rumpled!

Towards the end of the run we found ourselves in competition with a musical comedy called *Fings Ain't Wot They Used T'Be*. It was touch and go which show would make it to the West End. Both shows were about working-class people. *Fings . . .* was written by Frank Norman, a well-known cockney writer famous for his murky past. It was also a marvellous show.

The day before I auditioned for *The Lily White Boys* I had auditioned for *Fings . . .* by director Joan Littlewood.

'No, love, I can't see somebody like you in our show. You don't look very working-class,' she said. The ironic thing was my family came from the East End where the story was set; in fact, the hospital I was born in was a mile from the theatre where the show was playing.

It was *Fings . . .* that made it to the West End and went on to a long run. I didn't think it was any better than our show, but it may have been a shade easier for the audience to accept – in its own way it probably showed more of what people expected to see of working-class life. That might have made it more commercial.

I was only temporarily disappointed. There was something even better waiting for me. Tony Richardson had told me during the shooting of *The Entertainer* that he had a good role for me in the next Woodfall movie based on the Alan Sillitoe novel *Saturday Night and Sunday Morning*. The story was about a character called Arthur Seaton (supposedly based on Alan's brother) who would be played by Albert Finney. I was to play Arthur Seaton's young girlfriend called Doreen. Karel Reisz, who I'd not yet met, was the director. He'd just made a short film that was very well-received. *Saturday Night and Sunday Morning* was his first feature film.

Tony was enthusiastic about my being in the film, but Karel took convincing. After all, we'd never met before and he knew nothing about me. However, he did come along to see me in *The Lily White Boys*.

112

Shooting actually started on *Saturday Night and Sunday Morning* while *The Lily White Boys* was still running. It was exhilarating, but was also wearing, racing from the film studio to the theatre for the show, especially while I was having trouble with my own performance. I only did it for about two or three days. Albert had been doing it for about two weeks, he had a lot of stamina.

We were given a car to get us back to the theatre on time every night. Jan, our driver, suggested we stop for a drink at the Polish Club. Albert and I had to be on stage that evening, but Jan assured us that one Polish drink would only help us. Three drinks arrived on a silver tray, with flames rising above each glass and nuts floating on the top. When he finally blew the flame out, it tasted very good. No sooner did we put our glasses down than Jan nodded his head and another would appear. I left the club feeling distinctly rosier. I arrived at the theatre very relaxed. Every laugh and every gag was right on. I hadn't given such a good performance from the first week. I was so pleased with the results I asked Albert why didn't we stop at the Polish Club again?

'No,' he said. 'This time you can do it on your own. It wasn't the drink that worked. It was just that you let yourself relax.'

We filmed on location in Nottingham, in the same terraced houses Alan Sillitoe grew up in, and in the Raleigh bicycle factory there. The film was on a tight budget, and when we shot other scenes at Twickenham, a small studio in the suburbs of London, Karel would sometimes pick Albert and me up in his van to give us a lift.

This time I was playing a working girl, so my look had to be different from the beauty queen I'd played in *The Entertainer*. Karel was very definite about what he wanted. He didn't want Doreen to be the fashionable girl of that period, with hair falling around her face and very definite makeup. So my hair was pulled straight back in a pony tail, I was left with a pale face, and only my eyes lightly made up. I thought I looked awful.

'No, you don't, you look real,' said my makeup man, who was a dear, kind man. When I look at the film today, I am grateful to Karel because the look has never dated. He was right!

Although Sir Laurence had told me to always look at the rushes, Karel did not want this. He thought it made the actors self-conscious. It was a bewildering time for me working with these strong talents who said opposing things. Much later I found as an actor you had to find your own way of doing things and hope you worked with people you could trust like Karel and Sir Laurence.

I remember on one of the first days playing a scene and not getting it right. It exasperated Karel and frustrated me. He got cross, and told me I wasn't listening properly. I was listening but it still didn't work straight away. There's no doubt, though, his direction was right for me.

We began filming with the light scenes first. It took me several days to get into the character of Doreen. But within a week, she was me, and I was her, and without knowing why, I became Doreen off-screen and on for at least three months. This has happened to me several times since. In fact, one later character I played, was, I think, the girl my husband fell in love with. I wish sometimes I could swap my screen characters with the real me. I'm often calm and dignified on screen, but rather volatile and excitable off.

The cast was terrific. Rachel Roberts played the married woman Arthur Seaton was having an affair with. She was a wonderful actress, and a great friend. She was Welsh and funny and very proud of her legs – a great character. Norman Rossington, as Arthur's best friend, was also Albert's close friend in real life. He was a little older than Albert, but looked younger than his age.

In our love scene, Albert and I had to roll off a sofa to the floor where we consummate our feelings for the first time. I suggested that Albert pull the clip that held my hair back so it would fall free. We fell off the sofa, lit only by firelight, on to the floor. It's a sweet moment where neither of us said a word.

Sometimes Albert would irritate me. He could be such a committed actor, I think he may have done it on purpose. In one scene Doreen gets upset with Arthur and hits out at him. I was furious with Albert that day, and it wasn't hard to play that scene. Many times friends have remarked since they can feel that punch.

By now I'd known Albert some time. We'd both made our debut in *The Entertainer* and done *The Lily White Boys* on stage. Although he could annoy me, it never lasted long. He was too much like the boys I'd grown up with in Lancashire.

While we were on location in Nottingham, Albert knocked on my door one evening. It was a surprise. I asked him in, and we sat and had a cup of tea. For once we weren't aggressive with each other. Perhaps we both left our egos outside the door. 'Would you like me to stay?' he asked. I don't know what I said, but he was there the next morning. I needn't have worried that it would affect our working relationship. It was just as good, in spite of the fact I'd broken my code, which meant never getting too close to the actor I was working with. The code I tried to follow was garnered from the popular magazines of those days. I didn't have anyone else to set me an example, so the agony aunts, like the Claire Rayners of today, set my guidelines. Albert behaved impeccably, which I hadn't expected. On a later film, Steve McQueen once asked me out while we were filming. I told him to ring me when the picture was over, and he did!

I was not in close touch with Albert after the film finished, but three or four years later, just before Christmas, he rang me up. Would I come and visit him for the holiday? He was a different Albert than I had known before. His agent Philip had just died, and he was devastated. I told Albert I couldn't come for Christmas because I spent it with my family, but I could come just after. Myself and Norman Rossington went to stay with him in Brighton at the house his agent had left him. We spent nearly a week there. It was a difficult time for Albert and I was glad he asked me to stay. He went to great lengths to make it a beautiful time for all of us and it *was*!

When *Saturday Night and Sunday Morning* came out the reaction was amazing. Albert became an overnight success, and Rachel and I got lots of attention too. It was funny how some people's attitudes now changed towards me. The success was rewarding, but it was also a difficult time to cope emotionally. When *Saturday Night and Sunday Morning* came out *The Entertainer* had only been out in the cinemas a few months. I'd had a terrific reception with that film, and now it was happening again, but even bigger.

It was funny to see my name twinkling away, in lights that stretched across the top of the marquee, and it gave me a warm feeling to meet people who'd been thrilled with what I'd done. Every morning it was a joy to wake up, with something new and exciting happening every day. I was twenty two years of age and it seemed I didn't have a moment to breathe!

CHAPTER FIVE

Just after finishing *Saturday Night and Sunday Morning* I was sent to Pinewood for an interview with director Basil Dearden and producer George Relph (both their sons are carrying on in their film tradition: Basil's son, James, later wrote *Fatal Attraction*; George's son, Simon, is now the head of British Screen). It was great to arrive for an interview having just starred in two successful films in a row. Basil told me the character was an innocent and funny strip tease artist. The film was to be called *Man In The Moon*, and would star Kenneth More.

When they described the role, I saw it as an opportunity to play a character like the ones I'd seen Marilyn Monroe create. I liked her very much, but a lot of the people I was working with were unenthusiastic about her. This annoyed me, I thought she was marvellous – funny and sweet. It seems that only after she died was she put on a pedestal.

Written by Bryan Forbes and Michael Relph, it was a story about a man who couldn't catch cold, a human guinea pig, who because of this is chosen to be the first astronaut. It wasn't until he fell in love with my character, Polly, that he became vulnerable to the virus. I knew immediately what I wanted Polly to look and sound like – platinum blonde hair, tight-fitting clothes, an undulating walk, with a cockney accent. Basil and George liked my idea about the way the character should look, but had different ideas for her voice. They wanted Polly speaking in a refined English accent. The result was a character wearing very little except for a few well-placed feathers, talking frightfully like a would-be Margaret Thatcher.

I began the film, hopeful that it would be a good experience, but the environment on the set was often tense. Basil believed strongly in discipline. That a film set should be run like the Army: instead of the first assistant shouting 'Action', I half expected Basil to blow a large bugle signalling *reveille*.

The atmosphere didn't help me feel I could do my best work. The film crew and the other actors were jumpy as well. The tension made people feel on edge. I had several wet scenes, and my hair was dripping wet between takes, and the hairdresser would rush to dry my hair.

'For God's sake, get the hairdresser off the set,' Basil would shout. 'She'd be much better concentrating on her work rather than the way she looks,' meaning me, of course.

Kenneth More knew exactly how to handle Basil. He wasn't intimidated by him and made fun of Basil, in a harmless way, by countermanding his orders and impersonating him in a gruff sergeant-major's voice. To Kenny More, acting was just a job. I hadn't worked with anyone like him before. He was calm and pleasant, like you expect your accountant or bank manager to be. With most actors, the ambience is all important, but Kenny More had the knack of creating his own.

One of the wet scenes was filmed in a water tank with an actor called Charles Gray, a charming and debonair man who played the best friend of Kenneth More's character. As the macho leader of the astronauts, he was meant to be more like Charles Atlas than Charles Gray, but Charles was not comfortable in water. He was supposed to rescue me, but half-drowned me in the attempt. By the time we got to the edge of the water tank I was holding Charles up, and attempting to look as if he was saving me. We got there in the end, but not before I'd swallowed half the tank in the ensuing panic.

As the filming progressed, the atmosphere got more tense still. I knew I'd have to do something about my insecurity, and maybe the problem was to do with my childhood. I also wanted to know where I came from and find out the mystery of my background. A doctor friend Leonard Henry was a practitioner of LSD therapy, and he recommended it for me. The treatment combined shots of lysergic acid with memory recall, in addition to group therapy sessions. LSD was not yet known as a 'hip' form of psychedelic release, and the clinic was perfectly legal.

It was at the weekends during the making of *Man In The Moon* that I started having these treatments. On Friday nights I would finish the week's work, and then I couldn't wait for Saturday to come when I'd be at Dr R. D. Laing's clinic in Chelsea. He was the owner of the clinic and known as a great pioneer, famous for his books, one of which I read called *The Divided Self*, and he had a revolutionary approach to psychiatry. There were ten or twelve of us in the group. We'd all check in around five o'clock, have a cup of tea and a chat, then Leonard and his nursing sister would assign us our rooms. It was a bit like visiting a small private hotel or health hydro – the rooms were pretty and comfortable, and all had private bathrooms. By six o'clock, myself and the other patients would be in bed waiting for our LSD shot.

At times the treatment was joyful; at others horrific. You'd hear screaming coming from one room, hysterical laughter from another. The drug induced a flood of memories and images. A flashback of myself as a small child, on the move with my mother and sisters looking for a place to live. Then I saw my mother and father fighting, as if they were in the room with me. Another image, riding up in the cab of my father's lorry, three years old and gleaming with excitement. Suddenly we swerved, tyres squealed, metal scraped and petrol exploded. I found myself sitting alone at night on a dark, lonely wide road with the 'cats eyes' down the middle of the road blinking at me. In my 'dream' my father went off to get help, but it was a very frightening long time before he returned. To this day I am still wary of cats, and sometimes frightened of the dark. For years I wouldn't let myself learn to drive.

When I was having LSD I could remember the locations of houses and places I'd been in as a very small child, aunts and uncles I hadn't met since then, friends of my mother's – all in specific detail. It was amazing. I'd phone my grandmother, who was about seventy five at the time and still lived in the East End of London, and ask her about the things I recalled on LSD. I told her about the day I tried to carry my cousin Sheila down the stairs: I was only one and a half years old myself and I was happy because she was smaller than me; and how I'd dropped her and she'd bounced down every step right to the bottom. I told my grandmother she'd lost her temper and slapped my legs hard to punish me. When she asked, 'How can you remember that?' I just said I was doing some memory treatments. She didn't question me further. Having chosen to be an actress, she felt I was bound to be doing something strange.

In the morning after the treatment the twelve of us would have breakfast together before groggily going home. One of the patients was called Arthur. He was a chef by profession. His wife and daughter would drop him at the hospital and sometimes he'd walk in, in complete female dress. After seeing Arthur in sequins and high-heels, at six feet two inches, with stubble on his chin and long hairy legs, I thought perhaps my own problems weren't that bad. I got used to seeing Arthur this way. He was a kind sensitive man who explained to me he wasn't gay, he just felt much better, and more sensuous when he was wearing feminine clothes. He was generous as well, bringing large bottles of champagne to have with our breakfast so we'd feel better after having had those horrific experiences of the night before.

Another patient was called Betty, a beautiful girl, a professional pin-up model who posed for some of the magazines I once had. I liked her, and she had come from a strict religious background too. She felt badly about her work and I told her to be proud of what she was doing, and if she couldn't be proud then not to pose that way. She wanted the therapy because she was embarrassed about her job, but the extravagant transparent nightgowns she wore for the treatment sessions were far more revealing than any of her modelling pictures I'd seen.

I heard that Cary Grant was another patient of the clinic. Bad luck for me that he was there on different nights, being treated by Dr Laing himself. He had been having the treatment for several years. I had told the doctor how I wished I could be there when Cary Grant was. 'Oh, no you wouldn't,' he'd reply.

After three months or so my reaction to the LSD became violent and I would end up crying for hours, unable to be comforted. Leonard was afraid I would regress so much that he wouldn't be able to control it. He called in Doctor Laing and together they decided that the treatment was too intense for me and it would have to stop. This really upset me. Every weekend, for months afterwards, I hung around outside the hospital, making a nuisance of myself, asking them to continue my treatment. I wanted the LSD, and was frustrated because I couldn't have it now. It had stirred up a lot of horror but I needed to go on. It didn't seem worth it if I couldn't finish the therapy. Regrettably, the doctors said no, assuring me it was non-addictive, and finally letting me help in the clinic with the other patients whose reactions were less violent than mine.

Meanwhile I was trying not to lose my temper at work. It was the last week of filming *Man In The Moon* and, no matter what happened, I'd kept calm – until Basil screamed at me one day and I screamed right back. With his eyes shining with excitement he said, 'That's the girl I want. Why weren't you like this at the beginning?'

Quietly, I said, 'I was afraid of you, Basil, that's why.' The next thing he said really threw me off my guard.

'I shout and scream because I'm afraid of everybody else. My job is to be in charge and run everything like a military operation. That's the way I was brought up.' I hadn't known until then that his childhood had been spent in a children's home too. I wanted to go to him then, and tell him I understood, that I knew how he felt. How could I not know? I'd been brought up that way myself.

I thought at the time my performance could have been stronger, but I like it now. There's a lightness about the film and my character that remains. It was announced that *Man In The*

Moon was to be a Royal Command Film Performance. For this I would need a very special dress. I went to Bermans, a film costumier, immediately and they made me the most beautiful white dress and lace coat. At the rehearsal before the premiere, I was walking down the aisle to my seat when a young man sitting beside Joan Collins, stretched his legs out. I couldn't tell whether he intended to trip me up or not. As he helped me to my feet he said, 'I just wanted to tell you how good you are.' He looked like a handsome college student to me. 'Hi,' he said. 'I'm Warren Beatty. I liked you very much in *Saturday Night and Sunday Morning*.'

The next day I was at a small jewellery shop in South Molton Street looking for earrings to go with my dress, when I bumped into Warren Beatty with Joan Collins again. We were both obviously in a panic trying to get our outfits right for the Royal occasion. Joan was being presented that night as well, along with the rest of us. Warren was going as her escort.

A limousine was sent and Brian, my brother and myself, in my new white dress, were driven to the premiere in luxury. As we got to Leicester Square Brian stopped the car and pulled me outside. 'Look,' he said excitedly. All round the square I saw my name up in lights. One cinema displayed Shirley Anne Field in *Beat Girl*, another had my name over the top of *Saturday Night and Sunday Morning* and the third had lights blinking away outside the canopy for the Royal premiere of *Man In The Moon*.

There was a huge crowd at the barrier and as I stepped out it was a shock to find so many people shouting my name and snapping photographs. It was the first time it had happened, but I didn't have time to be nervous. The crowds waiting at the cinema applauded and I realized it was for me.

I found the Royal Family very impressive. I hadn't expected this. Like most English people, I'd been brought up thinking I knew all about them. The Queen was beautiful, smaller than I imagined, with a good figure. She talked to me for a few minutes, then I spoke with Prince Philip, who laughed and joked. There were a lot of pictures being taken and later people would ask me all sorts of things about this, many of which were just silly questions. I had been presented and thought it was wonderful meeting the Royal Family in this way.

After the premiere, I was invited to a splendid dinner at the Dorchester Hotel by Earl St John, who was the then executive producer at Pinewood. Brian escorted me. We sat at a long formal table, fifteen people on each side. We started the dinner with bowls of red gazpacho soup. Brian, who always had impeccable manners, had sprinkled some pepper on top of his soup and a little must have gone up his nose, because the next thing he did was to sneeze over his soup spoon thereby spraying the red soup over half the dinner table. It was a tricky moment, with guests trying to save their best clothes from being stained. I later told my brother about it and we both laughed hysterically.

When I first signed with London Management, Dennis van Thal's new agency, my life was a whirlwind of activity. Meetings with film executives for prospective jobs, appearances for the films I'd been in, trains half way across England and back in a day. What a difference from my childhood years where everything was so well-planned you knew what you'd be eating three Thursdays forward. It was a panic rushing here, there and everywhere, grabbing taxis, trains and planes and having to look perfectly groomed all the time. I found some people were delighted to meet me, while others were deliberately rude. Many times I was told in no uncertain terms I was only a youngster and not to get above myself.

Then a calming influence came into my life. Dennis's personal assistant was a woman called Jean Diamond. She was a little older than me, with fair shortish hair, good features and warm brownish eyes that had a twinkle in them. Her organized manner was the best thing for my hectic life style. She came from a large, close, loving family in the north of England but was separated from them, working in London. Her husband worked outside the entertainment industry and, in a way, Jean was on her own in London like me. We formed a bond. With myself, everything always seemed to be going on all at once, life was chaotic, and usually unpredictable; Jean was steady and reliable – she planned things carefully. I was the rebel, kicking over the traces as I went along; Jean was more reserved, but just as ambitious and we both had a strong sense of humour.

More and more Jean helped me with my schedule and appointments. We either met or spoke every day and if I didn't go into the office and have lunch with her, we'd just talk and joke on the phone. She got her friend Vicky to help me answer all the correspondence I was now getting. Over lunch one day she told me I was now officially her first client – Dennis had told her she could become the junior agent at London Management. We were both delighted. Soon we heard that a movie called *The War Lover* with Steve McQueen and Robert Wagner was in pre-production and they wanted me for the female lead.

I was leading a complicated private life now, with Brian as my steadying influence, and seeing Terry once again romantically. Just before the film began, I got sick, which frightened me. *The War Lover* was to be my big American debut and I didn't want anything to spoil it. A thorough medical exam was required to make sure I was fit for insurance purposes. The first question the doctor asked was could I be pregnant? No, I answered. My doctor didn't know why I felt sick or what was wrong, but he was sure it wasn't because I was pregnant. The insurance doctor suggested I go to the London Clinic for tests to find out exactly why I wasn't feeling well.

The studio paid for my stay in this luxurious clinic. I had an examination under anaesthetic. When I woke up five hours later I was told that my doctor had been wrong and I was indeed about eight weeks pregnant. Now I had a dilemma on my hands. I badly wanted to do the film, and if I was pregnant they wouldn't hesitate to replace me. There was only the weekend to make up my mind, if I was to play the part of Daphne in *The War Lover*. Filming was to begin on Monday. I talked it over with my doctors and advisors, and decided to stay in the clinic to have a termination. They said it was probably for the best, because of all the medical treatment and pills I had in the last few weeks. After it was over, Jean came to visit me and told me that she'd seen Terry. Apparently he was very upset and had told her he wanted to marry me and have the child. What a pity he told her instead of me. All I felt was furious and drained. It had been an awful time, with medicines, that made me throw up all the time, tests and examinations, and doctors telling me it was all psychosomatic, only to end up this way.

After the clinic, I felt emotionally exhausted and empty and would cry often for no reason. I went back to Brian. I didn't feel I could manage without him. What happened had made me very unhappy and I stopped seeing Terry. I didn't know what else to do but I still missed him.

The War Lover was the first American production I'd worked on. What luxury: I had a large trailer on the set with my name on it, and every time I stepped outside there would be a chair waiting for me. The comfort was nice, but there wasn't much time to enjoy it. I found the Americans worked at twice the pace we did. One good bonus: my friend, David Hurn, was the film's official stills photographer.

The picture was a big investment for the studio. The head of Columbia in England, Mike Frankovich, was a marvellous man who put me under contract to Columbia while shooting the picture. It had all the ingredients of a hit in the making – the veteran producer Arthur Hornblow Jnr – a shy, charming man – a romantic story set in wartime England from the novel by John Hersey, and two big American stars. Watching as a young woman, I could see what a good actor Steve McQueen was. But he could be difficult. Until then he had been a television star in a western show called *Have Gun Will Travel*, and was keen to become a major movie star. He'd practise his gun tricks endlessly, challenging anyone around to outdraw him. How I wished I could have. One day at lunch time he took his landrover out for a drive, to limp back two hours later on foot, telling us his jeep had sunk in the mud. The crew just left it there, and when we'd finished work at about eight that night Steve had to get the local garage to help pull it out. It was easy to like Steve when he was charming, but when he turned or became a show-off he was his own worst enemy.

I think the director, Philip Leacock, was too soft with Steve. If a problem came up, he would always placate him. I think Steve needed people as strong as himself around, otherwise he didn't feel any respect for them. Robert Wagner was great with Steve. I was enchanted with his perfect manners and it didn't hurt that he was also very handsome. However Steve behaved, and he could be impossible, Robert Wagner would always find a way to calm him down. I told Philip one day I hoped I would grow to be like Robert Wagner.

'No,' he replied, 'you're too much like Steve.' I didn't know if he was talking about a physical resemblance or did he mean our characters were alike? I didn't ask him because I was afraid of the answer.

As the film progressed Steve told me about his childhood. This is when I liked him very much. We'd sit in his caravan and he'd tell me story after story. He was proud of his tough upbringing, how he'd been left and brought up in the slums, how he had had no money and had served time in a reform school. I loved these stories, and would sit enraptured, but I did notice that on some days the details of his stories would change depending on what mood Steve was in. He would even pick up a news article and weave it into his stories. A mayor elected in Harlem – did I know his uncle had served a term? A baby found abandoned in the street – that was Steve at the age of five months. The more I questioned him, the more outrageous the stories became. With a solemn face, he'd describe his wife to me, as a Polynesian princess. The next week she had grown up in a tough neighbourhood like his, and was a Puerto Rican girl from New York. One of the things I liked about Steve was that whenever I pointed out the discrepancies he wasn't put out in the least. I was to come across this same quality again and again in a certain type of actor – Yul Brynner was one of them, and he was just as outrageous as Steve.

Under the surface there was an insecurity about Steve that was surprising. If a newspaper printed a photo of Robert Wagner and myself in a scene together, Steve would sulk for the rest of the day.

Robert Wagner was very easy to get along with, and very attractive too. He was quiet and charming, as calm and smooth as Steve was turbulent and unpredictable. When I'd say nice things to Steve about RJ, as we called him, Steve would say with a grin, 'Wait until you see us on screen. Then you'll think I'm the pretty one.'

In one scene, Steve visits my character, Daphne, at home. I am in a dressing gown with my back to the audience, facing Steve, and he was meant to rip it off down to my waist. I was nervous about how I would feel standing there only half dressed. The rehearsals went well when I was wearing something underneath the dressing gown, but when we came to shoot the scene, we couldn't get the gown to split. The wardrobe mistress explained that Steve had asked her to reinforce the stitching so it wouldn't come apart. Steve said he didn't want me to feel awkward being exposed. The following part of his explanation was probably nearer the truth. 'Besides,' he said, 'if you're standing there half-naked, who the hell's going to look at what I'm doing.' At the end of the same scene Steve had to throw me on to a sofa about eight feet away.

'Let's not rehearse,' he said. 'I don't want to hurt her.' When we came to shoot it, he threw me right across the room, and I landed behind the sofa and out of shot. Eight times more we repeated it, and each time I landed farther and farther away behind the sofa, and more out of shot than before. One side of my face was bleeding and I was beginning to feel dizzy. But I didn't get mad as I was trying hard to follow RJ's example by keeping calm at all times. Luckily for me, my dearest makeup man, John, couldn't stand it any more. He came to repair my face and stop the bleeding, and he said to me:

'Next time, bite the bugger's lip when he kisses you. That should stop him.' I did as John told me. Guess what? We got the take in one go, perfectly. I looked up at Steve afterwards and he gave me the thumbs-up sign and winked.

'Good work, kid,' he said. 'Good work.'

When I saw the film I thought of Steve McQueen's words. I was disappointed to find the film was not what I expected. I thought we would light up the screen because I thought RJ was magical, but the ingredients weren't mixed in the right way to let us shine.

Just before Christmas, during the pre-production weeks of filming, my sister Sunny rang me from America in great distress. It was three in the morning and she was crying hysterically. She was married again, to Ronald, a police officer from Washington DC, and told me she had two new babies called Scott and Lisa. Scott was eighteen months and Lisa was eight months of age. After an ugly fight with Ronald she had no money, and nowhere to live.

I was in despair after the phone call, up most of the night, panicking about my sister. If I hadn't been signed for *The War Lover* I would have flown to her straight away. I wanted to help by sending anything I could. Brian wouldn't lend me money, saying sensibly to wait and see what she really needed, so I wired her £100. It was the only money I had. Sunny said it had helped, but she still couldn't afford the air fares. Luckily my first cheque from the film came through the next week and I sent some more to her. The following week she arrived in London with her children.

I was glad to see Sunny, but was shocked by her appearance. My sister who'd once been the beauty of the family was showing signs of a hard life. She was white as a sheet, and her hair was very short and ragged and standing on end, as if she'd cut it herself without looking. Also she was as thin as a rake. She told me she had lost her other children, but these two she would keep no matter what. With her she brought a large sack of nappies, and another of used baby clothes. We would need a launderette and quickly. She was amazed I didn't own a washing machine, still a luxury in England in those days.

I had a hotel booked for her next door, with cots for the children, but Sunny wanted to be all together. Brian agreed even though it was impractical as his flat was not really big enough. We thought she'd come back home permanently and had left America for good. What we didn't realize was she'd only come for a visit. I had booked the hotel as a treat until we could find a more permanent home for her.

We made makeshift beds in Brian's flat for the babies and got them off to sleep. I was fascinated by eight-month-old Lisa and how lovely she was to feed and hold. Sunny showed me how to change nappies and make formulas so I could help with the children. She was exhausted, but couldn't sleep. She was always a night person, and very excited to be back home in England. We rang my grandmother, and spoke to Auntie Elsie and my cousin Sheila. Except for Sheila, whom my grandmother had brought up, Sunny was my grandmother's favourite. They got on well, and had a rapport. Sunny made arrangements to see them in the next few days. Nan and Aunt Elsie wouldn't give our dad a message as they'd had an argument with him and weren't speaking to him, so I sent him a telegram. When he received it, he did ring, and I was relieved he was nice to me on the phone. Sunny made plans to meet him.

We talked far into the night. I hadn't seen her for almost eight years, but we'd kept in touch. There was so much catching up to

127

do. Her life in America was fascinating and awful to hear about. Contrary to her phone call, Ronald turned out to be a loving man. Before Ronald, Sunny had been married to Jimmy, the father of two of Sunny's other children who were now living with Jimmy's mother in Florida. Sunny felt they were better off there. Her oldest child, Joy, was living in Texas with her first husband's, David's, mother.

'That's why Lisa and Scottie are so important to me,' Sunny said. 'Now I'm ready to be a mother.' I understood what she meant, but wasn't sure how Ronald would cope with her and the children living back in England. 'Let's not think about that now,' Sunny said.

When Sunny became furious at the memory of our mother, 'Ivy' as Sunny called her, and our sister Joy I just didn't know what to do. I was as lost as she was but always hoping there would be some explanation for why they'd disappeared. I reassured Sunny that our mother hadn't picked Joy over us. We both huddled together and cried, trying to ease the pain, even though many years had gone past.

It was impractical in Brian's flat – as he had feared he was working during the day, and with everyone sharing together, it was chaotic. I again thought the hotel next door would be the perfect solution while Sunny and myself looked for a more permanent home for her. It had nursery facilities for the kids, which would help Sunny recover from all the strain she'd been through. The hotel rang me a few days later.

'Where's your sister, Miss Field? We're looking after these children and they're crying for their mother. We can't find her.'

When Freddie, my friendly neighbour from Abbey Road, offered to put them up I was relieved. There were two large bedrooms in his flat, and I thought that would be the solution because he was a fatherly man. After a week Freddie rang me.

'I can't look after Sunny any more. She goes out and leaves me alone with these two tiny children, I'm an old man and my flat's all in a mess.' Freddie was meticulous and now he had wet nappies drying everywhere, toys over the floor, and Scott had drawn pictures on the walls. I was torn, I loved Sunny but I could see Freddie's point of view.

Sunny told me it was the first time she had had anyone helping her with her kids. 'You don't know what it's like,' she said. 'I've

(Left) My father as a young man, a football hero

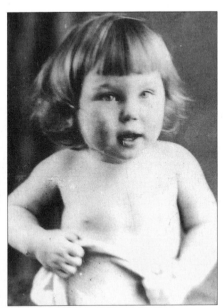

(Above) Myself at not quite two

Three little girls in Sunday best. In fact, the clothes cost my mother a month's rent. I'm in the middle, with Joy on the left and Sunny on the right

(Right) My mother, Ivy, with Bill, her second husband

(Below) The 'family' at Blackburn. I'm in the front row cuddling a little boy called Godfrey

(Right) A school picture of me, aged nine

(Far right) With Sister Jessie, at a reunion. She was the games mistress at Edgeworth and also Sister Hilda's deputy

(*Above*) My first 'glamour' portrait, aged eighteen

(*Left*) An early personal appearance for the troops, after a show organized by Harry Secombe

(Above) With Brian Peters, who was my first important boyfriend and who became my family

(Right) A still from one of my first films, *Once More With Feeling*, in which I played a beatnik student *(Martin C. Holzapfel)*

(Below) Rehearsing the love scene from *The Entertainer* with Sir Laurence Olivier and Tony Richardson *(British Lion Films Ltd)*

(Above) The fight scene from *The Lily White Boys*, with Georgia Brown *(centre)* and Ann Lynn *(The Hulton Picture Company)*

(Left) A 'snap' taken by Terry O'Neill

(Below) Albert Finney and myself in the fairground scene from *Saturday Night and Sunday Morning* *(British Lion Films Ltd)*

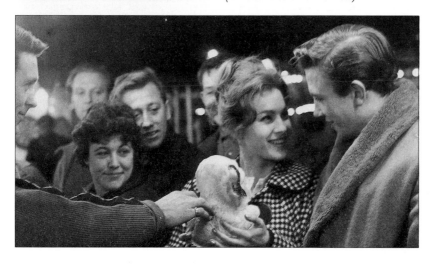

(Right) Albert and me jiving at the first-night party for *Saturday Night and Sunday Morning* *(PIC Photos Ltd)*

(Below) Norman Rossington and me in Germany on a publicity tour for *Saturday Night and Sunday Morning*, trying to read the German reviews (all good!)

(Left) With Kenneth
More in *Man in the
Moon* – it was my
tribute to Marilyn
Monroe
*(Rank Film
Distributors)*

(Below) Being
presented to the
Queen at the Royal
Premiere for *Man in
the Moon*
(P.A. Reuter)

(Above left) A Cecil Beaton shoot for American *Vogue* with the *Beyond the Fringe* team. From left: Dudley Moore, Peter Cook, Alan Bennett, Jonathan Miller
(Cecil Beaton photograph, courtesy of Sotheby's, London)

(Above right) With Robert Wagner in *The War Lover*
(The Kobal Collection)

(Below) With Robert Wagner, Steve McQueen and Philip Leacock (the director on the set of *The War Lover*)
(The Hulton Picture Company)

(Left) With
MacDonald Carey in
The Damned
(The Kobal Collection)

(Above) With Yul Brynner in *Kings
of the Sun*

(Left) Recovering from LSD
treatment at R.D. Laing's clinic
(Terry O'Neill)

(Right) The cover of
Nova, May 1965
(IPC)

(Below) With Robert
Stephens in *The Lunch
Hour*, directed by James
Hill and written by John
Mortimer

(Left) With James Robertson Justice and Leslie Phillipps (*on the right*) in *Doctor in Clover* (*The Kobal Collection*)

(Above) With Michael Caine in *Alfie* (*The Kobal Collection*)

(Left) Charlie Crichton-Stuart, my handsome hero

(Above) Our wedding day,
7 July 1967
(Daily Mail)

(Right) My sister Sunny, with
her children Lisa and Scott

(Left) With Nicola, at three days old. Isn't she beautiful?
(Daily Mail)

(Below) Back at work, in a production of Noel Coward's *Private Lives*. Alan Freeman, making his stage début, on the right of the sofa
(Malcolm Powell)

(Top right) Charlie and me with Nicola, just after her third birthday

(Right) Nicola with Lita, her South African nanny, in South Africa in 1973

(Below) Breaking the law in South Africa, visiting a township

(Top left) With Victor, in the
last year of his life

(Bottom left) In Alan
Ayckbourn's *How the Other
Half Loves* at the Theatre
Clwyd
(Brian Tarr)

(Bottom right) With Saeed
Jaffrey in *My Beautiful
Laundrette*
(The Kobal Collection)

(*Above*) I finally meet my mother

(*Right*) My mother, myself and
Nicola: three generations – I never
would have believed it possible

had one baby after another for eight years. I need a break.' I could easily understand her feelings. Sunny was enjoying herself, perhaps for the first time in a long while.

We had some marvellous moments together on this trip. A couple of my friends called Jack and Bunty gave an annual New Year's Eve party in Eaton Square Mews, with myself as the joint hostess, and they asked me to invite the guests. They had the impression, because of my job, that I knew all the outrageous people in London. I did know a few. Eaton Square Mews was a beautiful place. They had a lovely house and they hired staff especially for the night, some of whom worked at Buckingham Palace and were earning extra money. We filled it to the rafters with anyone who was remotely interesting. Only by invitation though, otherwise the party was invaded by gatecrashers. One year Michael Caine and Terry Stamp came without an invitation. I knew them only slightly, but nevertheless they stayed. That year the party was more of a success than ever. Great music, good food and a wonderful assortment of lively people. Someone put on Chubby Checker's 'Let's do the Twist'. The dance was the latest craze, and the only one who could do the new dance was Sunny. As she started we formed a circle round her. She was radiantly happy, wearing a short white, strapless chiffon dress, and dancing across the floor as everyone clapped. She had been a dance instructor in one of her numerous jobs. We may have been the first people in England who knew how to twist properly, thanks to Sunny's instruction.

Midnight struck, and as everyone kissed, Sunny and I found each other and held each other tight. We vowed to look after one another always. It was a promise neither of us would break. I'm glad we had these few good times together because our lives took very different directions in the next few years.

Sometimes Sunny would visit me on the set. She had loved Steve McQueen in his television series in the States. Just before a film take he would ask for a mirror to check his hair, and that small detail annoyed Sunny. It wasn't because he wasn't masculine, I told her, it was just part of his job. As Steve would shout to his makeup man, 'This haircut's going to be up there a long time.' She was convinced he was effeminate, the one thing Steve most certainly wasn't. It made me realize how different our lifestyles were becoming. I knew that Steve was just being professional but Sunny saw film work in terms of the fan magazines. Another misconception was that Robert Wagner and Philip Leacock thought that Scott and Lisa were my children and that Sunny was really their nanny. Apparently I had a secret life that I wasn't telling anyone about.

Sunny had other misconceptions as well. She'd expected to find me living the life of a big star, with a grand house and lots of money and in reality I was a young woman just starting to make my mark in films. I wasn't living the high life – there wasn't the time, or the money. This was England, not Hollywood. I was filming all day and, unless Sunny joined me, we couldn't spend as much time together as we would have liked. I spent time with Scott and Lisa when I wasn't filming. They were great, and being with them brought back memories of Rupert and some of the kids I'd grown up with.

I was terrified of having children like Sunny had done, away from home, with little or no money, no relatives except in-laws, and changing husbands. No wonder she had no energy to cope with life. When she was tired, she could be harsh with everyone, including her own children.

Sunny didn't get a chance to see our brother. He had emigrated to Australia to seek a better life. Before he left he had changed his name to Guy. At his advertising job that's what he had been called and he liked the name. He had never liked Ernie.

After a few meetings with our dad at his home, where Gypsy would forbid him to mention my name, that were uncomfortable for her, Sunny became less pleased with the idea of visiting there.

When she told me she'd wanted to go back to the States I wasn't surprised. I knew life was easier for her back there. The fight with her husband, that I thought had destroyed her life, had been over the next day, and forgotten. She missed him and wanted to return. Brian helped me organize the travel arrangements, and Terry came with us to the airport and took pictures of Sunny and the children. Despite Sunny leaving we were both happy we'd seen each other, but sad to part. No matter how different our lives, the bond was unbreakable. Seeing my sister again, laughing and crying together, was worth everything.

*

130

I became good friends with Bob Huke, our cinematographer on *The War Lover*, and his wife, Joy. They were an interesting couple who had lived a lot of their lives in South America, and both spoke fluent Portuguese. Joy was aged about thirty five years, had lovely golden hair and a pretty face and figure. Bob was older, tanned, with silver hair and perfect manners. They had a holiday apartment in Marbella right in Orange Square and said I should buy an apartment there as well. It was a sleepy little fishing village then, and if I'd followed their advice the apartment would be worth a small fortune today.

Sometimes I joined them in Marbella on holiday. The only hotel in town was along the seafront owned by a local man called Tomaniso. We'd have a terrific time at the bar there drinking delicious sherry, eating calamary and singing songs.

They were always urging me to live more grandly. If I was to be thought of as a star, they said, I should act like one. Back in London, I organized a dinner party for them, and invited Jean and her husband Martin as well. Terry, who had become a friend, and I had a good idea. I would appear to take their advice seriously, dressing Terry up as my new butler. He was to be the latest addition to my new starry lifestyle. Jean and Martin were aware of the joke and knew Terry well.

When Bob and Joy arrived they were delighted with my new found help. Joy thought he was perhaps a little young, but said he seemed quite willing! Terry poured it on with a shovel. He bowed and scraped and used our surnames when speaking to us. Then he began to flirt with Joy, showering her with compliments and asking what scent she was wearing. We began to include our 'butler' in the conversation and, as the evening wore on, he got, seemingly, more familiar and appeared to be getting rather drunk. After the main course, Terry capped his performance by bringing in the bathroom stool to join us at the table.

'I'm sorry, madame,' he said to me. 'This is the only chair I can find.' He asked Joy if he could sit next to her, then served an extra helping for himself. When Terry disappeared into the kitchen for the next course, I asked Joy what she thought.

'I don't want him eating with us,' I said.

'You should have been clearer at the beginning,' she replied. 'You can't hurt his feelings now.'

The joke worked so well the rest of us had to suppress our laughter. In the end I couldn't tell Bob and Joy the truth, since they had been so sweet and kind to my clumsy 'butler' and I felt rather mean at having deceived them.

Before *The War Lover* was released I went off to a quiet Edwardian seaside town called Weymouth, for a film called *The Damned*. It was a horror story about children who were being conditioned to live with radiation when the holocaust came. Oliver Reed and myself were the leaders of a gang of twelve youths who came into contact with the children. Riding our motorbikes up and down the small streets in our black leather outfits, we caused quite a stir.

Our director Joe Losey had left America in 1951 after being named as a communist. In the McCarthy hearings someone who had been in a Marxist class with him had given his name to the congressional committee investigating 'un-American activities', and Joe had refused to testify. He had to leave America and his home and work in Europe, he remained there for two decades. *The Damned* was one of several films he made in England at that period. Just after that film he had a big success with *The Servant*, which ironically got him an invitation to work back in America again.

I liked Joe very much. He appeared eccentric and vague yet didn't miss a thing. He didn't say much, or give you a lot of direction, except to tell you to do it over and over and over until you got it right. He seemed to look at everything but you when working – the sky, the landscapes, birds flying past – and still get the results.

With helicopters flying overhead for our safety, early one dawn Oliver, myself and MacDonald Carey who was playing the other leading role, were roped together and lowered to the bottom of a deep ravine for a dramatic scene. Unfortunately for us, the light changed while we were there, so Joe and the whole crew, plus helicopters, left to film somewhere else, ignoring the three of us still at the bottom where they'd lowered us so carefully earlier in the day. I was furious. In the three hours it took us to climb out of there I learned an important lesson. As MacDonald Carey kept saying, 'Don't ever take it seriously, my dear, they only give us the star treatment when it's necessary for the job.' When we got back to the hotel, footsore and weary, Joe asked where we'd been.

It shouldn't have taken so long to get back, he said. It didn't occur to Joe that it had taken an hour and a half to lower us down that morning with ropes, pulleys, as well as manpower. I felt like I'd just climbed Everest and told him so. He just laughed and said the exercise would do me good.

Oliver and myself played an incestuous brother and sister, with MacDonald Carey as the other main part. Tony Valentine was one of the gang, as was Kenneth Cope, who would later play in many things, including *Coronation Street*. I was working with twelve talented and attractive young men, most of whom became big successes later on. It could have been worse.

Oliver was one of the most beautiful men I'd seen – a strong face, flawless olive skin, black hair and blue eyes, fringed with long dark lashes. I liked looking at Oliver, but that was that. His voice sounded affected to me as if he had a plum in it, like a lot of old actors from the previous school of British Film Acting. Oliver was genuinely posh, of course, which I didn't know then, so it may have been his normal way of speaking.

As I've said, Tony Valentine was another member of the gang. He was funny, charming and full of personality. I couldn't tell where he came from. His voice was deep and great to listen to. To my astonishment he came from Blackburn where I had spent two years of my childhood. I don't remember many people from there sounding like Tony. He was attractive, warm and very attentive. I was attracted by Tony, but I steered away from him because of my already complicated love life.

I became very self conscious of the way I sounded at this stage. The people in charge had decided I finally looked all right, that I was even photogenic, but now I was heavily criticized for my voice. There was still a British insistence then on everyone sounding like the BBC, *Saturday Night and Sunday Morning* being the first exception. I was keen not to sound plummy, as the BBC announcers sounded then. I disliked that sound and it is rarely used nowadays. Joe Losey was American and couldn't hear the regional differences anyway. What's more he couldn't have cared less. As long as you made yourself clear that was enough. My beliefs about sounding real had been so criticized by now that I'd got self-conscious so, in self-defence, I adopted a flat monotone. As a result, my acting was not as free as it should have been.

On the location there was so much background noise that the sound became impossible to record, so most of the dialogue was put on after the film was finished. Adding the sound afterwards can be dreadful if you don't recreate the emotions of the part. When Jean and I saw the film, we were both cringing at the way I sounded. The funny thing is I don't mind it now, but then I had very little faith in my own ability.

I had a quarrel with Joe one day when I kept falling off my large unwieldy motorbike. I couldn't manage it very well. For a start, the kick pedal needed the force of my whole weight just to turn the engine over. Then the damn thing would fall over on to me. It wasn't so much the riding that scared me, it was just that most of the boys started before I did, they'd mastered their kick starters. When I looked ahead to see them falling off one by one, hitting the ground with an almighty thump, naturally it didn't do too much for my confidence. Joe reluctantly came up with a compromise and had the bike tied to the back of the van. Then he was able to get the close-ups he wanted of me as I was pulled along.

Anything involving climbing or falling I could do easily. I had been good at gymnastics at Edgeworth, and prided myself on being agile. There was a scene where my character had to jump about fifty feet down on to a boat and Joe decided to use a male double. The stunt man was a darling bloke who had imitated my way of running fairly well, but was about twice my size. I told Joe that I would do it myself and, to his surprise, I ran along the seafront, jumped straight off the quayside on to the boat fifty feet below, and started speaking my dialogue immediately. I didn't hear another word from Joe about motorbikes after that.

Back from Weymouth, I received a phone call from Mike Frankovich to ask if I would like to go on a publicity tour of America for *The War Lover*. It was a marvellous opportunity. Like most English girls who had been brought up in the war, America was a dream place. I couldn't wait to get there.

The huge skyscrapers and the majestic views of New York took my breath away. There was no time for jet lag, although my head did spin, and if I wasn't nearly falling asleep on my feet, I felt high all the time. The strange exhilaration of New York, coupled with so many smart upper crust occasions and charity events, made me feel as though my feet were hardly touching the ground.

Arthur Hornblow Jnr and his wife were determined this would be a trip I would enjoy and always remember. I was surrounded by luxury. A wonderful suite in the Sherry Netherlands Hotel in New York, all the food I could eat and room service round the clock. There wasn't enough time to relish it – a reception at eleven in the morning, two press conferences in the afternoon, a formal dinner in the evening, with a similar schedule each day for the next two weeks. Assigned to look after me was a publicist called Bud Rosenthal. He was in charge of the publicity for *The War Lover* and arranged my schedule. He was only a couple of years older than me and had a terrific sense of humour and a fast New York way of talking.

Some of the occasions I was invited to, including stage and television appearances, required full evening dress, and the publicists suggested I shop at the boutique in the hotel and charge it to the company. When I saw the prices, I decided not to buy. It was a strange dilemma for a young actress. My childhood ethics were still strong – I felt that one shouldn't spend other people's money, but looking back now, perhaps I should have. It was essential, and in the company's best interest, that I looked just right for these appearances.

I answered the telephone in my suite one afternoon to hear a man announce himself as the top photographer from *Life* magazine. Could he make an appointment to photograph me? I was delighted. It didn't occur to me he hadn't gone through the usual channels. He started talking quietly, telling me how good my work was, then he got quite personal and told me what a great shape I had. I still didn't think anything was amiss, I just thought this was his American way of being more forthright. However, as the conversation progressed I began to realize something wasn't quite right. Most photographers would ask your size, but they wouldn't specify details. As soon as I realized he wasn't genuine I reacted in shock. At this, the man gabbled something incoherently, some of which I gathered, most of which I fortunately didn't. His conversation had made me feel really grubby and I immediately called the hotel operator and asked if she knew where the phone call had come from. They couldn't trace it, but said they would monitor my calls from now on and watch my door. It wasn't a nice feeling to be in this strange, magnificent town, thinking there was some awful man out there who knew far too much about me and, what's more, where I was staying.

Bud arranged lots of radio and television appearances. They were all fun, and the presenters were fantastically good and very quick, a different style from back home. One was the *Johnny Carson Show*, which in those days was done from New York. It was great fun. On the same show with me were Jimmy Durante and Zsa Zsa Gabor. Johnny didn't meet his guests before the show, I think he wanted to keep it spontaneous when he met you live on the air. His way of flirting relaxed me and made me forget about the viewers. The show must have gone well because the station had a number of calls about me afterwards. When they said one was from the White House I thought they were joking.

Bud was anxious for me not to feel homesick, not that I had the time. He told me about a marvellous group of English people who were in *Beyond The Fringe*. I knew them. Just before I'd arrived in New York I'd been photographed for American *Vogue* by Cecil Beaton with them. Dudley Moore and I got in touch with each other. When I returned one of his phone calls at the theatre and said who I was, it wasn't Dudley but Peter Cook who answered the phone. I'm not sure if he believed me. He called out to Dudley in a grotesquely funny cockney accent, which I don't think I was supposed to hear, 'Oh, I've got that bleeding Shirley Anne Field on the phone again. I suppose you're going to have Ursula Andress or Marilyn Monroe calling you next, are you?' It became a running gag with them.

Dudley and I met at Reubens Delicatessen for a drink and I read his hand. I'd been studying a book about palm reading and, to my surprise, I kept hitting on the truth. He was mad about a girl called Celia Hammond, who was a successful model as Jean Shrimpton was at that time. I nicknamed her 'the vet' because she was crazy about animals. I told Dudley that according to his palm their relationship would last only three weeks, not thinking I would become involved with him. We were just friends at this stage.

After two weeks in New York, I left for the next stop: Boston. Bud stayed back in New York and another publicist from Columbia joined me. A suite of rooms was waiting for me at the hotel. I checked in and had a rest, and two hours later I was woken by the publicist calling to tell me I was scheduled to do a television broadcast that evening, a discussion with a women's group. As I opened my door to leave I saw two large Marine guards on either side of the entrance. It was very impressive, but I was somewhat taken aback. I thanked them for watching my door but couldn't understand why they were there. The one on the left saluted.

'The President is coming in tonight, miss, to vote for his brother. The top floor has been vacated, but you've been cleared to stay.' The President's youngest brother, Edward, was running for a seat in the United States Senate, and he was coming back to his home state to cast his ballot. It was November 1962. When I met the publicist in the lobby I told him how excited I was and maybe we would see the President.

'Oh, no we won't,' he said. 'We're leaving tonight.' On the itinerary he'd given me I thought we were to stay in Boston another two days. He gave no explanation, and I was really disappointed, leaving my suite of rooms with my bags packed, and missing the arrival of the President by only a few hours.

The War Lover had its world premiere in Dallas, Texas. It was spectacularly presented by Columbia. Steve McQueen and Robert Wagner flew in from California and we all arrived at the cinema together. Outside huge arc lights made white circles in the sky. We walked into the cinema on a crescendo of music and moved slowly through the stalls to our seats with the audience standing, clapping and cheering. The whole place was jumping with excitement. RJ sat on one side of me, and David Resnick, Steve's publicity man, on the other. Steve sat next to him. I couldn't wait for the film to start.

The first scenes that came on screen were fine, but then it began to get slower and slower. There's something wrong, I thought. There I was up on the screen and I could see that Steve's comments had been proved right. There was no excitement in the film and no tension, except when he was on. My two or three scenes with him were good, but I had been expecting so much more. I was crushed. I sank lower and lower in my seat, squirming with embarrassment. I think Steve must have seen me out of the corner of his eye, because he did something I didn't expect. He changed seats with David Resnick and whispered to me under his breath, 'Don't let them see you like that. Hold your head up. You've done it now. Doesn't matter if it doesn't work. It's not my best movie either.'

When the final credits faded out I couldn't tell if the audience were clapping or not. I was too lost in my own feelings. The three of us were expected to go on stage, and I felt like there were weights holding me down in my seat. Steve got hold of my arm, and propelled me upwards on to the stage, all the time talking to me quietly, telling me to smile. RJ Wagner was terrific with the audience but I guessed he would be, he was funny and sweet, as well as being good to look at.

'Go to the centre of the stage, take your bow and tell them how great it is to be here,' said Steve. 'Then after we get out of here you can go and cry by yourself. As long as they don't see you.' It was the strangest thing: Steve, the hustler and show off, who could be violent, had now quite literally got me through the evening. It was a side to him I hadn't really seen before, a sensitive side that he'd always kept well hidden. Before that occasion I'd always remembered Steve being macho and difficult and saying during the shooting, 'Watch me, kid. I'm going to be the biggest star in the world.' As he helped me through that night's ordeal, I had a premonition that Steve's time would come. The very next film he made, *The Great Escape*, made him into the colossal star he always said he would be.

That night Steve took Jeanne Baldwin, my girlfriend visiting from New York, myself and David Resnick out to a club. We walked down the staircase to a basement where a modern jazz band was playing. We were a few of the only white people there. Steve was very much at home, more relaxed than I'd ever seen him, and knew a lot of the people there. Here was another Steve I hadn't seen before. Dave Resnick and I struck a rapport. He was tall, slim and attractive. Jeanne spent the evening talking to Steve.

The tour moved on to Washington DC, where I met up with Sunny. Her situation hadn't improved much, and I thought it might be nice to have lunch together at my hotel. She brought along a girlfriend of hers, a go-go dancer called Sharon. I wanted it to be just right. Unfortunately, it turned out to be a dreadful lunch. Sharon didn't like anything on the menu, and Sunny couldn't eat anything either. Ever since we were small, she found it difficult to eat if she was watched. Thinking back maybe Sunny was borderline anorexic. She was certainly very thin. Jeanne Baldwin was visiting me in Washington and I seemed to have more in common with her than Sunny. I was really upset that my sister didn't seem happy or like the luxurious hotel. It wasn't until we got back to her home much later that Sunny became her old self. When I met Ronald, he was handsome and charming, and loved Sunny, in spite of Sunny's middle of the night phone call months earlier, from which I'd imagined he would be an ogre.

The American towns and cities became just a whirlwind as we flew from one to another on our flying tour: Chicago, Philadelphia, Denver, Portland; even the luxury hotels began to look all the same when we got to the ninth or tenth. Only certain stops stand out. In San Francisco I did a radio interview from the top floor of the Mark Hopkins Hotel. In my room I remember turning on the television set and seeing Tony Bennett singing 'I Left My Heart In San Francisco'. How romantic to hear this great singer singing about San Francisco just as I arrived and was stepping through the door.

Our last stop was in Los Angeles. Getting off the plane into the balmy air was wonderful, so gentle after the hectic tour. Bud arranged for David Resnick to meet the plane and look after me while I was staying in Los Angeles. He escorted me in an enormous convertible limousine to the Beverly Hills Hotel. I'd never seen anything like it – large pink and green flowers painted in huge murals on the hotel corridor walls, and cottages lining the walkways where porters and waiters rolled their carts along under the sunshine. It was pure Hollywood. The rooms in the Beverly Hills Hotel were simple, painted in soft, restful pastels, and rather plain. It complemented the sunshine and flowers outside, which were in abundance on the terraces, and was quite a contrast to the overdone corridors. I walked through French windows to my own private terrace before I unpacked. As I sat outside in the soft afternoon sunshine, sipping a fresh orange juice, it seemed truly magical.

No sooner had I relaxed than the phone started ringing non-stop. There were people calling, and I had no idea how they knew I was in there. Nor did I know how to cope with them. I was elated with the first one or two calls, people welcoming me and offering me lunch or dinner, or whatever, or just to talk about work. But after about the tenth call I was in a panic. I was confused by people's friendliness and didn't know who was sincere and who wasn't. Nothing before in my working life had equipped me to deal with all this attention. I phoned Jean in London. I wanted her to help me sort through this maze of work, calls, social invitations and outright conmen. Dennis thought it was too extravagant to send her to America, besides, they needed her in London. So he arranged for a woman from LA, named Mina Wallace, to call on me. She was the sister of the producer Hal Wallace. Dennis said she had all the experience necessary to guide me through the hysteria of Hollywood.

Mina was a tiny woman of about seventy. Her voice was gravelly and nasal, with what sounded to me like a Brooklyn accent, and she spoke with the speed of a machine gun. I opened the door to her, and she greeted me with, 'I don't know why they've sent for you. We've got all these gorgeous girls here, what do we need you foreigners for? They could have got ten Natalie Woods for the part. She'd be perfect.'

Despite Mina's view, the phone still rang inviting me here, there, everywhere, and I was meeting a lot of people who told me they liked my work. That made me feel good. It was rewarding compared to the coolness I'd encountered back home. I think I was popular in England (judging by the response from the public). But the people who employed actors were sometimes cold. They often gave the impression I'd been lucky in getting a job because I'd fitted in with what they wanted the character to be like. This made me unsure of my work. The enthusiasm in America boosted my confidence.

Like all good fairy stories there had to be a catch. *The War Lover* hadn't been released yet. It was not to be a box office winner for Columbia. The doors opened wide for an actress when you were in popular movies, as I had been, but to appear in a film that wasn't box office was to find them firmly shut. It was another tough lesson to learn.

One person I saw a lot of was David Resnick. We became close friends. He didn't drink, but he did smoke dope (marijuana), and I smoked with him. After my experiences with LSD it was very mild, but it did calm me and made me laugh a lot. At the parties we went to I noticed the people who smoked were often the gentlest – no spilled drinks, no aggression – and mostly just falling asleep on the floor or the sofas as the evening wore on. I thought dope was a lot better than many of the pills that were everywhere in the sixties. I never liked valium or librium, pills that were meant to relax you. I found they made me feel stupid or slow, and the next day I'd have a gigantic hangover, and I'd be worse tempered. These drugs appeared more dangerous than marijuana to me, yet they were prescribed legally. I don't advocate marijuana for long-time use though, as I still have friends from then who've been smoking habitually most of their lives, and I've noticed they can be slow to respond, as if their brains have stopped being as quick as they used to be.

One afternoon David took me to tea at Paul Newman's and Joanne Woodward's house. Joanne was a gracious hostess, a nice-looking woman with light hair and fair skin. I think she was doing needlepoint at the time. She was delighted that I was English. They both commented that my accent reminded them of Joan Collins, who they'd just finished a film with. Paul reminded me of Steve McQueen in some ways. When I met him he was sitting in the garden drinking a beer dressed in what looked like an orange flying suit. He had an interesting face with piercing eyes and very short hair, and was as handsome as he looks in his pictures, but more contained. Initially he was very quiet, and I got the impression he didn't like strangers. When I got to know Paul and Joanne, though not for very long, I found them delightful. They invited me to a dinner at their house where I met Paul's younger brother Arthur, who is now a film producer.

I met Warren Beatty again, in Hollywood, through Charles Feldman. Charlie owned Famous Artists, Mina Wallace's agency, and was a great Hollywood character – he often wore red socks, and was aged about fifty five or more and was terrifically charming. He had quite a reputation. One Sunday afternoon he invited me for English tea. Charlie told me it was his way of making us foreigners in Hollywood feel at home. He pointed out his new Modigliani – I believe it was worth two million pounds at the time – hanging in his entrance hall as we walked through to the sitting room that overlooked the swimming pool.

Ursula Andress was also a guest. A very English tea arrived, with crumpets, toast and jam, all served by an English butler.

Charlie intermittently answered the phone every two minutes or so. One call went something like this:

'Hey, come on over. I've got her here.' A long pause. 'Yes, she's great. Yeah, I'm sure she'd be glad to see you ... Yeah, she's very cute, just like you said. If you weren't coming over, I'd take her out myself.' Charlie put down the phone. I thought he'd been talking about Ursula, and I don't know what she thought. Five minutes later a sports car came roaring up the drive and a young, handsome man came bounding into the room. He greeted Charlie, then came straight over to the table and greeted me.

'Hi, remember me? I'm Warren.' I looked back up at him and laughed.

'Why should I forget you?' I said. 'You tripped me up.'

He was much more attractive than when I'd seen him in London, and with his tan and casual clothes, he looked younger somehow. Within two minutes he asked me where I was staying. 'You don't have a car do you?'

I said, 'No, I don't.' I didn't tell him I couldn't drive.

'I'll give you a lift back,' he said quickly. I'd only been in the house fifteen minutes, it was one of the shortest teas I'd ever been invited to.

I was in no hurry to leave, but Charlie shushed me to the door and said, 'Come back again next week.'

We got into Warren's car and roared off along Mulholland Drive, I thought in the direction of the Beverly Hills Hotel. It was one of those stunning California late afternoons, with a breathtaking view of the valley and San Gabriel mountains in the distance. 'Would you like to see my new house?' he asked. Warren seemed eager to show it to me and said very few people had seen it. We drove up a couple more hills, and down a little hidden road to a house you couldn't see unless you knew it was there. He stopped the car and we got out. 'This is it,' he said. After fumbling with his keys he opened the door to a completely empty house. Bare floors, white walls, no furniture and no pictures on the walls. 'This is the sitting room,' he said. 'Let me show you the rest.'

We walked through an empty kitchen and study, then on to a guest bedroom, but still no furniture. Finally he opened a door to the last room and said, 'This is going to be my bedroom.' It had the only piece of furniture in the whole house: a large king size bed. I laughed. And he laughed too. We sat down on the bed, the only place to sit, and talked. With the evening sun making patterns across Warren's face, I felt breathless. It was a most exciting feeling, the gentle way he touched and flirted with me. But I didn't want to progress further. Something made me stop. It felt so good, still and quiet with just the sound of my heart racing, anything else would have spoiled this delicate feeling. It was like time was suspended.

After about an hour or so he took me back to the hotel. I hugged him and gave him a kiss and he asked me why I hadn't responded like that when we were alone. I just laughed, stroked his hair and went into the hotel, giving him a wave. He said he'd call. In about half an hour, the phone rang. It was Warren. We talked quietly for a longish time. When David Resnick came to take me to dinner, I told Warren I had to go and said goodbye. I have had many phone calls from Warren like that over the years. There were a few other things that happened too, but they came later.

Seeing my old friend again, the director J. Lee Thompson, was great. I'd worked with him on *Yield To The Night* and *The Good Companions* years earlier. He was funny and enthusiastic and very warm, and gave me some good advice.

'Don't waste your time in LA,' he said. 'There's all this interest in you. You should get yourself an American agent and a job.' When I told him about Mina Wallace's reaction we laughed, and I think that's when Lee decided I could play his Mayan princess in the epic he was preparing, provisionally called *The Mound Builders*. I was in the room when Lee rang Yul Brynner, who was to star in the film, about my being in the film. Yul said:

'I've photographed her a million times. She's got reddish hair and freckles. She's not a typical Indian princess.'

Lee paused and said, 'I know, but she's in demand at the moment. I think it would be good if we get her while we can.' On reflection, I think Lee wanted English friends around him. He was often homesick I think.

I was so thrilled to get a job in a big American picture that I didn't stop to think what it entailed. One agent I'd met called Kurt Frings – his only two clients were Elizabeth Taylor and Audrey Hepburn – told me I was making a mistake.

'You're still a Hollywood virgin, picturewise,' he said. 'Wait for a better offer.' Later he was proved right.

Just after I signed the contract for *The Mound Builders* I was asked to an interview for another movie. The producer was Pandro Berman, a man with a terrific film reputation whom I liked immensely. I remember his courteous manner and him telling me he'd seen most of my work. He said he had a great subject in Irving Wallace's award-winning book called *The Prize*. It was to star Paul Newman. I wanted to do it very much, but couldn't because the schedules would have conflicted. It's one of the things that all actors will recognize, as you finally get one job, you're offered another straight away. And then, of course, you can't do both. So Elke Sommer played the role in *The Prize* and I went off to Mexico.

Kings Of The Sun, as *The Mound Builders* was finally called, was a big budget film. The story involved a Mayan tribe that emigrates from Mexico to Texas and makes peace with the local Indian chief there, played by Yul. I played George Chakiris's promised bride and was the love interest for Yul in the film too. We shot almost all of it in Mexico, with hundreds of extras and whole villages recreated for the film. I know the film company hurt the feelings of the local people. The fact that we imported the drinking water, wouldn't eat their food, and put up large Coca-Cola machines did not endear us to the Mexicans. Some of the services could have been supplied by the people there, but this was a big American company, full of tactless bonhomie and confidence. They didn't seem to realize they were stepping on people's toes.

Of course, I'd known Yul since making *Once More With Feeling* in Paris a few years back. I had worked on some photography sessions with him after the film. He didn't pay, he just gave you some of the photographs. Some years later, as we looked at one of the glossy covers he'd sold he said, 'I should have paid you, but I didn't want to offend your pride.' I wished he had, it would have helped with the bills. All the same, it was great fun being photographed by Yul. With Yul it could be a seductive experience. He went out of his way to make it so. And the pictures were good too. Now he was a much bigger star, and still a dangerous flirt. I had a warm regard for him, but I was anxious to prove to everyone, Yul included, that I'd been picked for my talent and not for any other reasons. The irony was my role in this film was hardly likely to prove this.

When Yul would be flirtatious with me during the shooting I was a little stand-offish. I didn't want to get involved whilst we were making the film. He was also married. Like Steve McQueen, Yul would embroider his past on the spur of the moment. One minute he would say he was half-Mongolian, the next he was a Hungarian Jew who had escaped in the war, the next he was born in outer Siberia into a gypsy family. I was never sure what to believe. On the set one day he introduced me to a woman he said was his mother. From what Yul had told me, I'd thought his mother was a gypsy who had died giving birth to Yul. Without missing a beat, Yul replied, 'Oh, that's another relative.'

George Chakiris was a slim, athletic man with a handsome Grecian face and a rather private personality, shy at times, out-going at others. Dancing was very important to him and though he was not a large man he was very strong. Yul and George had a sword fight scene and George held his own, much to everyone's surprise. Sometimes we did warm up exercises together. George was always complimentary about my suppleness and said I could have been a good dancer if I had taken lessons.

On Sunday nights Yul and his wife would have the cast and crew over for drinks and buffet food – it was really the only time we all mixed together. I found there was a formal hierarchy in big American films. It wasn't like in England where the carpenter would greet me and tell me about his wife and family, or the electricians talked politics. I was often lonely, and when I'd ask my makeup man why people were aloof after I had been friendly with them, he would reply, 'They're in awe of you. That's the price you pay for starring in a film and being paid so much money.' It seemed like an odd set of values to me.

One Sunday evening I was talking to our cameraman Joe MacDonald. We were great friends until that night. He'd told me he liked me because I looked Irish. 'I love your Irish President,' I said, 'President Kennedy.' Suddenly the conversation came to an abrupt stop. His face flushed and he began to shout all sorts of awful things about President Kennedy.

'Believe me, I never thought I'd see the day when this country would have a Catholic President. How can you admire anyone who's father was a fascist on the side of the Germans? If Joe

Kennedy had his way you wouldn't be alive today, young lady, because you wouldn't have had the might of America in the last war on your side.' I felt bewildered by the intensity of Joe's feelings. It was the first time I'd come up against this kind of attitude. Until then Joe had photographed me exquisitely. Some of the shots were so beautiful I hardly recognized myself. But after our 'discussion', I was never to photograph as well again.

From Mexico City, the production moved to Mazatland, and from there south to the Yucatan peninsula. The sun grew hotter the closer we got to the equator, and several of us suffered. Yul used to carry oxygen canisters with him to the higher reaches where the air was thinner. Some days the temperatures would rise as high as 140 degrees Fahrenheit. On a boat, where we were filming a scene, with the sun's reflection on the water the temperature rose higher still. With my face covered in darker makeup to look Indian, and a hat to shield myself from the sun, I thought my skin was protected enough, what I did not realize was that the reflection of the sun on water is the most dangerous of all. I got burnt so badly that I was rushed to hospital immediately by helicopter. I was given shots of medication like Silver Sun and covered in vitamin cream. I was lucky. It could have been worse. A whole layer of skin peeled off my face, but there was no serious damage. I had hundreds of freckles till then, like my daughter does now, but that day most of them disappeared with that first layer of skin.

I was back at work within the week, but the sun wasn't the only thing that exhausted me. Lee Thompson is a dear friend but when he was drinking he was very different. Lee will admit himself that he wasn't a rational person when he used to drink. I know he hasn't touched alcohol for many years now. During the day he was a formal and reserved Englishman. Sometimes he would get cross with me if I looked tired, but that was the extent of any problem between us on the set. Ironically I was often tired because of Lee. Late at night he would knock on my door. 'Come to get my little one to join the party,' he'd shout. 'Come out and make us all sparkle.' If I didn't open the door he would make such a noise he could wake up the whole hotel. He'd fall into my room and I didn't know what to do with my sweet friend and director. I'd cajole and plead with him, but he would carry on like a tornado, regardless. Frequently changing hotels didn't help. He'd always find out where I was. Once or twice he'd have Richard Basehart with him, at other times he'd arrive with a whole party of strange people. I don't know where he found them, or where he got his stamina from.

Lee could often be a delight, singing and telling me funny stories. It would have been great if we didn't have a film to make the next day. But in another moment, his mood would turn melancholy and he'd ask to stay. He would promise not to be any trouble as long as he didn't have to be alone. It was an impossible position to be in. Just as I'd get to screaming pitch in anger, he'd fall dead asleep wherever he happened to be sitting or lying, often straight out on the floor. By that time I was worn out myself. The next day on the set, bright and early, Lee would be the most together person you'd ever seen.

I did make a new friend while I was in Mexico. In the market one day I stopped to buy some *tamales*, a Mexican pancake, at a cooking stall run by a little girl called Lupita, aged about nine. When she bit off an end of the wrapper and spat it out before putting the *tamales* in a bag I knew she wasn't what she appeared to be. She was tough and was in a rush. She said she couldn't waste time with formalities because she had a business to run. I asked Lupita if she'd like a job on the film.

'I don't work with Americans,' she snapped. I told her I came from a country called England. 'Where is that?' she asked. I told her it was a long way away and that I sometimes got homesick. When she heard that, she wouldn't charge me for the *tamales*. 'Maybe I come and work with you if you pay more than I make with my *tamale* business,' Lupita said. I realized with a start that she was the breadwinner for her entire family. I took this feisty nine-year-old to work and she became the youngest player in the film. In a day she earned more working on the movie than she earned in a month on her *tamale* stand.

On a few occasions Lupita stayed in the hotel with me. She was a bit nervous in unfamiliar surroundings. The one thing she really loved was the shower, she'd wash herself over and over, so much so that after an hour I had to stop her. She was so shy she refused to take her underwear off. I felt for this tough little girl. I'd had a strange childhood, too, and knew how she was feeling. That was why she had endeared herself to me when I'd first met her.

147

At Lupita's invitation, George Chakiris and I went to her home for tea. It turned out to be no more than a shed, a lean-to with a corrugated iron roof propped up against a wall. It was very sobering to see how little her family had, but both of us kept quiet. They'd gone to great trouble for our visit. Fresh flowers were everywhere, but the only furniture they had was the cooker for the *tamales*. It was one medium-sized room with a dirt floor, containing a bed with no mattress or springs, and chairs with frames but no middles. A small altar rested high above the bed. Lupita had a mother and five brothers and sisters who lived there too. Apparently the father was alive, but hiding in the mountains from the police trying to stay one step ahead of the law.

On my last day in Mexico, I received an unexpected visit from Lupita's mother. She thought this was a chance for Lupita to have a better life if I took her back home with me. I wasn't sure what to do. My makeup man said I wouldn't want her when I got her back to England, but he didn't know how I felt. I talked to Lupita and her mother for several hours, and finally asked Lupita what she wanted.

'I want you to be my mother now.' I couldn't speak. This little girl had just melted my heart. I looked at her mother. Her face was expressionless.

'She'll be better off with you,' she said.

With her little sack and suitcase, Lupita came to the airport all ready to fly to California with me, but the American authorities wouldn't allow it. Even when I said that I was going to take her back to England eventually, they refused. 'If you still feel like that in three years' time when her papers are in order, come back then.'

Lupita sat very still on my lap. She cried, then I cried, then she was comforting me. She said, 'I will go back to my business and buy another two stalls with the money from the movie.' She was a realist above all else. I thought for a moment, and decided to cancel my flight. I wanted to do something positive for Lupita. I told her I'd buy one stall to begin with and if she agreed to go to school for one year, half a day, I would leave enough money for her to buy another stall, at the end of the year. Knowing Lupita and her family, I decided to stay a few days longer and go to the school myself to pay the fees and make sure she was registered. The nun in charge told me that if Lupita didn't show up, she wouldn't give her the money I'd left for the extra *tamale* stall. This was a bribe, but I hoped now Lupita would learn to read and write. I thought this business-like threat would encourage her to go to school, if only for the year.

The English community in Los Angeles was very chummy and after my return from Mexico, Peter Lawford rang up one day and invited me to a party he was having at his beach house in Malibu. He was charming and reminded me of the dinner with Frank Sinatra in London when I had spilled my drink down his wife's dress. He told me this party would be one I would always remember. Be sure to come, he said, because someone very special will be arriving. That was all he would tell me for now. He added that this special person would be the most attractive person I could ever hope to meet.

I knew it wasn't just another party when two security men frisked me as I walked through the door. After about an hour, quite suddenly President Kennedy was there. He walked over to me with two Marine guards on either side of him, the Marines scrutinizing me from top to toe. The President shushed them away and we talked for a little while. He told me I was an elusive person to meet. I wasn't sure what he meant, but later remembered the supposed phone call from the White House after the Carson show. And the two Marine guards outside my hotel door in Boston.

The President, close-to, had a stunning presence. He was dynamic, and very attractive, and his eyes were mesmerizing. He leaned forward whilst we were speaking so his head was only inches away from my face. It was more comfortable for him to stand this way, he said, because he had a back injury he'd got in the war. I answered that because of a fall I'd had when I was younger, I was beginning to have problems with my back too. He told me about the rocking chair he used and said that's what I should try. Much later on, when I got back home to England, a man from British Customs rang me to say they had a big parcel for me. I went to claim it and found it was a large rocking chair, identical to the one President Kennedy used in the White House, with a note saying, 'This chair is specially for backache. Regards, from the President.' I still have it in my living room.

That evening passed in a whirl of excitement as I talked to President Kennedy. He had to fly off somewhere else and left earlyish, but asked if I'd like to be a guest at a lunch party in the next few weeks.

Peter Lawford called the next day and said I had been a big success. There was going to be a party on his yacht the following month and he hoped the President would be able to be there.

At the time, I was staying in Malibu as a guest of a lawyer called Jimmy Cohen. He was the friend of my business manager and when we'd first met, he had helped me quite a bit. I respected his advice, not realizing it could be in his own interests. He was dead set against me going to the proposed yacht party. He threw a huge tantrum.

'You'd better take yourself seriously as an actress, or you'll get a reputation as a party girl around town. Besides, you mustn't go the first time you're asked. Wait until they ask you again.' It was a strange logic, but it tied in with the double standard we'd all been taught. On the day of the yacht party I had to go for a job interview, and Jimmy persuaded me to keep it. If I cancelled he said I wouldn't be asked again. It would count against me for future work commitments. I let him influence me. I've always regretted that I didn't go.

I spent a few months more in Los Angeles, but the time dragged by and I felt restless and homesick. It didn't make it any easier to see newspapers and television every day about the youth explosion in London, which they referred to as the 'Swinging Sixties'. I was longing to get home and be part of it all. I felt I was missing out on something important in my beloved London; it was the place to be, and I wasn't there.

CHAPTER SIX

I could have stayed on in California, but after making two American films in a row I was afraid of becoming just another actor sitting around LA waiting for the 'big break'. When I'd first arrived just a few months earlier, I'd been the unknown English actress with two critical favourites to her name. Now, I was established, but I didn't want to lose my working drive. With the California sunshine and temptations all around me, I realized I had to get home. The very beauty that had first enchanted me was now dangerously seductive.

For the second time in my life, I had earned a good salary, and this time I wanted to try and keep it. Most of my earnings from *The War Lover* had been absorbed by various fees and commissions and, of course, a huge chunk had been swallowed up by the Inland Revenue. I needed advice. English tax laws were complicated in the sixties, not only for actors like me, but also for foreign companies wanting to make films here. As it became less profitable for them to do so, American companies had second thoughts on working in England. In fact, some of them pulled out.

While he was in England, Robert Wagner had introduced me to his business manager, Andy Morgan-Maree, and before I left Los Angeles he offered to help me. I decided to wait until I got home, which may have been a mistake. Through my advisors in England I met the chairman of an investment company. I understood from him that his company took care of film actors' financial affairs, tax, savings and investments. I signed the contract. Sure enough, the company invested my money, but I felt they totally neglected my interests. Some years later I got my savings back but by now they were worth less. I wish I had chosen different advisors. Not only did people now know my name, but they assumed I was well-off. The truth was that everything I had earned was tied up making a profit for others. I was back to square one and looking for a job.

I think it's a good idea for any actor to learn about handling and investing money to prevent this kind of thing from happening. We have to be aware of the periods of unemployment. It's important to realize that the big money is made only by about ten per cent of the industry and, even for an actor who is 'known', the time spent not working can eventually use up any savings. I'm not grumbling, I'm stating a fact. We get paid for doing what we like. Sometimes it's not enough, and sometimes it's too much.

There was a small movie for me to consider, written and co-produced by John Mortimer, who was just having his first successes. I met John with Jean Diamond at the Dorchester for tea. We discussed the script and all agreed on the terms, and, before the bill even arrived, John said he'd be delighted if I'd do the film. I wish all my work could be that easy and civilized to set up!

John had written the film script of his play called *Lunch Hour*, a simple story about a man who meets a girl from his office, and books a room for an afternoon romance. The idea was a little like Billy Wilder's *The Apartment*. Unlike that film, we were working on a small budget, with a tiny crew and just a few sets, so the work was very concentrated. It was a world away from the epic I'd just made, and was the happiest experience, workwise, I'd ever had. On *Lunch Hour* I relaxed and enjoyed the work. The atmosphere was so happy that my nervousness disappeared. Our director was James Hill, a warm, funny and attractive person. James was the co-producer along with John, who was writing new scenes daily. For the next four or five weeks the few of us made our movie in a lovely working atmosphere. Each day I couldn't wait to get to work at six in the morning.

John became a dear friend. Not only was his work a joy to act, but he had a marvellous wit, and seemed to absorb everything. If you told him an anecdote at lunch one day it could easily come back the next day – rewritten, polished and incorporated into the storyline, of course. He had a 'day job' as a divorce barrister. Delivering new pages of dialogue, he would casually say, 'I'm just off to divorce a couple of people this morning. I'll be back in time for lunch.' At the time, he was married to Penelope Mortimer who was a writer too. She wrote *The Pumpkin Eater*, amongst other things. Their house in Hampstead was filled with books. John had enormous energy to work at two thriving careers and be a father to six children as well.

Robert Stephens was also good to work with. He was so attentive and charming it was easy for me to confuse the part he was playing with the real man. He later became a leading man at the National Theatre, where he had many successes and married Maggie Smith while they were working there together.

The unusual length of the film – one hour – prevented it from being released in cinema theatres. However, there was an afterlife for *Lunch Hour*. It went on to become a cult film, and occasionally plays at the National Film Theatre. John Mortimer's later successes speak for themselves.

For several years in a row, Brian and myself were invited by Jack Frye and his wife Bunty – who'd thrown the New Year's Eve parties – to spend a month's holiday on their yacht. Bunty could be strikingly beautiful, half-English and half-Indian, about twenty eight years of age. Jack was in his fifties, a self-made tycoon, blond, tanned and fit with a dynamic personality that could turn aggressive. He ran the boat singlehanded without a crew, and maybe that explained it. He was responsible for our safety. Brian and I had fights about going in the first place. He couldn't understand why I did not want to be away for a month. It was a wonderful holiday, and free he'd point out. But my career was very important to me and it wasn't easy keeping in touch with London, I didn't want to miss anything by being away.

Being on a boat with the same people for a month can be claustrophobic, and when things occasionally got tense it was difficult to get away even though the boat was sixty five feet long.

'Why were Brian and I always invited?' I asked Bunty.

'Because,' she replied, 'you're the only people Jack and myself can stand for a month!' I didn't know whether to be flattered or give myself a brownie point for good behaviour. There were some days when Jack would tease me unmercifully. This usually generous man could reduce me to tears by making awfully unkind remarks, especially if I happened to be beating him at table tennis.

In the South of France, they have a powerful wind that comes up in a storm they call 'a mistral' and, one day while out at sea, we found ourselves in the middle of one. We'd been through this in port, but now we had to deal with fifteen- to twenty-feet high waves that crashed over our heads and tossed the boat from side to side like a tiny cork. It was impossible to sit in the cabin, as the rocking made us unbelievably sick, so there was nothing to do but lash ourselves to the boat. The storm lasted for several hours and Jack guided us through. No whimpering. No complaining.

'If you feel sick,' he said, 'make sure it's over the side, and tie yourself to the boat with a rope.' His two sons were with us and Jack was even tougher on them. Nicky was thirteen and Michael sixteen.

Jack's Italian friend, Marla, and her husband, were also on board that day. She was praying throughout the storm, chanting Hail Marys into the wind. When she didn't think that was good enough, she started bargaining with her prayers, offering to give up cigarettes for six months, then alcohol, then finally her lover, if the Lord promised to keep us safe. Her husband seemed as surprised by this promise as the rest of us! But her prayers worked, the dangerous storm subsided, and the boat was stable for the first time in six hours. We were all OK, although soaked from head to toe. At the same time, I think Marla had some questions to answer when we finally reached dry land. I don't know about the lover, but I do know she gave up smoking and drinking for six months. Marla is now Lady Dashwood and, when I see her name in the papers occasionally, I remember her unexpected revelations during that time in the storm.

No-one could have been more relieved than I was when we were finally safe. It had seemed as if none of us could survive, and I don't think we would have done without Jack. Maybe that's why we accepted him, even if he did insult you when you won at table tennis.

Terence Donovan was a photographer friend who I had worked with several times. He was the son of a lorry driver from the East End and he and David Bailey were busy making a name for themselves in London social circles as part of the sixties working-class revolution. Terence always seemed to be planning or producing something, usually to do with advertising.

He visited me at my lovely flat in quiet Edwardes Square. To my dismay he said he thought it was small and cramped. I could do much better, he said, and should invest in a better flat for my image, and for my future. He knew of a large apartment available in West Hampstead in a block called Douglas Court. He'd bought a flat there and encouraged me to do the same. The location, just 100 yards from Kilburn High Street, wasn't as nice as Edwardes Square, but after seeing the place for myself and considering Terence's advice, I decided to move. It was a boomerang-shaped, spacious four-bedroomed flat with two big bathrooms and high Edwardian ceilings. With help from two women friends who were interested in interior design, I furnished and decorated it from shops around London. It was beautiful when we had finished.

I think Terence had an arrangement with the landlords because he introduced several people to these apartments. At one stage the building was full of what would be called artistic people. Terence lived beneath me, and had lots of the advertising crowd popping in, as well as hairdressers and models working there. David Puttnam was his photographic agent at that time – this was before he became a film maker – and Terence tried to avoid our meeting. He told me all David would do was talk about films and not get any work done. I'd see this attractive man disappearing into the lift and ask Terence who it was.

'Oh, you don't need to know him,' he said. 'He's just my agent.'

David Hurn was another good friend. He was one of my favourites because I loved his pictures. His manner was gentle and he worked only to get good pictures, not for any other reasons. He gave me a lot of photographs that helped me in my work.

In 1964 a group of people from the film industry, including myself and Peter Finch, were invited to the Soviet Union. They were honouring two films, *Saturday Night and Sunday Morning* and *The Trials of Oscar Wilde*, which Peter starred in. It was an interesting time to visit. Nikita Kruschev was in power, and the Cold War was still in full swing.

Moscow was unlike any city I'd ever been to. It was fantastic, full of the warmest people who, at night, seemed to emerge from nowhere. The city could look sombre and drab, and at other times be dazzling. After dark it was very black and still with no neon signs or advertisements to light it up. But when the sun shone, hitting the domes of the Kremlin, they would gleam pale gold. Then it was absolutely magnificent.

Necessities were in short supply. The large hotel we stayed in had a woman on every floor who guarded the keys for the rooms. Every time you arrived or left you had to deal with her. The bathrooms were impressive to look at, but nothing quite worked. The shower was an icy trickle, and with no plug to stop the water running away it was difficult to take a hot bath. I think the key woman kept the only plug, which was always in use when I wanted to borrow it. Bathroom tissue was limited. What there was of it was coarse compared to Western standards. Breakfast was a different story. We sat at long tables and were served plates of caviar, with large amounts of vodka in exquisite thimble-sized glasses, to drink. There were some things the Russians never seemed short of.

As we were shepherded all over Moscow and Leningrad with guides and interpreters, I noticed there was always someone hovering, even when there was no need. After a while, most of us became paranoid. Our English delegation was convinced there were sound bugs in our rooms, and we'd spend hours searching for the microphones. After a dinner date Ken Hughes (the director of *Oscar Wilde*) had with his Russian interpreter, he told us that when he returned to her flat, he saw there was a big mirror over the bed. Peter Finch said he didn't think it was there as an erotic accessory – he thought Kenneth might have been photographed for blackmail purposes.

Peter told me very sweetly I would be better off spending a romantic time with him than with any of our handsome Russian guides. I agreed, and thanked him, but said I wasn't feeling very well, and wondered if he would ask me again when I was feeling better. He was utterly charming.

'Oh, my dear,' he said, 'I will always ask you.'

Our films were shown and very well-received. At the screening of *The Trials of Oscar Wilde*, as we sat together in the dark, Peter clutched my hand crying, 'Oh, God. Isn't that sad?' It was amazing to see how moved he was by the story, which he must have known inside out. He wasn't a bit vain about his work, just very emotional.

We were both invited to the Kremlin for dinner. Mr Kruschev had a twinkle in his eye and looked like a wise old man. His English was a little faltering, but I'm sure he understood everything we were saying. Mrs Kruschev appeared motherly and Peter and I had an animated conversation with her. It felt like we could have been anywhere in the world chatting with older relatives. Everyone else in the Kremlin was warm and hospitable. They showed us round some of the palaces and we saw a few of the famous Fabergé eggs, encrusted with sapphires, diamonds and emeralds. I was told they were worth a quarter of a million pounds each! When I heard that, I felt I could understand then why there had been a revolution. One princess's small Easter gift could have probably fed a whole province for three months.

The table was set exquisitely, with place cards and gold plates that had belonged to the last tsar. When the dinner was served, however, it was somewhat disorganized, not like you'd imagine a dinner party at Buckingham Palace or the White House to be. The people serving the dinner kept bumping into one another, and would have heated discussions behind our chairs, which gave me the giggles. I was afraid to catch Peter's eye, as I knew it would be impolite to laugh out loud in front of the Kruschevs.

As the evening wore on, the dinner seemed to get more and more chaotic, and the guests became very jolly. I couldn't tell if it was from the wine or the vodka, or because everything we said was relayed back and forth through interpreters. Mr Kruschev was keen on jokes, and Peter was at his best. He was at pains to find easy ones to tell, and they were received enthusiastically, with hoots of laughter. I thought everybody, even the Russians, must have heard such old stories before.

Jean and I found my next job in Italy. Fernando Ghia was Jean's Roman counterpart – he later co-produced *Chariots of Fire* – and together they got an Italian movie for me, a feature called *Marcia Nuziale*, that was to be three stories compressed into two hours. I played the lead in one of them opposite Ugo Tognazzi, and was directed by Marco Ferreri. It was truly a multi-national film. The director was Italian, and also spoke Spanish and French, the makeup man was Greek, and I spoke what I thought was enough Italian to understand the direction. 'Triste. Triste!' Marco would shout. I thought he was referring to a place, when what he really meant was he wanted to see more *sadness* in the scene.

It was great fun working in Italy. We'd start at twelve noon and not stop for lunch or tea, going on until about seven in the evening. If we were hungry, there was a delicious food trolley just outside the sound stage where we could grab something quickly and then just get on with the work. In the evenings we'd dine in the open in the lovely restaurants that bordered the beautiful Italian squares.

A few days after I started the film I returned to my hotel room one evening to find it filled with flowers. 'This is from the man along the corridor' the note read. I thought it must be some terrible Italian wolf, and I became a little apprehensive. Like a lot of English girls, I thought of all Italian men as predators. It was a joy to discover on this trip that not only were they very attractive, but often very considerate. The flowers continued to arrive for a few more days, always signed the same way. On the fourth day, the little note attached asked, 'How would you like to meet the man who keeps sending the flowers? I'm just along the corridor.' I figured out by now that anyone who was so persistent and generous couldn't be all that bad, so I rang the hotel desk and asked them to put me through to the room along the corridor. A strange continental voice answered.

'Oh, hello senorita. I am so glad you called. I will ring and introduce myself in one hour.'

A very curious hour later I answered the knock on the door. What a surprise! I opened it, and standing there was Albert Finney. I hadn't seen him much since my visit to Brighton after his agent had died. What an unexpected surprise – Albert being in Rome and being the sender of the flowers. He'd just had a big success on Broadway with *Luther* and was travelling here, there and everywhere with his friend and former stand-in, Terry, who'd been with us on *Saturday Night and Sunday Morning*. As a friend of Fernando, Albert had heard I was in Rome working. It was marvellous to see him and we went to dinner in a lovely restaurant. At the weekend I asked Albert and Terry to be my guests on the producer's yacht for a trip round the Italian islands.

Another surprise reunion in Rome was with Dudley Moore, who was on holiday. We met in one of the places frequented by the English working abroad. Later in the week he picked me up at my hotel for dinner doing an outrageous loud and effeminate impersonation – 'How do you like my outfit? Is it too busy?' He was funny and adorable, and I didn't know whether to laugh or believe him. He'd be puffing up the cushions, acting like Dame Edna, and practically sitting on top of me all at the same time. He made me laugh so much, and that's when I started to look at Dudley in a more romantic light.

Sure enough, my palm reading had proved right about his girlfriend Celia Hammond. She had left New York after a short stay, and, strangely enough, was now having a relationship with Terence Donovan. The world seemed to be getting smaller and smaller all the time.

Dudley and I got to know each other much better back in England after I returned from the film. It was not like any re-lationship I'd known before, romantic but different. We did have some heated moments. Sometimes it was like a roller coaster. One moment Dudley was very serious, the next he'd be hysterically funny, and at other moments he'd withdraw. When Dudley wanted to be private he'd play the piano. I had a grand piano, a Bechstein, in my flat, and when an argument loomed it was there that Dudley would go. He'd go and play beautiful tunes he'd make up. One day he wrote a lovely jazz song called 'Field Day for Shirley'.

I had my own black days, and kept them at bay by keeping myself busy. There were many distractions to be found, especially in the sixties in London.

London was a glorious place to be, thriving with energy and change. It was a joy to walk down the King's Road or along Carnaby Street, exchanging information and watching everyone else parading up and down, admiring each other's outfits, or eating out in one of the more fashionable restaurants. It reminded me of the late afternoon parades in some of the Mediterranean countries. Our clothes were a vision to behold. The tiny mini-skirts went well with the way we combed our hair, high and straight. White lipstick, which I didn't much like, was fashionable and we wore as many pairs of eyelashes as we could stick on. I wore floating, very feminine clothes – long dresses, when I wasn't wearing a mini, and, yes, flowers in my hair! The exception was a black velvet suit I owned that was cut completely like a boy's that I bought from Biba's, the trend-setting clothes shop of the day. It was very inexpensive to dress and live well then. Most nights I'd be out at a restaurant or a club, frequently the Ad-Lib, which overlooked Leicester Square. Many of the artistic crowd gathered there, people like the Beatles and the Rolling Stones, and my old friends John Barry and Adam Faith. It was run by a man called Brian Morris.

I'd first met Brian a few years earlier, as the youngest barman at Les Ambassadeurs. One evening I was dining with Otto Preminger and Otto asked what I'd have to drink. I said I didn't drink. 'In that case, champagne is the only thing for a young lady to have,' and he immediately ordered a large bottle from Brian. I took a sip and when Otto wasn't looking I switched my glass for an empty one. Without a word between us, Brian filled it with fizzy water. At our table whenever Otto refilled my glass, Brian watched with amusement waiting for Otto to turn away for a moment when I would empty my drink into the nearest pot plant!

I liked Brian and he was much sought after as host of the Ad-Lib. He became something of a tragedy of the sixties, but at that moment, he was one of the most popular people in town. You had to have his blessing to get into this very private and exclusive club. There was a reason for this. Once inside, there were no holds barred. Everyone who was anyone was there, most of us high on something. Nothing injected, of course, just pot or pills, and cocaine wasn't around then. I stayed fairly straight. My experiences with LSD had scared me enough in hospital, and I didn't want to have that reaction again, especially in public. Sometimes I felt a little dull compared to some of them at the club who were busy getting high and seeing how many adventures they could have in one night. I felt I'd already had enough adventures for the time being.

I'd seen the Beatles performing three years earlier in Hamburg, before Ringo Starr was playing with them. They had seemed then like a wild, uninhibited bunch of young men, North Country, working-class, similar to the boys I'd gone to school with. One night at the Ad-Lib John Lennon said to me, 'You probably wouldn't go for somebody like me, would you?'

'No, not right now,' I replied. Damn, I thought, he would ask me when we were both with other people. By now, of course, they were already tremendously successful. At a party one night at Shirley Bassey's house, I was sitting on the sofa with John and Paul McCartney. Johnny Mathis, whom I'd always admired, was there and I wanted to go and speak to him, but I was holding back. John and Paul were laughing hysterically.

'Of all the people in this room you want to approach, why pick him? You can get to know anyone here you want except him.' I replied stiffly that I loved his voice and wanted to tell him so. This only made them laugh more hysterically. I couldn't see the joke!

I liked Paul and John, but George Harrison appealed to me the most because he seemed quieter than the others and had a handsome, sensitive face. When *My Beautiful Laundrette* won the Evening Standard Best Film Award in 1986, George smiled and waved before the ceremony, and I thought he was signalling to someone else. How silly I felt, not realizing he was waving to me!

'I've got a surprise for you,' Terence Donovan announced one evening as he came to take me out. He wouldn't tell me where we were going. We arrived at a Bayswater club called the White

Raven that, from the outside, looked to me like any other club. Inside, I sensed the place was different. A sea of heads turned and watched as we walked down the steps. I wasn't sure if the stares were friendly or not, and I was reminded of the time I first walked into Les Ambassadeurs with David Niven – that feeling of being in a strange place and not knowing if the natives were friendly. Terence, on the other hand, was delighted with all the attention we were getting, and he was on friendly terms with everyone, including the owner, a woman called Frieda. He explained to me he often came here to relax and get away from people propositioning him for work. One thing was sure. No-one was likely to proposition Terence here for work or anything else, in this place.

Two women came over to the table and Terence introduced us. The first was Brenda, fortyish, small, with short blonde hair. Her friend Colin was about two stones heavier than her.

'What are you drinking, sweetheart?' she asked, ignoring Terence completely. These women reminded me of the older girls at Edgeworth, but now there was no animosity towards me. Glancing around this packed cellar club it seemed like there were hundreds of people there, a lot of them dancing. Then I realized with a start that they were nearly all women.

We moved into another room with a bar along one side with a small dance floor. It was packed solid. Many women were dancing close together. Terry squeezed my arm.

'I love this place,' he said. 'Aren't they exciting, all these lovely girls?' I thought it was an odd remark, but he was completely serious. Just the same, it was intriguing.

Occasionally amongst this large crowd I'd spot an unusual couple. A beautiful girl dressed in the conventional evening wear of the day would stand out against her companion, dressed in jeans and cowboy boots and a tailored shirt. In another corner there was a stunning, dark-haired girl with a woman dressed in a man's striped three-piece suit with a very short haircut. She looked striking, but in a very different way. The woman in the suit gave Terence a wave.

'Hi, I'm Steve,' she said. 'Why don't you introduce me to your lady?'

Some months later, I was invited to a private party by Frieda who owned the club. She said she had been in the Land Army, and that was where she found she preferred women. I found the atmosphere to be full of suppressed tension, if you talked to one woman quite often another would get upset! That particular evening those moments seemed funny. Then, a few days later, Frieda rang me. She said that one of the girls I'd been talking to had had all her clothes torn up by her partner. It was because she had been talking to me. I felt sorry for the girl and upset at this turn of events and wished I could do something to help her.

I wondered how I could make an income when I wasn't acting. I'd been interested in antique furniture for a while. Why not open a shop of my own? The first step was to find a place, and I found a small stall to rent in the Blue Dolphin arcade just off the Portobello Road. The next thing I needed was a business partner, someone with flair who could drive, because I didn't, and someone who wasn't in the same line as myself, so that if I had a film or a play, they could keep the business going. I had a friend called Vicky, a very attractive girl whose own apartment in Knightsbridge was beautiful. But she didn't need to work, nor did she drive.

At a party at Vicky's home one of the guests turned out to be Romie, the girl whose clothes had been ripped up because she had talked to me. Romie told me she'd been having a miserable time at home and was going to enrol in art school when she had enough money. Romie did indeed go to art school later and became a very good artist, but at the moment, she was working delivering fish and fish tanks. I talked to her about my idea for an antique stall and asked what she thought. Would she consider doing the driving and help me look for the antiques I'd need to buy? She liked the idea. Laughing I said, 'If it goes well, you'll be able to replace some of the clothes you lost.'

In the next arcade to ours was an Australian girl called Anoushka Hempel and her German husband who ran another antique stall. If my customers couldn't find what they wanted with me I'd send them to their stall. She was a part-time actress and had had a few roles. Years later, after her first husband died, Anoushka married again to a fabulously wealthy man and now they live in identical houses in absolute luxury. She is now a fashion designer and runs a luxury hotel. It's a long way from her little stall.

We didn't really make a success of the antique stall. I was busy with my acting career and Romie would work only when

I was there too. Sometimes I didn't want to sell the pieces I had bought either, I liked them so much that I kept them. It was my first business venture and I lost money. I should have been more businesslike and I resolved the next time I would be. Still, it was a lot of fun and I acquired some lovely lamps and furniture. My home looked stunning. The stall did get some unexpected publicity. Terry O'Neill, whom I hadn't seen for many months, came to visit with a well-known American photographer called Sam Shaw, and a photograph of me working at Portobello Antique Market appeared in *Life* magazine.

Doctor in Clover was part of a series of films that had begun ten years earlier in the fifties, with Dirk Bogarde. They were similar to the *Carry On* films – funny domestic comedies with a continuing central character. I had a role as a nurse who swallows laughing gas and, along with everyone else, winds up laughing hysterically. John Fraser, a handsome, dear man, and James Robertson Justice were starring in the film. I'd known James as a very sweet man in earlier years. That's why I couldn't understand his stand-offish behaviour towards me during the shooting of this picture. Had he believed the rubbish that was printed about me and every other actress at that time? I hoped not. Or perhaps it was as simple as not having top billing this time. I couldn't think of any other explanation.

My next role was in what was to be a considerably more successful film. The director, Lewis Gilbert, has made it a point of taking good stage shows, adapting them and making them into even better films. He and his wife Hilda would go to the theatre looking for suitable plays, then buy the film rights to make them into movies. Most recently they have made *Educating Rita* and *Shirley Valentine*, and earlier there was *Colour My Name With Pride*. Lewis has also directed several James Bond films. *Alfie*, by Bill Naughton, was a huge success on stage in the West End. I had seen it three times, all with different men in the lead as the cockney womanizer: John Neville, Keith Michell and my friend Michael Medwin. It is a wonderful vehicle for any actor. I'd known Michael Caine casually for a long time, and had seen him in many of the fashionable restaurants and clubs around London. After his first major film role in *Zulu*, he'd taken me

164

to the cinema to see his performance. He was right to be proud of it, and he also looked very dishy in his bright red uniform.

There is a story told that after *Zulu*, Michael decided to become a film star. I've heard it several times from people who quote Michael as saying, 'I think I'll become a film star now. It's much easier than being an actor.' He must have said it tongue-in-cheek because he was a good actor and had been working hard in rep for years. Michael understood that to succeed in the film business you had to play by the rules, and that's exactly what he did. In the early sixties, Michael and I had filmed a love scene together as a screen test for director Ken Anakin for *Those Magnificent Men in Their Flying Machines*. Neither of us got the roles that eventually went to James Fox and Sarah Miles. I remember one conversation I had with Michael. It went something like this:

Michael: Do you fancy me?
Me: Hmmmm . . . Well, hmmmmmmm . . . well.
Michael: Oh, that's all right, because if you don't, you'll like Tel [Terry Stamp]. We share a house and we found between us we've got it covered, cos if they don't fancy me, they fancy Terry, and vice versa! Between us we've got it made.

Perhaps it didn't occur to Michael there were other types too!

My character was a nurse who becomes involved with Alfie. Jean encouraged me to accept the role and had a feeling it would be a hit film. Lewis filled it with good actresses, Shelley Winters, Millicent Martin, Jane Asher, Julia Foster, Vivien Merchant and Eleanor Bron. All the women's roles were smallish except for Julia's and Jane's. And Vivien Merchant was exceptional as the married woman who went through a very painful ordeal.

Michael and I did have one lovely scene together. We were lying in a single bed, head to toe, as that was the only way the characters could get any sleep. I was waiting for the alarm to go off, and only our heads and feet are in the shot. Otto Preminger had seen the film and rang me to tell me how funny he thought it was.

During the editing, I received a phone call from Lewis Gilbert, telling me that the scene was not staying in the film. In the story it came just before a scene where Vivien Merchant has an abortion, and Lewis felt it wasn't right for a humorous moment to precede it. Ironically, stills from that scene appeared on the front and back covers of the paperback book. I was sad that, after the cut, there was not much left of my role. I understood why Lewis did it, thanks to his phone call, but it was disappointing. All the same, from my billing it looked as if I had a substantial role. I would have liked to have been sparkling in *Alfie*, not only because it was a big hit but because Lewis and his wife, Hilda, are exceptionally nice people. I'd have liked to have done credit to them as well as myself.

One thing connected with the film I didn't like was a photographic session arranged by the publicists for *Playboy*. Four years earlier, I had been photographed on the beach in Malibu by a photographer called Ivan Nagy, who is now a polished TV director. They were stunning shots, and I was as delighted with them as he was. Ivan was all set to do a deal with *Playboy* when Jimmy Cohen, who was my legal advisor, threw a spanner in the works by telling me – again! – that I would never be taken seriously as an actress if there were half-naked pictures of me in *Playboy*. He said he wanted Ivan to get rid of the pictures. Ivan asked me if he could save them so we'd have them at a later date. I said I hoped he would, because I knew the pictures were beautiful. I hope he's still got them somewhere. When I asked who would be photographing the publicity session for *Alfie*, the publicists said, 'We've got the best for you . . . David Bailey.' I knew David was a great fashion photographer, but surely this was rather different. With this kind of photography it's better that one has a rapport, which I had with both David Hurn and Terry O'Neill, and I asked for them. But this was at a time in the late sixties when photographers and hairdressers were treated more like stars than any of the actors they photographed, and the publicists felt that Bailey was better and more famous than either David or Terry. The irony was that Terry was adamant about not shooting any revealing photographs. He wanted to make sure his work would be taken seriously.

David Bailey arrived at my flat and was nice, but posing for an intimate session with someone I didn't know wasn't the ideal way to work. I asked David when could I see the results. He was on his honeymoon with Catherine Deneuve, hardly the best time either to shoot erotic pictures of another woman! and said the negatives would be sent directly to *Playboy*, as he didn't have time to process them. I immediately became doubtful, and wished then I'd been firm and said no to the session. When I saw the results I was upset. The photographs were disappointing, and they didn't do anything for me. To add insult to injury, I wasn't paid either. A short time later, it seemed that everyone I knew had seen the pictures. I felt I should have been able to look at them before they were published and pick the ones I liked. These were average photographs at best. That publicity episode made me feel exploited. That's the reason I've always been reluctant to praise *Alfie*, which, of course, was and is a very good film.

CHAPTER SEVEN

I missed the whirl of activity of earlier times. The more I had to do, the better organized I was and if I didn't have deadlines I was lost. The two films I'd just made had been fun, but how long does an actor's work last in a film? If you have the main part it's often months, but if not, only weeks, or sometimes just a few days. I resumed my social life, which earlier had revolved round my work. Now I was meeting people from other walks of life and I was beginning to feel not only was I marking time, but wasting it.

One day a friend of mine called Ian Bolton rang to say hullo and said he had someone he'd like me to meet and could we all go out to dinner. He described his friend as charming and well-connected, and added that he was an up-and-coming racing driver. He sounded wonderful. I told Ian I knew nothing about racing.

'Oh, that doesn't matter,' he said. 'Charlie's mad about films.' We made a dinner date for the following week.

My first impression of Charlie Crichton-Stuart was of an open, straightforward man, quite different from the folks I'd been meeting recently. Charlie was around the same age as myself. He had black hair and blue eyes, and a marvellous quality of enthusiasm. He said I had a lovely home, and that it suited me. I'd spent a lot of time decorating it and I was pleased to hear this. Other people hadn't been so warm about it. Charlie's charm was infectious; it was impossible not to like him.

He told me he'd just broken off his engagement to Sally Curzon, who was now going out with his friend Piers Courage, another racing driver, who was a handsome, dashing figure. Sadly, a few years later Piers was killed in a racing accident. Sally is now married to John Aspinall. Since his father died, Charlie had for some time made his home with his cousin, the Marquis of Bute, and his wife Nicola, with whom he was dear friends. Their home was called Mount Stuart, miles away, off the coast of Scotland opposite Glasgow on the Isle of Bute. I asked Charlie, wasn't it a long way to go back at the end of the day? He smiled and said he had a flat much nearer, in Harrow-on-the-Hill.

It seemed we had a great deal in common. Charlie was an orphan of sorts, as well. At the age of five his mother had died, and when he was seventeen so had his father. With his sister, Charlie had spent time caring for their father when he'd been ill. Much of Charlie's life had been without wealth, despite his titled connections. And, like myself, he was working in an incredibly competitive profession, fighting for his own success.

I remember going to a first night with Charlie soon after we met and noticing how uncomfortable he was in the spotlight. I hadn't expected this, he was the one with the social background, and was a very good racing driver in his own right. But I know how disturbing it can be to have microphones thrust in your face or people yelling at you for pictures. Charlie's unexpected reaction made me feel protective towards him.

We saw a lot of each other that summer. On my birthday, at the end of June, Charlie gave me the most exquisite plaited gold bracelet inscribed, 'With my love, for ever Charlie, 1966'. It took my breath away, it was the most beautiful gift. In August, he said he was due to race in the Monte Carlo Grand Prix.

'I'll be driving and it will be exciting and fun. Why don't you come with me, Shirley Anne, and have a holiday?' Charlie was the first person who used my full first name. It made me feel more individual, and much less like Shirley Broomfield.

He reserved a hotel just behind the seafront. Charlie had spent his childhood in Monte Carlo so he knew the city well, and naturally spoke French. We visited the house he'd grown up in and he told me about his childhood. His father had spent much of the time travelling, and Charlie and his sister had stayed in Monte Carlo in the family home.

This was the second time Charlie had raced in the Monte Carlo Grand Prix. After Monte Carlo, Charlie decided not to enter his final two races. There was some trouble with his engine and he couldn't compete properly until it was put right. He could have gone on to the race on the assumption that it would be repaired, but he suggested we stay behind. It was bad luck for his racing team, but good luck for us two – we spent the next fortnight on holiday, sunbathing on the beach, and eating fresh sardines for lunch caught by the local fishermen. It was beautiful and very peaceful, a world away from both of our hectic lifestyles, and Charlie was magical in this open air setting where he excelled at most sports, like waterskiing, which we did together.

The racing circuit was a fascinating, frantic world, and in complete contrast to the way I'd been marking time in London for the past year. After Monte Carlo I went to a number of races with Charlie and began to like it very much. The drivers and mechanics were a friendly bunch that looked out for each other. The racing drivers themselves were a small circle of men, often in a state of tension and excitement. I thought of them as modern day gladiators.

Charlie had spent his own money on his racing career, unlike most other drivers who were sponsored. But when he ran out of money he had to find a sponsor too, and found an industrialist from the north of England who provided it, a woman called Natalie. Natalie being the rare exception, the racing circuit was virtually all male. It was a man's world, and the women who followed racing were mostly friends or relatives. Only in the last few years, with women like American driver Shirley Muldowney, has the balance begun to change.

I certainly didn't have that kind of ability. I didn't even drive. Charlie let me try his E-type Jaguar one day. I didn't realize it was in gear and, as I turned the engine on, the car leapt forward and I hit a wall, damaging the nose. To Charlie's credit, he didn't complain. But he didn't let me drive again, either.

With autumn came the beginning of the theatre season. I had met Jimmy Logan through my good friend Annie Ross, the jazz singer who was also Jimmy's sister. When Jimmy offered me a couple of months' work at the Metropole Theatre in Glasgow in the play *The Hasty Heart* I was happy to have the work. A few months before I had decided, after talking with Jean, to give myself a new look. We wanted people to look at me in a new light, to cast me in different roles. Besides, every woman will recognize the feeling of being tired with the way she looks, hoping that a change of hairstyle will rejuvenate her. I've done this often, sometimes with disastrous results.

I went to Leonard's salon and asked him what he thought. Celine had been cutting my hair for sometime, so when Leonard suggested he would do it himself I thought, why not? I was optimistic. At that time Twiggy was famous for the hairstyle he had created for her. She was also, of course, famous for her stick-thin look. The haircut he devised for me was similar to hers, and it may have suited my face, but my body now appeared too round. Sitting in his chair, with my hair lying all over the floor, I suddenly realized that the 'sweet little boy' look only worked with a sweet little boy's body. I felt like a very muscular swimming instructor. In fact, I found it hard not to cry.

Charlie didn't say a word when he first saw me. I think he was in shock, or maybe, for once, he didn't know what to say. Perhaps I was really testing him, to see if he still liked me without my usual long hair. It really was a drastic change, from shoulder-length reddish brown, to light streaks that looked grey on my now very short head of hair.

While I was in Glasgow, Charlie took me to Mount Stuart on the Isle of Bute for the first time. It's a stately home rather like an old feudal mansion, owned by his cousin John, the present Marquis of Bute. The family can trace their ancestry back for hundreds of years. Apparently, Charlie's and John's grandfather used to pull all the blinds down in Mount Stuart when the late King visited Scotland. He felt that the Stuarts were the rightful heirs and wanted to express his disapproval of George V. Having read about it since, they may have a point!

When we arrived, the butler opened the large, thick front door and my little hold-all was whisked away from me, only to reappear later, unpacked by the housekeeper, with my clothes beautifully laid out on the bed ready to dress for dinner. I wished then I'd brought grander clothes.

During the Second World War Mount Stuart had been requisitioned as a hospital. The upper floors were lined with bedroom after bedroom, which the family never used and referred to as the YMCA. There were also three separate chapels in the house. The bedroom I was given had a four-poster bed, a fireplace with a real log fire burning, and an old-fashioned, comfortable bathroom. Mount Stuart was an enchanting place, rather like having a very attractive, slightly quaint hotel to yourself.

In one of the modern but simply-decorated sitting rooms Charlie and I had a drink with John. He was handsome and considerate, and a good host. He talked about the house, and a little bit about the family heritage. It was interesting to hear about medieval times referred to as if they were happening today. I remember Charlie and John talking about a battle and thinking they were talking about the last war when, in fact, they were talking about the famous Scottish Battle of Culloden as if it had happened only yesterday.

During the evening John talked about his expensive tree doctor who took care of the 500-year-old trees growing in abundance on his land. I didn't know there was such a thing as a doctor just for trees! It also had never occurred to me that having an inheritance like Mount Stuart could be a tremendous responsibility.

Only at meal times, in the 'small' dining room, large by anyone else's standards, was it uncomfortable. It was like being in a scene from *Fawlty Towers* where the maître d' with two waiters stands behind you frozen for the whole meal, able to hear every word. It was inhibiting to have two servants standing as if they were made of stone, less than five feet away. I didn't feel I could talk freely without including them in the conversation, but John was obviously used to it and carried on as if they weren't there.

The play was just a two-month run, but it was a wonderful interlude in Scotland. I'd had waterskiing lessons on Loch Lomond with the Scottish waterski champion, no less, called Duncan, and with the visits to Mount Stuart and the work in Glasgow it was a great time all round and it gave me a chance to re-charge my batteries away from London.

Back home in London, things were calm and organized for once. I had someone I cared about and who cared about me. And although I wasn't working every week, I still had enough to live on.

Then, in the early autumn, the calm was broken when the phone rang at dawn one morning with a call from the United States.

'Hi, this is your brother-in-law here, Bobby!' the voice announced.

'My brother-in-law is called Ronald,' I replied. 'Who is this, please?'

'I'm Bobby, Sunny's new husband and we've got a brand new baby boy of three weeks.' I was still taking this in when he dropped the most terrible bombshell. 'But that's not why I called you,' he went on. 'Your sister has cancer. She's in the hospital now. She didn't want me to phone. She thinks you won't believe her because she always calls when she's in trouble.'

It didn't seem that long since I had last spoken to Sunny. I was devastated by this news. I crouched in the hall, so I wouldn't wake Charlie, but he heard me and came out to ask what the trouble was. He could see my distress and spoke to Bobby himself. After the conversation Charlie and I discussed what to do, and I rang my brother, who was now back in England. Guy and I both wanted to go to Sunny, but I knew her better, so we agreed that I would make the trip. On the phone her doctor in Washington convinced me the situation was serious. Since I didn't have enough money to pay the fare there and back, I decided to break into the savings fund held for me by my financial advisors a year

173

earlier than they wanted me to. Within a week I was on the plane to America.

At National Airport in Washington I was met by Bobby's parents. They greeted me kindly, but I hadn't been in the car ten minutes when they told me how bewildered and hurt they were by their son's relationship with my sister. At twenty two, Bobby was eleven years younger than Sunny, and I don't think his parents understood the attraction they had for each other. They were also worn out from the emotional turmoil and the financial drain of the last few months. They really loved their new-born grandson, Bobby Jr, whom I saw as soon as we arrived at Sunny's flat. He was so small and fragile I was afraid to even hold him. Due to Sunny's illness, he had weighed very little at birth, but tiny though he was, he was fighting fit now.

The doctors told me there had been a possibility of arresting my sister's cancer if she'd terminated her pregnancy in the early stages. At that time in the United States, abortions were legal only in cases where the mother's life was threatened. Her doctors advised a termination and were prepared to go ahead, but Sunny said no and continued her pregnancy. Sunny knew the risks involved. I loved little Bobby very much, but she had five other children she couldn't take care of, and now it looked as if this new baby would be motherless too. Sunny had always been a gambler, and it was as if she was deliberately playing Russian roulette with her life.

Hours later, Bobby came bounding into the room, straight from his job at a local grocery store. Perhaps he had a marvellous personality, but I failed to see what my sister saw in him – he was large and awkward and not immediately attractive. Certainly his parents shouldn't be too worried, I thought. On first impression, he seemed to be the lucky one.

On the way to the hospital Bobby told me not to be too put out with his mother and father. They were upset that he had postponed college for a year because he wanted to be with Sunny and help with her expenses. Her health insurance had expired and there was still $4,000 outstanding on the hospital account. I told Bobby I would pay. He was obviously doing all he could, working long hours to help cover the bills.

I didn't know how I expected to find Sunny, but I was surprised when I did see her. She looked soft and pretty lying

174

against the pillows in a pink nightdress, and better than when I'd last seen her in England. She showed me the scar, a long line from her chest downwards, where they'd operated. That was when I learned she had stomach cancer. She was glad to see me, but also defensive about my having come to America. It was not her idea to send for me, she cried. She didn't want me to think that she only wanted me in a crisis.

'Sunny, if you can't call me now, who can you call?' I said, hugging her.

She pushed me away. 'Well, we do have a father, you know, and we did have a mother . . . *once*. God knows where she is now. I notice she took Joy with her and not us!' Sunny hadn't mentioned Joy for the longest time, and her anger surprised me. A nurse told me that the medication often made the patients' hidden aggression surface.

When I was finally alone with my sister, I sat and listened as she began a dreadful litany of the last two years, and all she'd been through: her separation from Ronald; their fights over the children, Scott and Lisa; living on her own, and then meeting Bobby; his parents' complete disapproval of her; her pregnancy and her sickness, one right after the other; and the doctors' insistence that if she went on with her pregnancy she would endanger her life. I asked her quietly why she'd gone through with it, as she already had five other children.

'I'm not sure I want to go on,' she said quickly. 'And anyway, he *is* ten years younger than me. If we have a child together, there will always be a bond.'

Sunny had two doctors looking after her. One was in his late twenties, a nice man who had a soft spot for Sunny. The other doctor was much older, and he was the one who summoned me to his office after I first saw her.

'Look,' he said. 'You want to know the truth? Your sister is dying.' I couldn't believe my ears. This was a thirty-three-year-old woman he was talking about.

'How long has she got?' I asked. 'And is there any hope?'

'Two years at the most, but it could be just a few months. We opened her up and took out what we could, but the cancer has spread because of her pregnancy.' He told me that the cancer cells grew as the baby developed. 'She's an impossible woman in every way,' he continued. 'We probably could have arrested

175

the disease if she'd listened to me.' I sat down hard on the chair. I felt numb. The doctor kept on talking and talking. He was a volatile man. I didn't like him much, maybe because he was so hard about Sunny. I thought he was my friend when I had first spoken to him on the telephone from England, but now I wasn't sure. He asked me my medical history and if there had been cancer in my family before, as well as lots of personal questions. He said he'd give me an examination to make sure I was healthy, and I said I could come back the following week when I could cope with my feelings. 'In the meantime,' he said, 'you'd better think about getting your sister back to England. She can't afford the hospital treatment here or the medication, and at least in England she can get it free.' He explained to me, that when the pain got severe, the only thing that could ease it would be the strongest drugs, like morphine or heroin, drugs that were against the law in America, even for terminally ill patients, because of the escalating drug problem.

Sunny's condition deteriorated during the eight weeks I spent in Washington. She couldn't swallow any food, so they put a tube through her side straight into her stomach. What amazed me was that no treatment was given unless they knew you had the money, and I had to break my trust again for this to be done. Before they released Sunny from the hospital we also had to settle the outstanding bill, which was now over $4,000. I got the distinct impression the hospital had been marking time with Sunny until her bill was paid. They certainly had cut back on her pain medication.

I didn't know that the doctors had told Sunny very little about her illness. One day she screamed at me as I arrived at the hospital.

'You've been lying to me, haven't you?' I stood there immobilized. I didn't know what she would say or do next. 'I'm going to die, aren't I?' Her bluntness stunned and frightened me. I didn't know what to say or do. Sunny had always been the strong one. I replied it wasn't that I was trying to hide things. I'd only been told myself recently.

'It was just that the doctors had told me it was better not to tell you.'

'OK,' she said. 'How long?' I gave the longest answer I could, two years, praying silently that it *would* be that long. 'All right,

176

I'm going to make my plans. I'm going home with you this Christmas, and then I'm coming back to spend my last Christmas here with the children.'

One of the nurses on duty, an Iranian woman called Kay, heard Sunny talking and volunteered to return with us to England to help me take care of Sunny, if I would pay her fare. I knew this could be a terrific help, and I was relieved. I was dreading the plane journey, wondering how I was going to manage if Sunny needed medication or if she couldn't walk.

As soon as the nurse left the room, Sunny grabbed me. 'Don't take her, please. I don't trust her.' I was very sorry later that I hadn't listened to my sister. I just thought she was being demanding, and her older doctor had convinced me of it when he said aggressively:

'If she had her way she'd have Florence Nightingale looking after her by now and no-one else. If this nurse has volunteered, I'd take her.' If only I'd known her true motives.

We moved Sunny back to her apartment for the time being, where we could nurse and look after her. On her first night home, Sunny let me know how pleased she was that I was there with her. She'd been dreading the time when her insurance would run out and she would be forced to go to a charity hospital. She loved the attention and being cared for and badly needed it. I did whatever I could. I'd try to get her to eat, even though I knew she'd probably throw it all up. Bobby, on the other hand, felt I was in the way. He wanted to resume his love life with Sunny, and said so, which put me in an awkward position. I phoned Charlie, whom I'd been calling regularly, and we discussed the whole situation. I said I thought the only thing to do was to bring Sunny back to London, as the doctor had advised, because at least she could get free medical care back home in England.

I wanted to take her baby son with us, but Bobby's parents gave me no choice: either Sunny or the baby. However, they were not able to accept the responsibility of caring for little Bobby. Sunny had a wonderful neighbour living opposite who had helped me with the baby and said she would take him into her family and look after him. I agreed to pay her a small monthly fostering fee. It was a solution for the time being.

Bobby was in two minds about Sunny's leaving for England. It was as if he couldn't believe she would get worse, yet he wanted her to have all the medical help she could to make her feel better. Sometimes I wasn't sure what he wanted. And neither was he.

Sunny's courage was enormous. She got out of the wheelchair and walked on to the plane herself, despite her condition. Kay gave her pain killers, but they didn't help much. When the pain came, it was unbearable for Sunny. I couldn't stand to see her like that and I asked Kay if she could double the medication. She did and it made Sunny more comfortable. The extra medication kept her drowsy, for which I was grateful. At least she wasn't suffering. When we touched down in England she forced herself one more time to walk off the plane, with the nurse and me on either side of her. The airport staff had a wheelchair waiting. It was the last time Sunny would walk any distance again.

Charlie and Guy were there to meet us, and as soon as Sunny saw them her personality changed. I couldn't understand it. She started ordering Kay and myself around, and in the car on the ride back she kept grumbling, it was a mistake her coming back ... England looked so poor compared to America ... she missed her baby and Bobby ... she didn't like the woman I'd found to look after young Bobby ... her husband would start going out with another woman. Nothing pleased her. I was disappointed that Charlie and Guy had to see Sunny acting this way. By the time we got back to Douglas Court I was hurt and angry.

'Let's all keep a united front,' Charlie said. 'It'll be all right.' In the meantime, my brother was becoming furious with me. He didn't think I was sympathetic enough with Sunny. He didn't know the half of it.

I was beginning to wonder if I'd done the right thing in bringing her back, and just as I was getting to the end of my tether, Sunny became calm again. The atmosphere at home seemed to reassure and quieten her, and she told me how cosy it was. This was the place she expected me to have had on her last visit. She was glad to be with me. I tucked her up on the sofa, with a telephone at hand, so she could ring her relatives, and gave her a hug. I heaved a sigh of relief, after having fought so hard to get her back, knowing now at least I'd done what Sunny wanted and needed.

After making appointments with a private doctor and with my old friend, Leonard, I sat down to arrange a schedule with Kay so that we could look after Sunny in turns. She gave me a strange look, which at the time I didn't understand. Sunny stayed up all that day, and went to bed at about ten o'clock that evening. It was just a few days before Christmas, and was to be the last normal day of her life.

The following day brought an unwanted twist to events when Kay informed me that her son was dying of smallpox in Iran, and said she had to go to him. I was presented with a *fait accompli*, and there was little I could do. She showed me how to give the injections, and then she was off. 'She just wanted a free plane ticket,' Sunny observed.

My life became a three-ring circus in the next few weeks, with people constantly in the flat – doctors and nurses, friends and family. All of us were running the whole range of emotions. It was a period of extremes, like a hideous seesaw with highs and lows. All of the coming and going created a lot of muddle, and people were extremely helpful or extremely difficult: there was no inbetween. The last thing I wanted was for there to be any stress. Romie would ring at strange hours, usually in the middle of the night, to talk about the business or our friendship, or anything but Sunny. It made her upset that I wasn't sympathetic to her problems. I felt exasperated. I didn't have the time for this now. It was a gigantic effort to even think about my own needs, let alone anyone else's.

Guy didn't want to accept his sister's condition either, and would sit at her bedside and cry. Even with her illness, Sunny was strong mentally, and she hated this. When her friend Sharon arrived from the States, she and Guy clung to each other, which only complicated things more. Guy's long-time girlfriend, Madeline, was often in the flat helping out, and naturally began to sense their relationship.

There was a wonderful nursing sister I engaged called Irene who was a great comfort to Sunny and myself. When the tensions in the house became too much, Irene would gently say that some people reacted badly in a crisis. It was their way of grieving and she would pray for them. I don't know how she kept calm, because if anyone behaved badly in front of Sunny, I was beside myself.

Having a large flat made it a little easier. If Sunny couldn't face visitors, they could stay in the sitting room. The Broomfields

179

were supportive and made frequent visits. My dad came nearly every day, and Aunt Elsie and my cousin Sheila bought cakes and made tea. My grandmother, who was now eighty, was good throughout. They wanted to help in any way they could. Even Gypsy was civil, or tried to be.

'You've changed your tune,' she said to me one day.

'That's not true,' I replied. 'I'm just the same. You just saw me differently.'

It was hard on everyone. This was a person we had known, a few of us had loved, and now she was slowly dying. There was nothing anyone could do.

One afternoon, when Sunny was not in pain, my father, myself and Guy were gathered round Sunny's bed. She looked at my dad and asked him which one was his favourite. 'Between you and Shirley, I can't choose,' he said. 'Well, you've always been special Sunny . . .' There was a long silence. 'As for the boy,' he said, 'I can't say. I don't know him, do I?' I could feel Guy tense up. My father went on, 'Cause I think he could have been a bit different since you've been ill.' Guy was turning white with anger. I thought he was going to scream out or hit his father. It was a good thing he didn't because I don't know what would have happened. They were emotional opposites and, after this incident, things were never good between them. I don't think Guy ever forgave Dad.

Charlie was great during this emergency, and did a lot in the first few weeks to help me nurse Sunny round the clock. He would sit at her bedside and light cigarettes for her, and when she became unconscious or fell asleep and they'd drop out of her mouth, he'd pick them up and wait until she came to, then put them back. Charlie and I were very close in these days. Our feelings were stretched so tight it was like being on an emotional tightrope. Nothing felt quite real.

One day I asked Sunny if there was anything I could do for her. 'Yes, there is,' she said. 'I think it's time you got married and settled down with Charlie.' We told her we were going to eventually, but Sunny said she wanted us to marry straight away in front of her so she could see for herself. Charlie asked the local priest if he would perform the ceremony in my flat in Sunny's bedroom. To our sadness and disappointment he refused, saying he would only conduct it in a church.

There was one moment when I realized that Sunny had very little time left. She hadn't eaten anything for weeks and her physical strength was all but gone. I noticed a sweet, sickly odour in her room. As I was washing her with a soft cloth I saw that one of her toes had turned black. At first I thought she'd bruised it, but when I looked closer I could see that the colour was really blueish-green, and as I began to wash her foot the toe came off in my hand. I quickly put on heavy socks so she wouldn't see it, and phoned the doctor immediately. By this time I was praying that it would soon be over for Sunny. I was afraid of anything worse happening. She weighed only as much as an eleven-year-old child by now and seeing her toes that way had panicked me. There was no-one to turn to. Irene had gone home to rest, and Charlie had left for the Argentine, where he was competing in a race and it was far too early for any visitors. I felt completely alone.

Exhausted, crying quietly, I sat in the kitchen wondering what to do next. I sat there for what seemed ages with my head on the table, trying not to be sick. Just as I got to the edge of despair, I heard Sunny's voice ringing out loud and clear from her bedroom. 'What are you doing in there, Shirley? Get back in here quick! I'm not gone yet!' Trust my Sunny, she got me back on course. I couldn't let her see I was afraid.

Before Charlie left for the Argentine, he'd arranged an undertaker in case the worst did happen. He'd also left me a ticket to join him.

Brian and his wife Jackie were marvellous and used to come and stay at the flat. They were a great moral support. Brian thought I needed a break after three weeks of being with Sunny constantly and one evening he and Jackie took me out to dinner. When we returned Sunny was hysterical. 'Please don't leave me again, please!' she cried. It was one of the only times I saw my sister show any fear. I held her close, crying myself, and promised I would never leave her again, ever.

Sunny and I had made a solemn pact. I promised her that if the pain became unbearable, I would have a jar of pills ready for her to take. Thankfully, the heroin that was prescribed took away most of the pain and we avoided such a measure. Either Irene or myself would inject her intra-muscularly, but on the night after I'd been to the restaurant, Irene rang Leonard and was told to give

181

Sunny the injection herself *intravenously*. This time she sent me out of the room. When I came back, Sunny had calmed down considerably, and was conscious and comfortable. We laughed and talked for a little while about our childhood and her kids in America, and she made me promise again to marry and settle down. After fifteen minutes or so, Sunny dropped into a deep sleep. I held her hand and sat very still with her for some time in case she woke up.

'Go to bed, go to bed,' urged Irene. She gave me two very strong Nembutals to help me sleep. I should have slept right through the night after taking those pills, but two hours later I was up and wide awake. Irene came into my room. 'She's just gone.'

'I know,' I said quietly.

'How?' she asked. I didn't know how I knew, but I went into my sister's room and saw that the pain had all been wiped from her face. I was glad to see Sunny at peace. I felt calm, as though she was still with me. Irene was busy tying something around her jaw.

'I'm arranging this so her face will be in repose,' she explained. It was just three days before Sunny's thirty fourth birthday.

I spent the rest of that night taking care of Sunny's appearance. Most days I had been getting her ready before anybody came to visit, as she was unhappy about the way she looked since she'd been ill. I bathed her face and put her favourite long-sleeved nightgown on her. It covered her arms so you couldn't see how thin she'd got. Then I brushed her hair, which had become very thin, and added a hairpiece of mine she'd always wanted, and gently made up her face. It was as if I was doing it without thinking. Sunny was always so proud, and I was determined that she would look beautiful. Her skin was cold by the time I finished.

Leonard arrived in the morning. 'What an act of love,' he said. 'She looks lovely.' The undertaker felt the same way, he said he didn't need to do a thing with her.

My friends and relatives were kind when they heard the news. Aunt Elsie gave me some money for the funeral and John Bute sent £500 to help with expenses. Sunny had been very definite about wanting to be cremated.

Two days after Sunny died, Kay, the nurse who had flown to England with us, knocked on my door. She was standing there with a small boy.

'What are you doing here?' I asked. 'It's too late now. Your patient has *died*.' I was so furious I could have strangled her. Here she was, back again three weeks after having run out on Sunny at the most crucial time. I looked at the boy. 'This is your son with smallpox, is it?' I asked. 'Where are his marks, then?' She told me she had got it wrong, that it had been *chicken*-pox instead. What followed convinced me that Sunny had been right about her. She said I owed her for the flight back to America, her return ticket had expired as she was late. I was astounded. Not only had she lied about her son and borrowed money from me to fly to Iran, worst of all she had run out on a dying woman.

'Not a chance,' I replied. 'Our agreement was that you made the trip with me, looked after Sunny until I could get other help, and then went back to America. You'll have to find your own way of getting back.'

She said her son was wet. Could he use the bathroom? I reluctantly let them in, as I really didn't want her in my home. Then she asked if she could use the telephone to call the airport. I told her to use the one in the kitchen. After she made the call she asked if she could stay for an hour because her flight wasn't until the evening. Her son was whimpering throughout all this. I had to go to the funeral parlour to see Sunny's body and make arrangements for the service, and with some hesitation I let her stay. Unfortunately, Jackie and Brian weren't back. They'd gone to their own home for a break and a fresh change of clothes. When I returned, she'd gone. There was no note, nothing. Jackie came back shortly afterwards. Her engagement ring, worth £2,000 or more, was missing from the dresser. I knew it had to be the nurse.

Immediately, we phoned the police and gave them her name and description. They phoned the airport and tried to stop her, but were too late at this end, she had already boarded a plane. They thought she must have pawned the ring on the way to the airport. We rang through to the FBI in Washington, and they intercepted her as she stepped into the terminal. She was questioned for quite some time. Later I heard the story she told the FBI. Supposedly I was a heroin user and had nursed my sister in order to get hold of the drug! She picked on the right ingredient, the authorities in America were paranoid about drugs. I realized, with a shock, that I was up against an expert. Even though they discovered she had a record, the case was her word against mine. To press charges overseas would have taken a great deal of time and money. I phoned the doctor at the hospital. He sympathized with me and assured me that nursing would be a closed door to her from now on. I was rushing to join Charlie in the Argentine and so I let it rest at that. I hadn't the energy left to fight any more.

The nurse was released on insufficient evidence, and the only tiny bit of consolation was that at least Jackie had been insured for her ring and got some compensation.

I went to Sunny's funeral in a haze. Charlie's arrangements had made sure that everything was taken care of. Emotionally it wasn't so smooth. My brother and I had fallen out over his attachment to Sharon during Sunny's illness. I was furious about the extra tension, and he thought it was none of my business. During the ceremony I couldn't see where Guy was standing, but I could feel the strain between him and his father.

When the family got back to the house my dad became jolly, despite the sombre occasion, reminiscing and telling jokes, which annoyed me. I didn't feel it was right. He hadn't spoken to his mother or his sister for fifteen years, nor had he visited his family during that time. Maybe that explained his jokey behaviour.

Two days later I flew to join Charlie in Buenos Aires and watch him race. I'd been to the Argentine a few years earlier – when I'd had an emergency appendix operation! – for a film festival where *Saturday Night and Sunday Morning* had won the Best Picture award. It was the height of summer when I arrived this time. Inside the racing cars, the temperature was dangerously high. Charlie led most of the way until, halfway through, the officials suspended the race because of a technical problem. I sat on the grass with him during the interim. He was hot, exhausted, and very pale. I thought he was going to be sick and was praying there would be a long break so he could recover. Thankfully, my prayers were answered. To my great relief, the officials called the rest of the race off, and Charlie was declared the winner.

After we got back from South America, Charlie mostly stayed with me at Douglas Court. We found we wanted to be together all the time now, especially after what we'd been through in the last year, and round about March I became pregnant. We were both delighted and decided on a summer wedding that would be very small.

One afternoon at the antique stall – we were still there two days a week – I had a frightening experience. The previous weekend I'd had a party at my flat and someone had brought a bottle of pear brandy as a gift. My friend Vicky was pregnant also and a day after the party she had a miscarriage. We didn't know if it was from the pear brandy or not, but on the following Saturday I got terrible stomach pains and started to bleed. I could hardly stand up. Romie drove me back to the flat and Charlie, who was out at Elstree giving flying lessons, raced home. I lay on the sofa while we waited for an ambulance.

The week in the clinic saved my baby. I stayed in bed, my doctor told me not to move, only if it were absolutely necessary. All the same, it was nearly catastrophic. One day two nurses came in and physically turned the mattress over with me on it. I fell on the floor on the other side yelling in a panic, 'What are you doing?' They thought I was there to have an abortion, and were stunned when they learned it was the other way round. Gingerly, they put me back into bed. These were the same nurses who, in a few months' time, would deliver my daughter.

While in the clinic I heard about a revolutionary new treatment. The idea was to allow the baby more room inside the mother in the later stages of pregnancy. Scientists had found this out while training astronauts. They used a weightless chair that enabled pure oxygen to enter the body which, when it reached the stomach, produced a lot more space inside the mother thus allowing the unborn child room to stretch and move much more freely than normally, and the research showed that many children whose mothers had received this treatment were more intelligent. It was called the decompression chamber. I don't know if it worked but it did make my pregnancy easier, it got rid of aches and pains and incidentally, my daughter *is* very bright.

Home life for Charlie and myself was peaceful, and as we had a large flat I thought it would be great to have a dog. I bought a wonderful Afghan hound I really loved, called Washer. His real name was Washire, but after calling out his name several times in the park I shortened it to Washer. His parents were champions, and he should have been one too. But poor Washer had one cracked tooth, so he wasn't allowed to compete in the dog championships. Their loss was my gain. To me he was a great champion anyway, a little dozy but very beautiful with a loving nature. In profile he looked a bit like Vivien Leigh.

Like most Afghans, Washer could run at nearly forty miles an hour and almost every day I'd take him to Regent's Park, where he'd rush off as soon as I let him off his lead. There was no way I could keep up with him, and Washer knew it. He'd run and run, and I'd get exasperated when he wouldn't come when I called. I often left him in the park until Charlie came back later and we went in the car to collect him. Washer was so slim he could squeeze through the railings.

As a treat one afternoon, I took Washer to Hyde Park instead of Regents Park. He was thrilled to be in a new place, and even worse than usual in coming back. Luckily, there was a police station in the middle of Hyde Park and after failing to catch him during the day, the police told me they would try again after dark, so I left Washer happily galloping around. No-one could run as fast as my dog, and when the police drew close in their Land Rover he got frightened by the headlights. Washer ran away and another car hit him accidentally on his left front paw, breaking his elbow.

Washer was a sorry sight when we picked him up, limping and in some pain. The sound of a dog crying is so sad, like a baby's, but worse somehow. We couldn't get a vet to come out in the evening so we had to wait until morning. Poor Washer's paw was hurting so much that Charlie and I ended up sleeping on the floor while Washer got the king-sized bed to himself. The aspirins Charlie gave him to stop him crying were useless, and promptly at seven in the morning, Charlie took Washer to the vet and had his paw put in a sling. When they returned, Washer and I were so exhausted we slept all day.

Charlie and I decided to have the wedding in a register office. Somehow the priest, Father Bagnell, the same man who wouldn't perform the marriage ceremony in Sunny's bedroom, heard about our plans and proceeded to convince me otherwise.

'You want it to be special, don't you? You want it to last. These are strange times we're living in. You could set a good example. You should get married in a church.'

A few days before the wedding, Father Bagnell asked me to his church for a talk. He was a genuinely sincere man. 'Is there anything you want to tell me, my dear?'

'Like what, Father?' I said. This was breaking new ground for me. I wasn't used to a religious man offering to help me, especially one who asked me to confide in him.

'Well, I'm sure there is something,' he said gently.

'But, Father, I'm not a Catholic, and I don't want to change.'

'I know,' he said, 'but we're all Christians. That's the important thing.' I thought about our visit, and two nights before the wedding I went back to see Father Bagnell. I sat with him in a small room off the sanctuary and told him about my pregnancy.

'In that case,' he said, 'we should kneel down and pray together for the coming child.' Afterwards I felt calm and at peace. I was very glad he had persuaded us to have a church wedding.

We had wanted just a few friends and family, but the wedding party grew and grew when people kept ringing for invitations. I heard from people I hadn't seen in years. Then the newspapers reported it and, by the wedding day, there were at least 200 guests in the church, in addition to about thirty to forty photographers waiting outside. Vicky and her boyfriend, Don, had hired a cream Rolls Royce for us, which was a lovely surprise, but the wedding had turned into a grand social event that we'd been trying to avoid.

The church next door, in Kilburn, was hardly the neighbourhood for that kind of wedding. In fact, I'd often see several 'gentlemen of the road' sitting on the steps drinking VP wine, or bottles of cheap cider. On our wedding day they calmly moved across the road and toasted us as we went into the church.

Charlie went to stay the night before with his best man, David Greenland, in Radlett. I stayed at home with Washer, and woke up wishing for a cool English day. It wasn't to be, it was blazing hot, and the morning sickness I'd been having was worse than ever. On top of that, the high temperature made my feet and ankles swell. It was the only part of me showing and I was counting on them not to look plump!

I seemed to have an ability for chaos. I should have had a quiet morning getting ready. I wished Charlie was with me as he had been every morning for the last few months, keeping me calm and helping me when I felt sick. This particular morning he had his own nerves to deal with. Instead of Charlie I had every girlfriend dropping in to help me in one way or another. I managed to get dressed with various friends shouting advice and fussing over me, and generally getting in the way. Jan, one of my closest friends, brought endless cups of tea, which Romie kept swapping for boiled water with lemon when Jan wasn't looking, which she thought was better for me.

It was just as well that the pregnancy had given me a bit of a glow, because I wasn't left alone long enough to put my makeup on. My bedroom had turned into an all female social gathering. I was so confused by all the advice that was being bandied around, I just went on getting ready, hoping it would be all right. I put on too much eye makeup, hoping I'd look like Elizabeth Taylor. It didn't work, but fortunately in the heat it wore off. Luckily, with the veil over my face everything was a little misty and soft anyway. Juliet, another friend of mine, was the most practical. She went straight to the church. I began to wish my other friends had done the same. In spite of the distractions, I remained calm, one of the few times in my life I remember being so. Still, it was a huge relief to get to the church in one piece.

I had a beautiful long white dress, loose and easy to wear, that I should have worn for the ceremony, and if it was today I wouldn't hesitate to wear it. Carol, a friend who was an expert on loose-fitting, comfortable clothes, as her own weight varied from time to time, had bought it and urged me to wear it. But my other girlfriends thought I should be more stylish and talked me out of it. Vicky said I had wonderful legs and it was a pity to hide them. I thought it was sweet of her to say so, considering I could hardly fit into my shoes as my feet were beginning to swell. The dress I did wear was short and close fitting, with an empire line, right in the height of fashion, and was given to me by my close friend Bunty. If it hadn't been a gift I wouldn't have dreamt of wearing it, but I expected her to be in the front row and I didn't want to hurt her feelings. Two weeks earlier it had fitted, but now it was too tight. The dress was the same size. I wasn't. However, my hat was stunning, made of white voile with a veil. It was made for me by Madame Vernier, a famous French milliner. Earlier in my career I'd modelled hats for her, so she knew what suited me. My hair was now medium-length, grown back after my disastrous haircut, and back to my own colour of reddish-brown. I was glad my face still looked like me. In spite of my morning sickness and the chaos around me, I finally got myself ready. I heard one press photographer say to another as I entered the church: 'Focus on the face. That'll make a good picture.'

I'd asked my brother to give me away. I wanted to share my special day with him, as we'd been through a lot together, especially our childhood which I was saying goodbye to. Guy met me on the church steps, appearing tall, handsome and a little tense, and walked me down the aisle.

Halfway through the ceremony, Father Bagnell leaned over and whispered, 'Better sit down, my dear.' He had guessed I was feeling shaky and had arranged a small seat at the altar for me. All of us were a little nervous. Charlie had, unusually for him, taken a tranquillizer that morning.

We were on the front page of most of the papers the next day, and in some of the pictures even Washer was included! The society photographer that Nicola Bute had engaged to photograph us enjoyed himself so much during the wedding day that we never did get our album of pictures. In fact, if it wasn't for the press, we wouldn't have any pictures of our marriage at all! That day the press came up trumps. Next time – if there is one – I'll have it videotaped.

The whole of John Bute's house downstairs and the garden was filled to the brim at the reception in Chelsea Square. I finally changed into the long white dress. Thanks to Nicola Bute and her four wonderful children, the afternoon was a success. They were the most unspoiled, loving children I'd ever met. Everyone who'd been at the church piled back, as well as lots of others – plenty of fashionable people, Stirling Moss and others from the racing world, Adam Faith, film people and a lot of the Broomfields as well. They all got along famously, at least for that one afternoon.

Before we left the reception I changed into a beautiful green silk dress I'd bought with Carol. Outside, Charlie's blue Mini was waiting for us, with cans and streamers trailing from the bumper. We did a lap of honour round the square to the shouts and cheers of our guests, then we were off. Charlie wanted to keep our destination a secret and we drove for about an hour before pulling into the courtyard of a small country hotel. He had gone to great lengths to make sure it was special. In the room, fresh flowers were everywhere, and there was a huge basket of fruit along with pink champagne on ice from the management. Everything was perfect. We opened the champagne and then, for some reason, I began to cry and couldn't stop. Charlie tried to comfort me, but all my feelings became too much. I told him not to be concerned. I was crying because I was happy.

It's happened to me occasionally throughout my life. Whenever everything is just right, I cry because I'm afraid it can't last.

CHAPTER EIGHT

Charlie had planned a peaceful honeymoon for us sailing on the Norfolk Broads. We went off in a thirty-feet cabin cruiser he had rented, drifting along the river, talking to people on the shore and watching the world go by. Sometimes we stopped at a pub for a meal or we made sandwiches on the boat, that was what we liked best. Then, at the end of the day, we'd tie up to the nearest tree to sleep the night. It was a great summer and a great honeymoon. And, strangely enough, all my sickness disappeared on the boat.

I think Charlie was renegotiating his racing contract while we were away, as it had to be renewed each year. He didn't talk about it much but I had the feeling that things were at a standstill for the time being, or he'd have been in Europe competing. I assumed he would continue racing later in the year.

Just a little while after we returned from our honeymoon we made another trip to Mount Stuart to visit John and Nicola Bute. One evening Charlie and John were talking quietly on the steps of the grand staircase, at the bottom of which was a suit of shining armour standing to attention as if on guard. I heard words like 'sponsors' and 'expenses'. I wasn't sure of Charlie's finances, only that he wasn't racing at the moment, and that one day he would have an inheritance. I asked him what they were talking about.

'Nothing to worry about,' he said. 'I'm just trying to get advice on my business affairs.'

During our holiday at Mount Stuart, from various conversations, it appeared that his cousin had financed Charlie's racing somewhat. Now it looked as if it was coming to an end. I asked Charlie what I could do as I had a little money. John replied, 'You must keep your nest egg. In your position, you absolutely must.' It was upsetting to find that Charlie had these problems, but he didn't want me to worry. He wanted to resolve them himself.

One Saturday afternoon back in London, as we were watching television, two men in buff-coloured coats knocked on the door. They came in and greeted Charlie as though they were old friends, and slowly began to move the furniture into the hall. Charlie took no notice of them and sat watching the football match. The men went to move the telly.

'Excuse me,' Charlie said. 'That's rented. And be careful with the furniture, please. It all belongs to my missus.'

'Who are you?' I asked.

'Bailiffs, m'am. The court sent us to collect the furniture in lieu of unpaid bills.' I'd been born into a family who'd been known to pawn their Sunday suits on Monday and get them out again on Friday, and my grandmother had pawned her best sheets from time to time so they had something to live on until the next pay day. Charlie, on the other hand, had been born into comparative luxury. Strangely, he was the one who knew about bailiffs. I'd never had the dubious pleasure before.

When I first married Charlie I was invited by some of his relatives to their homes for dinner to welcome me into the family.

On some of our visits I noticed there would be one or two pieces of exquisite antique furniture which Charlie would touch lovingly. I was touched when I saw him stroke the sideboard in his uncle's drawing room. He told me he'd grown up with this piece of furniture in his home in Monte Carlo. When Charlie was seventeen his father had died. Charlie and his sister had been so distressed they hadn't worried about keeping their father's treasures. Softly, I asked him why he couldn't claim them back. Surely it was a good time, as we'd just got married. I thought Charlie should have had his father's things. I knew he'd loved his father very much and it would make him happy.

With all the ups and downs of our short married life, I wanted good fortune to be on our side, so I looked in an astrological book, to see what sign our baby would be born under. I already knew Charlie's and my signs were compatible. If it was an early November birth the baby would be Scorpio, which would be an affinity sign to my own of Cancer, and also to Charlie's of Pisces.

Physically, I found pregnancy a bit difficult. My skin was glowing and my hair was healthy, but I was often tired and would feel sick. Charlie would make me dry toast and black tea on the mornings when I felt unable to get up. He was wonderful. I don't think I could have got through my pregnancy without him. I felt tranquil, but fragile as well. It was great to know that he was with me.

Our child's expected date of arrival came and went, so it would be a Sagittarius baby after all and that sounded even better. It really didn't matter as long as the baby was healthy. One of the nurses advised me to take some castor oil to speed up the baby's arrival. A few nights later in bed I felt a strange punch in my stomach and went to get a glass of water.

'Come back to bed, darling,' Charlie called. 'You must have taken too much castor oil.'

Ten minutes later, back in bed, I felt a most peculiar feeling, nothing like I'd ever felt before. I screamed. It was the baby getting ready to be born. Charlie practically fell out of bed, I couldn't blame him, I almost fell out of the other side! The two of us must have looked like characters from a Marx Brothers' film.

There I was, scared and crouching on the floor in front of the fire, as the flat was freezing cold. Naturally, being England, the heat was switched off at night, even though it was in the middle of one of the coldest spells. In the meantime, Charlie was hurriedly trying to stuff my belongings into a suitcase. Talk about two more frantic people! I was in my oldest nightie, wearing thick socks and slippers, not at all what I'd planned. I'd pictured arriving at the hospital wearing the most beautiful nightdress with my hair beautifully washed and styled. It was nothing like that. Charlie threw his heavy coat over me and off we drove, helter-skelter like mad, to the hospital.

'Let's have a look at you,' the night nurse said casually. 'Oh, no need to panic. The baby won't be born for three or four days yet.' I was feeling uncomfortable and Charlie was doing his best to help but, if anything, he seemed more nervous than me. The nurse said he'd be better off going home and having a good night's sleep. I stayed in the hospital, impatiently waiting for my baby to be born.

In spite of what the nurse predicted, I thought the birth would be quite soon. In the early hours of the morning, as I lay on the bed groaning quietly with contractions, I could see, out of the corner of my eye, a man squatting on the floor on the other side of the room. He was adjusting one of the light switches.

'What are you doing?' I asked him curtly.

He replied, 'I'm the electrician, Miss Field. Just mending the lights,' and he smiled sweetly.

'You're a bit bloody late!' I said.

'Come now,' he said, carrying on with his work. 'You'd like them to see you clearly when your child's born, wouldn't you?' I replied that I couldn't care less, I just wanted to be private, without the company of strange men repairing the light fittings whilst I was having a baby!

'Don't be bad tempered, my dear,' he replied. 'We've all admired your work for years.' It's amazing, I thought. If I can't be bad-tempered in the middle of labour pains, when can I be? I was so exasperated with him I thought I'd explode.

'Get out! Get out of here!' I yelled.

'Don't worry, Miss Field,' he said calmly. 'I'm used to all this!' I told him in no uncertain terms that I *wasn't*, and that I would like him to leave, *immediately*. I'm often reminded of this by his wife, who works in the local chemist's shop, and we still laugh about it.

I wasn't comfortable in a lying position, so I moved to a chair, but that wasn't any good either. I tried crouching on the floor and that was better. I was fairly comfortable and could breathe properly. Two nurses and a doctor came in.

'Get up!' they ordered. 'You can't have a baby like some peasant woman in a field!'

'Leave me alone!' I snapped back. I felt OK where I was and didn't want to move. Then my own doctor came in. Dr Bierer was in his mid-sixties, quite frail and eccentric. He should have been retired but he didn't want to give up delivering babies. Even though he was old and shaky, I wanted him because he saved the baby for me.

'Well, she's all right,' he said. 'Just leave her alone. That's the way people all over the world have babies.' Thankfully, they left me in my comfortable position.

After a little while they came to check on my progress, and put me back on the delivery trolley. The pains started in earnest as soon as I was lying down again. The nurse holding my hand spoke with a strong Yorkshire accent.

'C'mon, Shirley, push, luv, push! They don't call this labour for nothing,' she shouted in my ear. 'Push a bit 'arder, luv!' At least I could laugh between the contractions. By now my doctor was trying to give me any medication he could. I refused an epidural shot in the spine. I did have some pain killers, but I was still quite clear as to what was happening. I'd read so many books on childbirth, I thought I'd be well prepared, until now. One thing I didn't want was my child to be drugged as it was born. The oxygen mask they kept putting over my face gave me claustrophobia, which was almost worse than the pains.

Charlie was back in the hospital by now, waiting in a nearby room. I wanted to see him very much. Just then a nurse came in and told me to please keep it quiet, because it was unnerving for Charlie. I didn't think I was making much noise, it must have been very little, because along the corridor I could clearly hear the screaming of another mother-to-be. She was yelling blue murder, not only at her own husband but at all men in general! I hoped to God Charlie wasn't hearing her and thinking it was me.

I surprised myself at how calm I was. I often get excited over small things, but when it came to having *my* baby it was different. Some of the hospital staff had been dreading the birth, presuming I'd be difficult. They told me they'd been trying to rearrange the rota to be off-duty at the time my baby was born. It amazed them, they said, as if they were paying me the biggest compliment ever, that I was such a good sport in spite of being an actress! If I hadn't been worn out with the labour pains, I would have told them I wasn't trying for any medals. I just wanted to have my child.

Dr Bierer was a little nervous. Tears streamed down his face as he delivered my daughter. 'She's perfect,' he said. 'I hadn't expected this after your near miscarriage earlier in the year.' After he dropped this bombshell, he practically dropped the baby as well, he was so overcome. Fortunately the midwife caught her in mid-air!

As Dr Bierer put her on my chest, I thought she was a miracle. Suddenly Charlie was there as well. He was speechless, giving me a kiss, and then the nurse gave him our baby to hold. We'd decided, if it was a girl, we'd call her Nicola, after Nicola Bute. She was funny and small, with dark hair and long fingernails, and looked a lot like Charlie. Dr Bierer was still in tears when he wasn't laughing with joy. I think he thought he was personally responsible for this baby.

Straight after Nicola was born, Dr Bierer decided it was best to put her in an incubator. I don't think it was strictly necessary, just a precaution on his part. I think he also wanted to make sure I would rest, after all this great excitement. Today I would do it differently, and I would keep my baby with me. I think it's good to have as much closeness with your child as soon as he or she is born. I also think it prepares one for the complete change one's life takes. I was now responsible for another human being.

Dr Bierer had my interests at heart. He wanted to make sure I rested for as long as possible. In fact, he only let me leave his nursing home the day before Christmas. It was a hectic time 'resting' in the clinic: visitors, gifts, newspaper covers with my baby and myself on the front page, learning to handle, feed and look after Nicola generally. Just the same, it was still a fairytale time.

All in all, perhaps Dr Bierer was wise, I certainly didn't have that back-up at home. I had just a very young au pair from

Czechoslovakia who'd been with me for about a month. I came home to a wonderful Christmas organized by Charlie and what was more extraordinary, he'd managed it on very little money. There was a beautiful Christmas tree he'd decorated and Brian and Jackie, together with Charlie, had organized the Christmas lunch. We had a brand new baby of our own and Jackie was about to have twins within the month. Everything was perfect. At last I had my own family.

When we left the nursing home, the nurses had waved us goodbye except for one tiny nurse called Helen from New Zealand. She offered to come and visit us as soon as we needed her. Nicola was dressed in a pink and white checked woollen dress and wrapped in a soft, white shawl. The shawl was a present from Juliet. I carried her on my lap and Charlie drove us home. She'd slept all the way.

When we got home, we put her to bed in her crib, given to us by Nicola Bute. Her bedroom was painted white and yellow and Charlie, with me helping a little, had put up pretty transfers on the wall and on her chest of drawers.

After Nicola had been asleep for at least three hours, both Charlie and myself got anxious. We kept peering over the crib wondering if she was still breathing, willing her to show some signs of life. We didn't know what to expect and, if we'd been more confident, we'd have left her well enough alone. We had a peaceful child but, like many new parents, we were anxious, which I'm sure communicated itself to our baby. This was when I missed having a family of my own, and, most of all, a mother. Just someone to be there and reassure me that everything was all right.

Everyone else's needs now came second to my baby's. Of course, I didn't mean to do this. And though I had an au pair girl, I was still too intense. Some days, I never quite got out of my night clothes. I tried to do everything by the book. I didn't have any relatives to talk to or help, except my grandmother of eighty. My girlfriends, most of them still without children, were all leading busy social lives as they had before. Charlie was out at Elstree most days training long hours for his new job to be a flight instructor.

One marvellous friend was Annie Ross, who'd ring me every-day around twelve o'clock lunch time, to ask if she could bath the baby. I loved Annie for helping me because, by this time, I'd be exhausted. I'd been up since six in the morning and often once or twice during the night, feeding Nicola myself every four hours. Annie was great with her, and would sing and croon to her. One time both of us were convinced that Nicola crooned right back.

I was often in a tizz, wondering if I was doing the right thing, so it was a great relief when the health visitor called. I didn't even have the courage to cut my baby's fingernails, she was so small. It worried me that she might scratch herself as she had done sometimes when I was feeding her. I think the health visitor was amazed at my welcome of her. She was a kind, lovely woman who called unofficially quite a lot.

The professional help I had came and went, depending on our circumstances, or what I could afford, or how they fitted into the household. It was a time of great change emotionally. I had a small baby dependent on me, without anyone around when the responsibility seemed overwhelming. This was a very different lifestyle to anything I'd ever experienced before. Although I wasn't the youngest mother, I could have been a teenager of fifteen for all the practical difference it made.

When Nicola was five months or so, I got a job in the theatre. I hadn't been on stage since I was a teenager. The play was Noel Coward's *Private Lives*. It was at East Grinstead, with a disc jockey called Alan Freeman, who'd never been on stage before, two other actors and myself. It was in a lovely setting, and I took Nicola with me to rehearsals and put her carry cot in the pretty grounds.

Later in the year I appeared at the Royal Court in a play as part of the Edward Bond season. It was an excellent production, breaking new ground, very contemporary, avant garde theatre, and rewarding for us as actors. *Early Morning* was a bleak, desolate look at human weaknesses and frailties, taking place in a kind of hellish wilderness. In one scene we were supposedly eating human bones. In another scene I sat on a laundry box wearing a crinoline, my speech was interrupted by Jack Shepherd's head suddenly appearing, revealed to the audience underneath my long skirt. It was difficult to concentrate with Jack's head there, and hysterically funny in rehearsals. Sometimes we couldn't stop laughing, which would exasperate our marvellous director Bill Gaskell.

On opening night Charlie came with Vicky and her boyfriend, Don. They didn't mince words, they all hated it and afterwards Charlie and Don said they'd been quite put off theatre. Edward Bond's plays do shock a lot of people, but I think he intends this to make them think about the injustices of life. It wasn't easy theatre on any level, and certainly not a show for polite dinner conversation afterwards.

When Charlie wasn't at home, he would be at Elstree, either giving lessons or spending time with his friends there. Sometimes he'd bring them home for dinner, which I liked, but often he'd stay at Elstree late into the evening. I felt stranded being on my own in the huge flat with just the baby.

Two people who became friends through Elstree Flying Club were Richard and Linda. In many ways, they were the opposite of Charlie and me. They were both dentists, Richard had an office in Harley Street, and they had been married for some years with two little boys of their own. They were impressed with Charlie's background and seemed just as excited with my being an actress. After being alone all day with no-one to talk to, they were welcome dinner guests. Richard was a flying pupil of Charlie's at Elstree, and the four of us had shared social activities there.

We all went on a holiday together to Majorca. It was quite different from anything Charlie or I had known before. The day's routine consisted of sunbathing around the pool, in fashionable matching swimwear. Some of the guests hardly got wet, let alone swam. Compared to the others, we seemed like Olympic swimmers. In the evening everyone would dress up again to show off newly-acquired suntans. I enjoyed the dancing very much. Richard could jive, which was great fun for me as it was my favourite. Both of us were flattered by their attentions but we hadn't known that Richard and Linda were having problems and that this holiday was a distraction for them from their own troubled marriage.

Linda flirted with Charlie and Richard would flirt with me. Flattering though it was, it was dangerous. We'd been married less than a year and they acted as if they weren't married at all. The added tension may have added spice to their marriage, but I knew it wasn't good for mine. We'd get jumpy with each other.

Then at dinner I'd feel stupid for being insecure and I'd think I'd imagined things.

The next year I did a season of plays at the Citizen's Theatre in Glasgow. It was the training I'd always wanted and never quite had. The pay was the minimum, and the work was intense and disciplined. I took Nicola with me with an au pair girl called Lilabell, a beautiful Swedish girl, about twenty two years of age, who was wonderful with Nicola, and a great help to me.

When one of the people I was working with took a shine to me, I was surprised. I hadn't realized how lonely I'd become. Charlie stayed behind in London. The girl living directly below us was called Stephanie, a tall blonde girl aged around eighteen, who told me that she'd look after Charlie while I was away. She did that all right. She introduced him to one of her girlfriends.

When I returned from Glasgow for Christmas the atmosphere was very strained. Charlie was ill with 'flu and stayed in bed for two weeks. The first night home I wanted to talk about the difficulties we were going through and mentioned it, but somehow I couldn't bring it up the next day when Charlie was feeling so bad. I kept thinking we would talk as soon as he got better.

When Charlie did get better, Stephanie was always around. Douglas Court had gone from being my own flat, to my married home, to what was virtually open house for my neighbour, often for most of the day and most of the evening. Stephanie would tell me how much she liked being in our flat because she couldn't stand the boys she was sharing with. If I wanted privacy with Charlie, there wasn't a chance. It did not help our marriage. But, when I'd say this, Charlie would reply that she was very young and only trying to help. She may have been helping Charlie, but not me. I found our home neither private nor peaceful. It was a bad contrast to the easy *bonhomie* of the theatre and the fun of my work.

The following summer I starred in *Ten Little Indians* on a tour around England, taking my daughter and a young girl to help me, not realizing what touring with a child of less than two and a young girl entailed. Not to mention trains and hotels, let alone first nights every week. This was the first commercial production I'd been in, and I found it very different from the Citizen's Theatre or the Royal Court. In rehearsals I found people were jumpy and somewhat on edge. Most of them had been stars at one time or another. When I replied with an 'um' instead of a 'yes' to one actor, who had been nice until then he became very nasty.

'If you can't stick to the lines,' he said, 'we'll never be able to do this dreadful play!' It scared me to think people could be so testy over one tiny word.

The two people in the cast I really liked were Desmond Walter Ellis, a master of farce, and Bill Kendall, who'd starred in the West End on stage for many years. They were not only gifted, but gentlemen in the most lovely old-fashioned way.

In Swansea, as I sat in my dressing room before the show I heard a loud knock on the door. 'Can I see Miss Field, please?' 'Who's there?' I called.

'I'm her uncle!' came the reply. I shouted back I didn't have an uncle any more. My Uncle George had died a few years earlier. 'Look at this photograph,' he yelled.

I opened the door just a little and the man showed me a picture of a little girl, aged about two. My heart skipped a beat. The photograph was old, but the girl in it looked exactly like Nicola, who was just about two herself at the time. The picture was of me. I stood very still as if I was frozen. To my amazement, the man said he was my mother's brother George. This was a new twist of fate, a relative from my mother's side of the family. I'd never met anyone before who'd been related to her, or who could give me any idea of her whereabouts at all. I asked him excitedly if he knew whether she was alive or dead. He looked at me with tears in his eyes.

'I was hoping you'd have some information for me,' he said. 'I've been searching for my sister ever since my mother was on her death bed. She wanted to say goodbye to Ivy and couldn't.'

It turned out my Uncle George had been trying to meet me for years, and had even driven from Wales to Pinewood Studios just outside London where I was shooting *Man in the Moon*. He had introduced himself as my uncle to Kenneth More.

'Yeah, I *bet* you bloody are,' Kenny had replied. 'That's what they all say.' Sadly for me, my uncle was intimidated

201

by Kenny's good-natured humour and got back in his car and drove home to Wales.

'Oh, well,' he said when he got back. 'She didn't want to know us after all.' How I wish he had not left without contacting me first. It would be another ten years before I'd finally meet my mother's family.

My uncle told me his family was outside. Could he bring them in? They all came rushing into my dressing room. His wife Hannah, a tiny woman with white hair, ran straight over to me. My cousins Anthea, who was somewhat like me, being red-headed with a very definite personality, George and Margaret were all there too. My aunt enclosed me in an iron grip of a hug.

'My God, it's wonderful, bach. Oh, it's like Ivy all over again!'

'Don't say that, Hannah,' Uncle George broke in. 'I told you not to mention her mother. It might upset her. She might not want anything to do with us if you carry on like that. She was left behind, you know.' The little woman, who I now realized was my uncle's wife, took a breath.

'I can't help myself, bach. I've always wanted to see Ivy again.'

I gently extracted myself from her hug. 'But I'm not Ivy,' I said quietly. 'I'm me.'

By now the stage calls had started. 'Half an hour, Miss Field, please . . . fifteen minutes, please!' I was about to go on stage in a thriller, but I felt I was in a much better one of my own, surrounded by this strange family who I'd never met before. Anthea's husband, Irwin, suggested they all stay and watch the show. Anthea made me promise to visit them the next day and I was delighted to be invited. My heart was pounding. How exciting it was, at last I was going to find out about my own mother. I'd been a small girl when I'd last seen her and now I was a woman, with a child of my own. I felt as if I was dancing on air and I breezed through the show.

The next day I was up bright and early, too excited to sleep the night before. I got Nicola ready and Anthea and Irwin collected us and took us to their home. It was on top of a hill overlooking a large Welsh valley. I had an immediate rapport with them – I knew instinctively we were related. There were too many similarities for it to be coincidence. We spent the day in celebration, crying and laughing. I took a great liking to my uncle. He was quiet and tall and looked a lot like my brother, Guy. It was a joy for me to hear about my mother in a good light. My father was never unkind about her, but everyone else had been critical.

I couldn't hear enough about my mother. Uncle George didn't know what had happened to her either. He said the last time he'd seen her was when she came to Wales with an American he thought was called Johnny. Could that be the same man who had visited Edgeworth with her the last time I'd seen her too. I promised my Uncle George that as soon as I got back to London, he and Auntie Hannah could come to visit.

The rest of that week went by in a hurried daze. Desmond and Bill were thrilled for me when they heard the news, but a lot of the other performers thought it was a publicity stunt, and not really true. I didn't know that my cousins, in their delight at having found me, had let the newspapers know and that several stories had been printed about our reunion. But I didn't care either. I could have told all those doubting Thomases truth is much stranger than fiction anytime.

John and Nicola Bute invited us to spend Christmas 1970 with them at Mount Stuart. Charlie and I had been separated for most of the year, but it hadn't really sunk in, nor had we discussed it. Most days I would invite Charlie for tea so he could see his daughter. Whatever we felt, I was anxious that Nicola would have a mother and a father.

When we got the invitation from Mount Stuart, Charlie seemed as pleased as I was. I thought this was a chance to work things out. But fate played a strange hand. On Christmas Eve, after eating oyster, I spent six hours being sicker than I've ever been in my whole life. As I stumbled to the bathroom and was sick over and over again, I thought I'd never get through the night. Nicola slept through it all, while Charlie appeared to be fast asleep. About six in the morning, I finally stopped being sick and collapsed back into bed without waking him up.

On Christmas morning the Bute children came running into our bedroom bright and early, wanting to dress and look after the baby. Weakly, I said yes. I was relieved that they wanted to take care of Nicola. The sickness had stopped by now but I felt empty and weak. Charlie was already up and celebrating the Christmas festivities with the family. The rest of the holiday passed in a whirl and, although we were sharing a room, we only saw each other at social occasions.

Suddenly it seemed clear that my husband didn't want a reconciliation, or even a discussion about our situation. I felt very sad remembering how it was only four years earlier when we'd brought our baby home from the hospital. He'd then arranged our first family Christmas together with only £16 and a lot of love. How could everything turn around so drastically in such a short time? It finally dawned on me that I would now be living with my daughter on my own. I racked my brains searching for a way to make an income that would allow me to be at home with her while she was so young and needed me. Renting my home and living in a smaller place could be a solution. Carol, the person who had shopped for my wedding dress with me, was going to America and had a small ground floor garden flat just along the road that I decided to rent from her. It was easy to run and had an enclosed garden for Nicola to play in, an ideal place for a woman on her own with a four-year-old child. Carol's flat was one of those lucky finds, safe, secure and cheap to run, and one that I could afford whether I was in work or not.

When I was offered a play in South Africa in 1972, I knew it would solve my financial worries, as the salary was marvellous. Carol was now in America starting a new life and, on the phone, we talked about her flat. She said she would sell it to me if I came up with the money and, with my solicitor, a man called Tubby, a dear person I'd been introduced to by Charlie, we started to negotiate. Her place would be a 'Godsend' for Nicola and myself when we got back from South Africa.

I didn't know I would end up spending a year in South Africa. Some of my friends were censorious about me going there because of the apartheid problem. One person who wasn't was Annie Ross.

'You go,' she said. 'You have a child to take care of and her future to think of.' The truth was I couldn't allow myself to worry about politics. I now had a four-year-old daughter and no steady income. I needed the work and, with the money I'd earn, I could buy Carol's flat as a home for Nicola and myself.

Uncle George and Auntie Hannah said they'd be delighted to come and look after Nicola in London until I could send for her from South Africa. Charlie thought that a good idea and said he would visit her almost every day and make sure that my aunt and uncle were managing all right. I was reluctant to ask him where he was staying, neither did he tell me, but I think he was living with his girlfriend. I'd have to face the fact that we were not going to work it out. I told Uncle George not to give the keys of Carol's small flat to anyone and on no account give the keys to Charlie. I was making arrangements for my return when I would be a mother on my own with a small child.

South Africa was a glorious place to be, very beautiful and temperate, like God's own garden. In its climate it was much like the South of France or California, except that in Johannesburg every day the clouds would open up between six and seven, watering the plants and cleaning the streets. To have a garden there must be pure pleasure!

The play was called *Waiting for Dark*, a suspense story of a blind girl who unknowingly has possession of a doll stuffed with illegal drugs. Audrey Hepburn had played in the film a few years before. This was only the second time I had done commercial theatre and it was a hard schedule, but I survived and even learned a thing or two. Our director, Anthony Sharp, a nice man and an old-fashioned actor, rehearsed us very quickly, like a lot of commercial productions, before we went into previews.

There was an extensive Indian population in South Africa, which kept mostly to themselves. Some of the Indian community were prosperous and many of the smart stylish clubs were run by the Indian people. At one of the clubs a waiter serving me said enthusiastically, 'I'm so glad to see you! You're my favourite. Look, I have a picture of you here.' And he began to fumble about in his pocket. 'Oh, no,' he said. 'Sorry, I haven't got it today, only my wife. Must have left you at home. Tomorrow!' The next day he was as good as his word and showed me several pictures of myself from *Kings of the Sun*, a film I found was surprisingly popular in South Africa. It amazed me how a film can surface like that and make you known where you least expect it. He was disappointed that I wasn't Indian in real life. 'Ohhh,' he complained, 'I liked you better with black hair and brown skin!'

At another restaurant, the owner said to me one evening, 'Course you wouldn't want to shake hands with me, would you? The brown might rub off.' I shook his hand. 'Just checking to see if you're prejudiced. I'd like to see your play. What can you do so I can see it?' I said I'd ask the producer for tickets. 'No, miss. Don't do that,' he said. 'I was just testing you. It won't be allowed.' I did ask our impresarios, Peter Torien and Shirley Firth, if we could have mixed audiences and they came up with a compromise. There would be several previews for different races.

One evening, during one of these shows, as we were in the blackout, I slipped off the edge of the stage right into someone's lap in the front row. It reminded me of a Peter Sellers' film when the man said, in a strong accent, 'Oh, I'm sorry, madame. I'm so very sorry!'

I shushed him, telling him it was I who should be sorry. 'I've fallen off the stage, not you!' I climbed back on to the stage rather clumsily, as fast as I could. I must have knocked myself silly because the next thing I knew was I started saying the other actor's lines instead of my own, which made the play even more confusing than it was meant to be. At the curtain call, I got a huge reception and I didn't know why. It couldn't have been from my brilliant performance. The audience was pleased I'd carried on with the play after falling off the stage. It certainly helped my popularity from then on with the Indian community. In every town I visited in South Africa there would be small gifts waiting. In Durban, in my hotel room, there was a beautiful white voile embroidered blouse, which I loved. It was a nice feeling knowing I had all those friends out there, even if I hadn't met them all.

When we first opened in the play, it was quite difficult technically. It's a very good thriller, but the plot depends on everything working efficiently. It builds suspense for the audience by plunging them into darkness. The tiniest technical mistake could cause it to become ridiculous, thereby losing the tight thread of suspense. I was so panicked by all these details – for a start, the girl I was playing was blind – that I couldn't relax in Johannesburg, but the night we opened in Durban the role suddenly became my own. It felt almost as if I really was Suzy, the blind girl. It was a marvellous feeling, one that I've had from time to time on the stage, when nothing is an effort and you have the freedom just to feel what you're doing, and the audience responds accordingly. That night, the local critic gave me a glowing review. He said it was a marvellous performance. I was pleased it had meant so much to him because it had meant a lot to me too. It was one of those times when my instincts were right. Once I got the character, it stayed with me and I found I could reproduce it every night – more or less.

When we'd opened in Johannesburg, the male lead, Kenneth Handel, was very familiar with the play and much the best. In London he had been the understudy and he had stayed in the play after that. Kenneth's reaction to my review was surprising. I didn't feel he was delighted for me.

For six weeks Nicola had stayed behind at Douglas Court in London with my aunt and uncle and I rang home nearly every other day. Nicola was only four but these phone calls were a routine I was to set up for the rest of her childhood. Whenever work separated her from me I rang her most days to tell her what I was doing and wish her goodnight. It was extravagant but it was important for me to let her know that I was only a phone call away and hadn't left her.

After six weeks apart, Nicola joined me. Her little figure rushed to me at the airport and gave me a big hug. It was lovely having her with me again. In her hand she clutched a small handbag with an important letter she told me was from her dad. It was a nice note wishing me well and asking if I'd mind if he borrowed the keys to the small flat. He wanted to lock Nicola's toys away to make the big flat ready for renting. His postscript asked if I would mind if he stayed just a week or two in the small flat while he got this sorted out. I was so delighted he was helping me, it seemed churlish to resent a short stay while he got on his feet. I phoned and thanked him for looking after things and said yes, he could stay there while he was arranging to rent out the big flat for me. Three months later Charlie was still there and I had rent demands from Carol, who was annoyed with me for letting Charlie stay there in the first place. I told her I thought he'd be there only a couple of weeks. I asked him to leave as she had. Tubby told me not to worry, that he would take care of it. Charlie was still there. Finally, I thought it was easier to let Charlie stay there for the time being. I was working thousands of miles away and had our lovely daughter with me. I knew things were tough for him back in England and I felt sure we'd sort it out when I returned and that, by then, he'd have found somewhere of his own to live. In the meantime I sent money back to my solicitor, Tubby, for Carol towards buying her flat when we had reached an agreement.

Nicola had arrived in South Africa with an English nanny I'd found through a friend called Johnny. Johnny, a merchant banker, had recommended his chauffeur's girlfriend but she hated South Africa and complained bitterly about 'all the black people', as well as missing her boyfriend. I explained to her rather sharply that this was Africa where black people were the majority – what did she expect? I accepted her grumbling for the first week or two, because I needed her there for Nicola. I hoped she would get over it. She looked after Nicola for a few hours in the evening when I was appearing at the theatre, but in the mornings she didn't get up. She complained of jet lag, which may have been true, but it didn't affect Nicola who was up at the crack of dawn every day. One evening, during the interval at the Intimate Theatre in Johannesburg, the doorman rushed into my dressing room with an urgent message saying it was something to do with my daughter. I was terrified, afraid she might have had an accident. Just then, my neighbour came bounding in to tell me he had the most awful news.

'Please tell me. Please tell me what's happened!' I shouted.

'Your nanny left two hours ago. She's caught the plane back to England, leaving Nicola with us.' He said she had been determined to go back from the first day and had persuaded him and his wife to give her a lift to the airport. In London I had bought her a round-trip ticket plus tickets for flights round South Africa where the tour was going. I immediately rang my flat and spoke to his wife and Nicola who thankfully was unaware of anything being amiss. The second half of the play I walked through in a daze. The show was ten minutes late because of this.

When I got back, my long leather coat with a fur collar that I'd let the nanny wear once or twice was missing, so was my camera. I phoned Johnny for help. 'I can't get involved,' he said abruptly. 'She's my chauffeur's girl. She doesn't like South Africa or you. In fact, she says you threw an iron at her.' I'd been ironing my daughter's dress the day before while the nanny lay on the sofa, with a cup of tea, grumbling about the heat. I did drop the iron on the floor, but not anywhere near her. To make matters worse, she cashed in the rest of her ticket, worth several hundred pounds. I heard she'd gone back to her parents' fish and chip shop. I hoped she worked harder at serving chips than at looking after children!

I tried to talk to Johnny about getting my coat, money and camera back but he again said he couldn't get involved and put the phone down. So much for the man who, two weeks earlier, had flown to South Africa for my birthday, proposing marriage to me with a large gold and turquoise bracelet worth hundreds of pounds. I was so disgusted with him I never wore the bracelet again and sold it later when I needed the money. I rang Tubby and asked him to pursue it, but he said it would cause a scandal and be in the papers, and didn't think it was worth the trouble!

The neighbours who had come to the theatre to tell me about the nanny leaving had a six-year-old girl of their own who became a friend for Nicola. They also looked after my daughter for me while I was working. I had no way of knowing whether they helped my English nanny on her way, but I had no option but to trust them.

They were under the impression, like some other people have been, that I had masses of money. The local newspaper had just run a story on me and this couple thought I'd been paid £10,000 for it. I informed them this was not the case. There was no way I'd be working nightly in a theatre with twice nightly Fridays and Saturdays, if I had £10,000.

'Oh, well,' they said. 'Never mind, we like you anyway, and we'll still look after your child until you find other help. But it's disappointing you're not well-heeled!' I liked their cheek and the fact they didn't hide that their first interest in me was financial. Needless to say, they were full of charm.

They may have been in it for the money, but they helped me. One day they asked if they could take Nicola to the ophthalmologist with them, as they were taking their own daughter anyway. I asked them why, and they said:

'Nicola is a pretty child, but when she gets tired one of her eyes looks slightly to the side.' I was glad they noticed that because I'd been to medical people in England who'd told me I'd either imagined it or it was only my unnecessary 'vanity'. The doctors in South Africa informed me it was vital to operate as soon as possible before my daughter got any older. Peter Torien advanced me several months' salary so I could have the operation performed straightaway.

Suddenly it was as if my daughter contracted every childhood illness going. The doctors told me changing continents made her vulnerable to the different kinds of germs. It was awful for her, and terrible for me to think that my decision to have her there with me may have been a mistake. First she had a very bad attack of measles with a very high temperature and a dreadful rash that covered her. It was impossible to keep her comfortable and it was a time of dreadful worry. Luckily I had an English friend called John, who was in a rival show, who was a terrific support and helped me when I got nervous.

The English girl who'd run away had, in the end, done me the biggest favour. Our new nanny was called Lita, a marvellous Zulu woman. She and I nursed Nicola in turns for four days, day and night, right around the clock, something I'm sure the girl who'd run away would never have done. Lita was always there whenever I got really scared. Nicola lost a lot of weight and it was a tough fight for her. She couldn't bear any light in the room, and couldn't seem to swallow anything but a little water. I felt devastated for my small daughter and helpless to ease her discomfort.

It was a gruelling two months. Her eye operation and measles came right after one another. But, no sooner had she recovered than she caught chicken pox. The English and South African friends I'd made couldn't do enough for either Nicola or me and, finally, her illnesses were over. Then Nicola just blossomed and blossomed in that great climate. She loved playing in the water, wearing water wings I had promised Charlie she would always wear. I could never get her out of the pool. Her skin had turned golden brown in the sun and her hair became a pretty silvery colour. For a small girl who liked the fresh air, the water and beautiful flowers, it was a wonderful place to be. The food was excellent, abundant and very cheap, as were most things. I found I could buy double what I could buy back in England. I felt like the Americans must have felt when they came to Britain during the war and their money was worth twice as much.

Lita could not believe that I would understand her. She thought I was soft because I didn't order her around, and so she stopped doing her job well. We'd had a big row because of this. It was difficult to explain to Lita that I wanted her to do her job but I didn't want a 'lackey'. She told me that unless I shouted at her, she didn't know where she stood. I told her that I didn't want to do that every day, I was enough of a shouter as it was, without doing it just because Lita expected it. She wasn't used to this and it confused her.

Through Lita I saw a side of Africa I'd never have seen if she hadn't been taking care of my child. I moved from the block of flats I'd been staying in to a new apartment with a large communal garden and swimming pool – better for Nicola, with more children to play with – and nice, friendly neighbours. When I went to the theatre, Lita stayed in the apartment with her and I'd given her a room of her own. Unknown to me, the local police had found out about it and, one night, very late, paid us a visit. At their knock, Lita dived under the bed. When this had happened before I'd always thought she was ridiculously nervous. Now I was to find out why.

Was it true that my nanny had stayed in the apartment at night? they asked me. If so, they would have to take her to the station with them as she was breaking the law. I was furious at their intrusion and to be told that her staying there was against the law. I lost my temper and that's when they arrested me, leaving Lita behind.

The station was a grim, awful place, made even more so by the hostility I met with. The Afrikaans officer in charge asked me what I was going to do about my situation. What *could* I do? I said. I was working every night and couldn't leave Nicola on her own while Lita returned to Soweto in time for the curfew. He replied sharply that she could sleep on the roof or in the cellar as the 'kaffirs were supposed to do'. What business was it of his, I asked, and who told him about my domestic arrangements? To my amazement, he said it was another English family who had emigrated to South Africa and now thought it was their duty to report it as I was breaking the law. I couldn't believe it! I knew this family and Nicola had played with their children. The officer

211

escorted me in to see his boss. I sat in a small, dingy office while the chief read me the riot act with another heavy-set policeman standing to attention just to the side of me. I was tired and hot and asked for a glass of water. The officer in charge ordered his subordinate to go and get me one.

When we were alone, he closed the door. 'Look, miss,' he said in a thick accent. 'Get smart. We have these laws here. Don't be seen to be breaking them. That's subversive behaviour.' He continued in a lower voice: 'I slept with my kaffir nanny until I was seven, and your child can do the same, as long as you're clever about it.'

I realized that the only way to get out of there was to appear to conform. I had already stated my case and antagonized a lot of people and it wouldn't help anyone to spend the night in jail. They would go back for Lita as well, and God knows what would have happened to her. My small daughter of four would have been left by herself. It didn't bear thinking about. For once in my life, reason prevailed. I promised the officer to obey the law and got out of there as quickly as I could. Lita was waiting for me at home very scared. I told her what had happened and not to be afraid, as she wasn't going to be arrested. I had no intention of her sleeping on the roof or in the cellar either. We'd just carry on as we had before, being careful not to let any of our seemingly friendly neighbours know what our household arrangements were. Lita made us tea and we both calmed down. She was always formal, and never ate with us when I would ask her to, but this night she did. We were just two women who'd been through an ordeal together. As we drank our tea, I could feel the tension disappearing. She was right to feel fear, I'd only been in the police station for a couple of hours and found it horrendous, and I was not really the one they wanted. Thankfully Nicola was unaware of the evening's events, she'd been fast asleep. She hadn't seen the two police officers or the van they'd taken me away in. By now, I'd been in South Africa for four months. I was becoming a little wiser.

After that evening, Lita and I formed a strong rapport. She showed me parts of the country I would never have seen without her, and we took Nicola with us, of course. The tour took us to various cities, and with her as my guide I got to see many of the black townships and villages which were definitely not on the tourist maps. At Lita's invitation, I went with her to a Methodist service in Soweto, as I knew it would please her. As we left the church, we were surrounded by a gang of local 'tombies', black thug-like boys who often carry bicycle chains and aggressively taunt people, particularly unescorted white 'do-gooders', as they thought I was. We left the church and saw several of them standing by the side. One of them started to whirl his chain over his head, making a horrible whooshing noise. Then Lita took control. She walked ahead slowly, keeping Nicola tightly in front of her, holding her shoulders firmly and moving through the group. It was probably because of Nicola that they didn't harm us. One of the younger boys reached out and touched her hair, in a very gentle way, almost as if he didn't think she was real. Finally, they stepped back and very slowly and carefully we walked past them. I thought in the future I'd be more careful. It was probably foolish of me to go to Soweto but how was I to know that?

I had been paying Lita roughly the equivalent of five pounds a week, the average rate. I didn't think it was very much, so I opened a bank account and put in the same amount again, so that when I left for England Lita would have a year's wages. My South African friends told me not to do this, as it would spoil the market rate for them, but I wanted to give Lita a year's freedom, if possible, as she had been wonderful for Nicola and for me. When I told her I was leaving and what I'd done she said she would give me the money back if I took her daughter and her two children with me when I left. It was like Lupita all over again.

'They'll live with you and look after you and your children in London,' she said. I was touched by Lita's faith in me, but there was no way I could. I tried to make her understand that Kilburn, London was very different from life in South Africa.

I was spending my free time with a chap called John, who was in another play in Johannesburg in competition with our own. He was great fun and very special. Most Sundays we'd visit somewhere beautiful together, taking Nicola with us. He was the friend who'd been so helpful when Nicola had been ill.

When we got to Cape Town, which was stunningly beautiful, I was offered the lead in a costume film called *House of the Living Dead*, thanks to Peter Torien, who had suggested me. After eight months of touring, I was pleased to be doing a film. Nicola was now almost five years of age and not in school. In South Africa, the children cannot start their schooling until the age of six or seven. I wrote to Charlie about sending her home so she could start school and received a nice letter back. He said he would love to have her, adding that he thought I was never coming home, that I would stay in South Africa and marry a millionaire! Obviously, I didn't know he felt this way. He must have surmised I'd left with our daughter to start a new life. We hadn't kept in touch for the last several months because I was concerned about him being in the small flat. Carol had been sending me letters, annoyed with the situation, needing her rent. There was no way I was going to pay the rent for Charlie and his girlfriend. Carol wouldn't sell me the flat while they were living there, so it was a stalemate. After six months of letters back and forth and Tubby flying out to visit me, I'd given up arguing with everybody. I had enough on my plate and it was too difficult to sort something out six thousand miles away. And so the flat situation drifted on.

I barely remember the story of the film, though it did win a prize at the Brazilian Film Festival. The director, Ray, was a former stunt man who'd recently moved on to directing. Apparently he wanted to move into a few other areas as well. He had been interested in me, he said, since he'd first seen me at Pinewood doing *Man in the Moon*. He told me he'd once arranged to bring a tray of tea to my dressing room while I was making that film. Did I remember him? I did remember him, but not in that context. I'd seen him around the studios occasionally, an athletic man usually performing quite dangerous stunts. I'd known his wife, Alison, a lovely girl with whom he'd had two children.

He said his marriage was in trouble. He told me he liked only women that he could worship. I could see that could be exciting and I got involved with him, only for him to end it two weeks before the film finished, in a very nasty way causing me days of pain. When my relationship with Ray was over, I met John again and realized the difference between the two men. One was a very nice person who cared for me, the other was just looking for a conquest.

This episode had an unusual ending. A few months' later, Ray arrived back in London from South Africa and rang me, telling me how much he'd missed me.

'Have you thought about us?' he asked. 'You said once that you'd like to live with me.' I hadn't said that, he had, when he first met me. He hadn't been in touch with me for at least three months, and now he wanted to stay with me in my flat. He obviously had nowhere to go and was chancing his luck. After the way he'd behaved, I didn't want to see him, which is unusual for me. If I've cared about anyone I usually can't bear to say goodbye.

CHAPTER NINE

Charlie met me at the airport with our daughter and Tubby. He said he was glad I was back, and that Nicola had been happy the two months she'd been home and had started well at school. He said my tenant friend had left Douglas Court in perfect shape. Tubby gave myself and Nicola a lift back and Charlie drove off in his own car. I returned to Douglas Court for the time being, thinking that later in the week I'd sort out the business of the small flat with Charlie.

Sure enough, my friend had left it immaculate, but that had been three months ago, and now a thin film of dust clung everywhere. It was clear not a soul had been in the place since she'd left. The laundry was stacked in neat piles, ready to be sent,

216

and the kitchen was completely bare. Being the Easter holidays, most of the shops were closed for the long weekend, and to add to the isolation, the phone was disconnected! I felt very cut off after Tubby left. Before I'd left England my life had been full of enquiries for work, appearances, social invitations; generally too much hustle and bustle. Now it was as if everyone had forgotten me. It had been an idyllic time in Africa, but this wall of silence didn't bode well for my career.

I was overjoyed to be with my daughter again, but I found it difficult to keep a conversation going with a five-year-old *and* keep her interested. There were just the two of us now, rattling around in this enormous flat. I sat Nicola down in front of the television, but she followed me around everywhere. It was her way of showing me how glad she was to see me, and, as she'd been used to a small, intimate flat, I think she felt as isolated as I did. I kept trying to make it more cosy for the two of us. There were no clean sheets for the beds, and not many toys for her to play with either. I decided we'd better stay together in the big bedroom, the one I'd once shared with her father. I thought we'd feel less lonely this way, especially as the size of the bedroom was almost as big as the small flat where she'd been living recently.

It worried me that my little daughter was bored and not getting enough fresh air, so we walked to a small park in Kilburn. It looked very drab and dark compared to the sunshine of South Africa, but I put her on the swings and made an effort. I talked to her about her dad, and her school and what she'd been doing while we'd been away from each other. From a phone box I called Vicky, hoping she'd be in to invite us round for tea. No luck, she was out. In four days I hadn't seen another soul. I felt completely cut off.

I phoned various friends to tell them I was back and that the phone wasn't working, and would they stop by and see me? Then I asked Charlie if he could ring and try and get the phone reconnected at Douglas Court. I let Nicola talk to him, saying that we were calling her daddy to say goodnight because our phone wasn't working. I was afraid of running out of things to keep her happy. I thought Tuesday would never come, when everything would return to normal at the end of the long weekend. On Sunday I took Nicola to see Victor. I thought Charlie would be sure to pop in to see her, but perhaps he was giving us the time to get re-adjusted.

During the first week I was back I found Charlie now regarded Carol's flat as his, and to anyone else it must have looked that way. He'd been living there for about a year from the time he'd first got the keys from my uncle. The small, inexpensive place I wanted as a home for my daughter and myself, was now Charlie's home. It was infuriating. Two hundred yards away from my bedroom window I could see the garden. The price of the property had doubled since I'd left and two months after I got back, I found out that Carol was now selling it to a friend of Charlie's. Charlie had his friend's permission to stay there, so the arrangements had worked out perfectly for everyone but me!

Soon after I arrived home I heard from my brother. He'd had an argument with his Australian girlfriend while in Germany, which led to him nearly being arrested. The German authorities notified me that if he wasn't put in hospital, they would have to keep him in custody, and he was released on condition that he received treatment. After he got back from Germany, I took Guy to various hospitals, none of which he liked. He said he didn't like the look of the other patients!

I encouraged Charlie to ring every evening to wish Nicola goodnight. One night my brother answered and Charlie asked me what he was doing there. After I told him the situation, he offered to take my brother into the small flat with him. It was hard to look after Guy and keep his deep depression from affecting me, and not to let it affect my daughter. We'd already had the fire engines out once when he was on the balcony and wouldn't come back inside.

'You can't look after him,' Charlie said. 'You've got enough to do looking after our daughter. I'll come and get him.' I was touched by his thoughtfulness, and was relieved when he persuaded Guy to stay with him instead. I thought he'd be safe with Charlie, especially as I knew he'd been kind to a relative of Nicola Bute's who was not the 'same' – and that's putting it mildly – as anyone else.

The next day I rang up to check how Guy was, but Charlie said he had gone. He said he went off with two people, 'who looked as daft as a brush'. What's more, he said he couldn't care less. Guy had been 'a pain' the whole twenty four hours he'd been there, acting like 'a wet rag'. I was furious with Charlie. Didn't he realize that was part of Guy's illness? I couldn't think what would happen to my brother now, and I had no means of finding him. I went over to see Charlie an hour later, seething. It was the first time I'd been near Carol's flat since I got back from Africa. I let myself into the garden to tell Charlie that I thought it was wrong to let Guy go like that, and not even get an address.

He didn't ask me inside. 'As I'm here,' I said, 'I'd like to collect my stuff.' He refused, saying he had no intention of letting me in his home. He said he was dealing directly with Carol now!

I was hopping mad and furious that he'd let my brother go off in his condition. I tried to get by him. At this, a man came to the French windows, the ones that I had paid for, and told me to clear out. It was going to be his flat now, he was buying it and he didn't need any hysterical women around. 'I'm negotiating to buy this flat. You're trespassing on *my* land. Get off at once!' At this my temper really boiled over. I wanted to thump Charlie, but the man stuck himself between us. 'Run inside, Charlie, run!' he yelled. I didn't know this man from Adam, but I told him I'd come to collect my things *and* any of Carol's things as well. He had put our clothes in boxes outside the flat including a statue, a small replica of a Michelangelo sculpture that was one of Carol's prized possessions. In the commotion it flew into the air and winged its way back into the flat it had occupied for so many years. It glanced off the side of his head. There was no chance of him catching it, he wasn't the least bit agile.

'My God, Charlie, call the police! This bloody woman has hit me!' Charlie was already in the house. A few minutes later a police van arrived and I was escorted home.

As luck would have it, the man I'd accidentally hit was a barrister. Not content with calling the police, he pressed charges against me for assault as well. When the policeman in the station read the charge out another officer overheard him. 'Oh, very good,' he said. 'She had a fight with two men in a garden, and they are going to bring a charge against *her*?'

For about three weeks Charlie phoned me on the quiet, we weren't supposed to talk because of the pending case, saying if I apologized to his friend, he would drop the charges. I didn't want to, I was worried sick about where my brother was and felt his friend had aggravated a situation that didn't involve him in the first place. I'd found a new solicitor called David Offenbach and to save me money, David assigned one of his young trainees to look after me.

On the day of the hearing Romie gave me a lift to the court. Since I had no-one to look after Nicola, she came along too. As we approached the police station, to my horror, I saw about twenty photographers waiting outside. I told Romie to drive on as fast as she could and take Nicola with her. I didn't want her exposed to this. I walked into the building with questions being thrown at me from all directions. In the court my lawyer told me there was good news, the charges against me would be dropped if I said nothing about the case publicly. He advised me to accept this to save the court costs and fees. The next day my picture was on the front pages, with headlines giving the impression I was a female wrestler.

When I'd gone to South Africa I'd left Tubby and my accountant, Mr Lux, in charge of my financial affairs. The rent had been paid at Douglas Court, but not the rates, which now amounted to several thousand pounds. I felt as if I were back at square one. I've wished since that I'd known about the Citizens Advice Bureau and asked them what to do.

I was buying vegetables from a stall in Quex Road one day when a short, rotund man approached me. He began by complimenting me on my work. It was flattering to have someone be so enthusiastic about my films, and it didn't cross my mind he wasn't genuine. I could hardly get a word in. He introduced himself to me and said he had an estate agency. The man on the stall was getting a little peeved.

'Could you move along and compliment the lady somewhere else, mister? I can't get any bleedin' business done with you rabbiting away at ten to the dozen!'

He walked on down the road with me, keeping up a string of compliments, recalling a scene from *Saturday Night and Sunday Morning* where I'd said to Albert, 'See you on Wednesday then, but not on back row.' He told me that when he was at school, he and his friends had loved this moment. This really threw me as I looked at this unprepossessing little man jogging along, trying to keep pace with me. It hadn't occurred to me that he was younger. He said I should get back to work at all costs, that the film industry was losing a valuable asset! He suddenly changed the subject.

'Why do you need such a big apartment just for yourself and your small daughter?' he asked. That should have struck me as strange, how did he know my situation and the size of my home? 'My partner and myself have just opened an agency, particularly for quality people like you. While you are having this quiet hiccup in your career, Miss Field, why not let your big apartment and take somewhere smaller for the child and yourself?' He said he'd like to see my home to give me an opinion on its value. He walked back with me to Douglas Court and he promised to come the next day to give me an estimate, as I told him I had been thinking of renting out my home anyway, to make ends meet.

Early the next morning he was at the door. My flat must have pleased him because, within two minutes, he told me he could let it in a week. I could have a thousand pounds, cash, in my hand by Friday, he said. Much as I liked the idea, it would help pay the huge rates bill, for a start, I told him to hang on: where would I go? I'd only let my home once before, and that had been to a friend while I'd been away.

'Don't worry, Shirley,' he said, 'I may call you by your first name, mayn't I?'

'In that case,' I replied, 'my name is Shirley Anne.'

He didn't miss a beat. 'We are anxious to make all our clients happy, Shirley Anne,' he answered. 'I'll be bringing you quality people like yourself, but it's entirely your decision.'

The first people he sent along saw my home and, within five minutes said they would like it. 'I couldn't possibly think of letting it at such short notice,' I replied. A few days later he rang again and said he could get twice as much if I would reconsider. It sounded very good. The money would help me clear my bills, but I still didn't feel like renting to strangers.

'Please forget about it for the time being,' I said eventually. 'I don't want to move. Where would I go?'

'Oh, we'd find you somewhere smaller and cheaper,' he replied. He didn't stop pestering me. However, when I objected to the flurry of calls, he'd say, 'Don't be like that, my dear. I only called to talk about films. And ask how you're managing.'

Three weeks later he rang again to ask if he could bring somebody to meet me whom I'd find terribly useful. He arrived with a whole family of people who complimented me on my apartment and asked if they could look around. The man and his wife asked him to make me an offer, stressing they would pay more than the market rate. I still didn't take it seriously. How they were meant to be useful to me I still wasn't clear. They assured me they would give me all the references I needed as they were part of the Jamaican High Commission. The next day the agency rang to say they had good news. The family wanted it in about a month's time for £1,000 a month and was that agreeable? I said the offer was tempting but I needed time to think about it. Three weeks later I had a phone call from the Jamaican High Commission stating that their van would arrive the next day with furniture. I told them to please hang on, I had not agreed to this and, besides, what were they thinking of paying.

'We've already paid you, Mrs Crichton-Stuart,' they replied. 'We've given the agency nearly two thousand pounds.' I called the estate agents immediately and they informed me they had accepted money on my behalf and when the family took possession of my flat, I would have the money.

By now I really had reservations about the whole thing. I went along to the agency and said I really didn't want to let my flat after all. The agent wiped his fat little forehead and pushed back his lank hair.

'Oh dear!' he said. 'We've got a bit of a quandary on our hands. We've already accepted these renters on your behalf.' His eyes suddenly gleamed. 'I know what! Why not let them have it for two months and you have a little holiday. After that, if you don't like it, you can always move back and, in the meantime, you'll have a bit of tide-me-over money.'

I rang David Offenbach. 'Unless you're sure, on no account deal with them,' he said. I put the phone down and phoned the estate agents, and said:

'Please tell your clients I am not going to rent my apartment to them.'

On Saturday morning, to my astonishment, a large pantechnicon arrived, packed with things from top to bottom. David Offenbach advised me to ignore it, but by this time I had the whole family sitting in my kitchen. I couldn't contact the agents. John, my friend from South Africa, came over, thank God, as did another friend called Conrad. Finally, the family, after much toing and froing, asked if they could leave their belongings for the weekend, until they could at least sort things out with the estate agents when they opened on Monday. Box after box came through the door. It was impossible to move or get close to the front door without tripping over large cartons.

'This is such a mess,' Conrad said, 'why don't you come and stay with me for the weekend? You'll have a peaceful weekend and everything will look better by Monday.'

I let the family carry on unloading and went off with my daughter to Conrad's flat. When I returned on Monday morning they had unpacked their boxes and moved in. It took me several months, even with all David Offenbach's professional help, to get just £300 of what had been paid to the agency for my flat. For three months they managed to keep the rest for so-called 'expenses', and deposit, etc. Meanwhile, I was the one with expenses and now, worst of all, I had no home!

This was one of my lowest times. I'd lost my beautiful home, and was now using two rooms in Conrad's flat for my daughter and myself. Thankfully I had good friends to help me through this. A friend called Jez painted the room Nicola was staying in, using the same colour as her room at home. I moved her bed and all her toys from Douglas Court into Conrad's flat, so her room would look more or less the same. It was the best I could do for the time being. In the hope of making Nicola feel this was a special adventure I put my fur coat on her bed as a cover. I cried almost every day, but was careful not to let her see me crying.

Two weeks later a script arrived from a small production company I hadn't heard of. A man called Ben rang to ask if I'd received it. He said he'd met me once before, but I couldn't remember.

'I came to your apartment in Douglas Court two months ago to deliver a different script, and a young girl of about eleven came to the door.' It was Jackie, Nellie's daughter, who looked after the flat for me. I remembered because Jackie had called out:

'Look, Shirley Anne, look, it's him! It's Gordon! He's always on the telly!'

We arranged to meet at his office just off Baker Street. It turned out to be a small house on two floors in a mews. I rang the doorbell and down the stairs bounded a young man wearing a colourful shirt and no shoes, looking about twenty five. He had dark hair and interesting eyes that sparkled and creased in a smile as he greeted me. 'I'm looking for Ben Cleggly,' I said. 'I've come to discuss a play.'

'I'm Ben,' he said. I was expecting a much older man. We went upstairs to his office. It was light and airy with no-one else there. The only interruption was a telephone that kept ringing.

'Don!' Ben called out. 'Can you get down here please? I want you to answer the phone. I'm talking to Miss Field.' Don came in. He looked about ten years older than Ben, and was rather untidily thrown together. In fact it seemed as if he'd slept in his clothes. He greeted me enthusiastically and went into the adjoining office to handle the phone calls.

Ben and I talked for some time. He suggested we had lunch, and we went to a small café just round the corner and talked for another couple of hours. He asked me all about my previous work, especially the films I'd been in – he said he was going to be a movie producer one day. I had to leave to pick up my daughter from school and he offered to drive me. I thanked him for lunch and said I'd take a cab. I wished I still had Douglas Court, and then I could have invited Ben back another time. We talked for so long I had about ten minutes left to get to Nicola's school.

The next day at nine o'clock in the morning Ben rang, asking if he could come by and visit. I said it wasn't possible as it was Nicola's half-day and it was Conrad's flat anyway. I explained to him again that I'd rented out my apartment. He said it didn't matter where I was living, he still wanted to come and see me and meet my daughter as well. I rushed about all morning, not sure of the local shops or the district yet, then promptly at midday the doorbell rang.

I was apprehensive about how my daughter would react. Since we had got back from South Africa, the only man she was happy with was her dad. When any man other than Charlie was around, she would cling to me and not leave my side. Ben strode into the room and made a bee-line for her and, within five minutes, they were chatting happily. He did exactly the right thing. Any man who was that good with children, especially mine, could only make a favourable impression.

I spread the lunch on a tablecloth on the floor of Conrad's sitting room, and Ben stayed all afternoon. He didn't talk much about work. Instead he talked about himself and told us very funny stories about two little girls he knew, slightly older than

Nicola, who he'd been living with until a few months ago. We were both utterly charmed.

Nicola went off to play and Ben then told me a little about his own situation. He'd been living with his older girlfriend and her two children. They had broken up, but last year she'd become pregnant and they had a baby girl who was now aged about six months. He said he loved his daughter and was always happy to look after her. This impressed me. After Charlie and I broke up, I was so unhappy that I thought if I was ever to let myself love anyone again, it would have to be someone very different from him. On the surface, Ben *was* very different. He was working-class from the north of England, and proud of it. And what's more, he came from Liverpool where Paul McCartney grew up. I knew Paul slightly and I'd seen how great he was with his wife, including her in everything and even making her part of his music. Ben was a few years younger than Paul and had been to the same school. I thought that was a good omen and that Ben would be as caring as Paul. I hadn't realized Paul McCartney was the exception, not the rule.

Ben was chauvinistic, like a lot of men from that background. But I didn't notice this and it didn't count, because he had one thing that was irresistible: the ability to make me feel that his life wasn't worth living without me. At the beginning, it was like being surrounded by a warm blanket of love. Was this what love really felt like? I wondered. I didn't know. Whatever it was even when things went badly wrong Ben still had the capacity to fold me in this imaginary blanket and make me feel safe.

Ben rang several times a day to talk about plays or anything else for that matter. He asked me if I could sing. I hadn't sung since *The Lily White Boys*, but Ben said that Saturday afternoon he'd listen to my singing and give me an opinion, as he had been an actor and a pop singer! I knew he had played in a famous telly series, but the pop singing was new. When I did sing for him he gave me the feeling I could sing anything. He arranged an audition for *Billy Liar*, a big new West End production. It was the first time it had been done as a musical and was to star Michael Crawford, who had appeared in *The War Lover*. I was encouraged by Ben's interest, and fired by his confidence in me.

My friend Jez was a good pianist and I rehearsed a few songs with him. When they were ready, we tried them out on Ben. 'No, no, no,' he said. 'Your material is far too old-fashioned. You sound like Mary Poppins. I'll find other songs for you.'

The audition the next day was a ghastly mistake. The theatre was dark and quite empty, except for two rows halfway back, which were full of people I'd known professionally one way or another for most of my career. My heart was in my boots. I didn't know the director, but by all accounts, he was very much 'up and coming'. I was wearing clothes that Ben had chosen – a green jumper and beige trousers that were attractive but slightly too tight, which didn't help. I hadn't had the time to learn the new numbers well and, as I stood on the darkened stage, I knew it was all a dreadful mistake. As soon as I'd finished the first song, before the director could say a word, Jez stopped playing and stood up. I beat a hasty retreat, with Jez hot on my heels. I don't think I ever felt so stupid in my life. Of course, now my ambition is to do a big, successful musical and surprise them all.

I'm sure Conrad appreciated having a few evenings to himself, this dear friend who'd suddenly had his home turned upside down by a woman with a small child. He would gladly babysit in the evenings, so I could have a break. After a little time, my friendship with Ben deepened. I remember our first romantic time together when he wore a darkish-blue shirt which, no matter what, he wouldn't take off. From that evening on, Ben and I talked at least six times a day, and most evenings we'd meet as well. I started work on the play he'd first offered me. We opened in the north of England and, every night, Ben would be on the plane from London to have dinner with me after the show and stay the night, even though he was afraid of flying! I'd never met anyone like him before.

One evening the director, Bill, invited us to his very attractive flat in Hampstead for dinner. I told him the saga of my last two years and how I missed my lovely home. He said he'd been to a party of mine several years ago and loved my paintings and remembered my wooden kitchen. I liked his flat and said if he ever wanted to sell it, could I have first refusal? He said he and his friend Patrick were very happy there but, if they changed their minds, I would be the first to know.

Ben was having financial problems with his business. I knew what it was like waiting for money that was owing. I had just made a soap advertisement and I don't know if I offered Ben my fee for this but, the next day he asked if he could borrow it until his deal went through. I phoned Tubby to ask if he could advance me some money until my fee arrived. He said, 'What for?' I said I wanted to lend it to Ben. There was a long silence. Then he said, 'Why would you want to do this? What do you know about him? What security can he offer you? Does he realize this is all you have, your first priority is a roof of your own over your head. You're a mother, there's more than just you to think of. If it's for you, yes. If you're going to give it to someone else, no. Ask him for his house as a guarantee.'

I asked Ben and he said, 'I can't do this as I've given it to Maggie.' (Maggie was Ben's ex-girlfriend.)

I phoned Tubby back. He said, 'In that case, ask him to sign over the car as a guarantee.'

I asked Ben again and he said, 'I can't I've given it to Maggie, she needs it to get to work.'

I felt badly not giving Ben this money, but Tubby was right. Less than three months later I used it to buy Bill's Hampstead flat. That flat became a home for Ben, as well as myself and Nicola. He never quite forgot about it, though. It remained a tiny niggle between us.

Neither of us had any money now. When I'd ask Ben to contribute towards the household expenses, he'd point out that I should ask my child's father for support, as he had to support his child. I couldn't argue with that, as I'd seen him struggle to pay the bills for his ex-lady and daughter.

Six months later our relationship was more intense than ever. I felt like I had two children instead of one. We'd argue a lot, often about money, because we didn't have any. I cared deeply about Ben, and think he cared deeply about me, but these arguments were spoiling everything.

I asked him to leave because I thought it would never work out. I was tired of carrying all the responsibilities alone. After three days of being apart we still spoke as much as we always had. It was as if we couldn't live with or without each other.

When the doorbell rang early one morning, I thought it was bound to be him. I put my head out of the window to invite him for breakfast to see a strange woman standing below. I was still in my nightie. I asked her what she wanted.

'My name's Maggie,' she said, 'and I have to talk to you. I believe you have my husband living here.' If anything, she was even more intense than Ben. I went downstairs, opened the door and let her in. She asked me to think about what I was doing. 'My husband and I have a baby now, and you're almost the same age as me. You should know better! He's an absolute bastard, you know, and you're enticing him away.' All this time I was trying to rush her up the stairs. I didn't want the people from the other apartments in the house to hear this. Nothing stopped her though. She went on and on without drawing breath. 'He's weak, and a compulsive gambler you know!' My head spun.

I got her inside the flat and finally sat her down. 'First of all,' I said, 'he's not your husband.'

'OK,' she replied, 'we're not legally married. It's just that we haven't got around to it yet. He comes home at weekends, and you're just making matters worse.' As he'd spent every Saturday and Sunday with me for the last eight weeks, I knew this couldn't be true.

I didn't want to live with Ben because it wasn't practical. Everything he earned seemed to go to Maggie's household, and he found that hard to keep up. But after this list of all his faults and misdemeanours, practicalities became unimportant. It was the worst thing she could have done because instead of turning me against him, it did exactly the reverse. She hadn't been out of the door five seconds when I phoned him. I was in tears. I'd been trying to forget all about him before she came to see me. Now all I wanted to do was help him. I didn't let myself think about the practical problems. He came back straight away and we had a loving reunion.

We did end up living together, and at first he was so absorbed in me *and* his work that I was never sure which he valued most. Fridays were toughest. He'd have bills to meet and his staff to pay. I couldn't get him to leave the house. For the longest time it was a hard battle for him. Once he got to work, though, I couldn't get him back and he would complicate things even more by ringing home every half-hour. 'I won't be long, babe, I won't be long,' he'd say. 'I'm just on the way.'

With the intensity of our relationship plus my child's routine, I didn't have any energy for myself or my career. My daughter wasn't difficult, she was a joy, but when Ben had a crisis with his work, which was often, I found myself on an emotional tightrope, trying to keep the tension away from home.

Ben worked hard, but he didn't have a suit – at least I'd never seen him in one. Thanks to David Offenbach's help I was at last getting some income from Douglas Court, and after receiving my first cheque I bought Ben a beautiful velvet suit. He looked wonderful in it. His mother said how smart he looked, ready to go places. When Ben 'decided' one day he was going to be a tycoon, I thought I'd buy him another suit for his business meetings. I bought one made of soft, grey wool but, blow me down, three weeks later he'd lost it! He said he'd left the car unlocked, with the suit hanging in the back of the car, and when he came back that evening the suit was gone. I couldn't believe he could be so vague, until two months later he managed to lose the car as well! He'd forgotten where he'd parked it, he said. Luckily it turned up some months later, from where I don't know. I'd bought the car to learn how to drive, but didn't get much chance as Ben was either driving or mislaying it. There was a bonus, however, because when the police called about payment for parking tickets – which Ben collected on a regular basis – I could reply with all honesty, 'I'm very sorry, officer, it can't be me. I don't even have a licence!'

One of Ben's biggest projects was a children's show based on a bestselling book that he was going to present in theatres all over the country. The show had dancers dressed up as brown furry animals. It was a tricky proposition to get right. One day Ben phoned and asked me to go and see Mrs Kohurt, our downstairs neighbour. Would I ask her if she'd like to sew a few costumes for him? He said to be sure to tell her he'd pay. Mrs Kohurt said thank you, but no thank you, she didn't think animal costumes were quite her line!

Ben had a general factotum called Jan, who made the costumes as well as doing everything else. When she ran out of brown fur material, she got a cheap bargain in coloured fur, blue, green, yellow and purple!

The promotion for the shows had gone on for almost six months, to open in time for the Christmas season, simultaneously all over the country. I saw Ben off at the station, happy that it was coming together for him at last, and relieved that I could now get ready for our own Christmas celebrations. I had invited friends to celebrate and have Christmas lunch with us. The turkey was prepared, the stockings were filled, and the tree decorated ready for Ben's homecoming. When I finally got Nic off to bed I sat down, tired and relieved, to watch *The Graduate* on television.

Later that evening Ben rang. He was hard to understand and sounded odd. He told me his whole empire had collapsed – I didn't know he had one! At the opening night in his home town, with his parents and his family in the audience, no-one could hear what his furry animals were saying with their big bear-like heads on. Ben called just as *The Graduate* was reaching the end. I asked him could he ring back in ten minutes. I couldn't hear him clearly and, as I was used to Ben having crises anyway, I presumed it would right itself as it usually did. We'd had so many calls just then, especially regarding his furry animals, the costumes, the sound, the head shapes, whether he should use actors or dancers, whether to put the zips in the back or the front, that when he did phone and say there had been a collapse, instead of realizing that this time it was important, I thought it was just another panicky call.

Off the train at five o'clock on Christmas morning, I met a pale, tired figure in a long coat borrowed from his father. He said he was going to lose his house in the country – he didn't have one, but he told me that, if his shows had been a success, he had planned on getting one. It was extraordinary for me to hear this. Although he shared his crises with me, I hadn't shared his plans or dreams.

We went home to what was a very sad Christmas. I tried hard to console him by telling him that at least all the theatres would be closed on Christmas Day. I wanted him to forget his shows just for that one day, for Nicola's sake particularly, and for our guests.

At six thirty, Nicola was sitting on the bed, anxious to open her stocking, and holding the great big one we had for Ben. I watched my little girl excitedly open hers while Ben mostly ignored his. Our guests arrived, my good friend Peggy, a girlfriend of hers called Jean and her boyfriend Bill. All day it was heavy going. Our guests tried to cheer Ben up, but as they got jollier, Ben got more morose. It was the only Christmas Day I spent with my daughter when I was glad her dad picked her up early. I wanted her to be in a normal atmosphere and Charlie was always wonderful with her.

Christmas had been the only special occasion of my childhood and, for me, it was always important. But for Ben I think it was just another day. The only Christmas feeling he needed was from his shows. But that Christmas morning there was no Christmas feeling at all. I was afraid Ben wasn't going to talk to anyone.

Whenever we'd hit a black patch like this and I thought we couldn't possibly work it out, Ben would always do something to make up for it. For example, later in the year I was in Coventry appearing in one of his shows and had Nicola with me, because it was the school holidays. Ben arrived out of the blue as a surprise for my birthday. He'd arranged a beautiful suite of rooms at a luxury hotel less than five minutes from the theatre, with a four-poster bed and anything else you could possibly imagine. He'd also reserved an adjoining room for Nicola and the au pair girl. The next day it was gloriously sunny and we ate lunch by the swimming pool. That weekend together was wonderful and we celebrated my birthday and swam with Nicola, which she adored. It was idyllic. My worries faded away.

Ben was always like that, one extreme or the other. Sometimes I was in despair because of the bills. I sold jewellery to buy curtains and a wardrobe for the bedroom. The worst thing was to sell my beautiful Persian carpet I'd managed to save from Douglas Court – that was much worse than selling my fur coat. But the gas bill was £800 and they would have cut us off if it hadn't been paid.

The last Christmas Ben and I spent together was chaotic. Ben was producing his first West End Christmas show and there weren't enough funds to meet the costs. I went to most of my friends swallowing my pride to ask them if they would like to invest or if they could help financially in some way. There was no response and, worse, to this day some of them are still wary of me. In dismay I talked to one girlfriend, whose name was Iraine. She said she couldn't bear to see me so tense and unhappy and although she had no wish to help Ben, for my sake, she would see what she could do. The next day, she said she would lend him £4,000 in cash and asked how he could guarantee this. Ben's solicitor, John, drew up an agreement whereby my property, the one I rented out to make an income, secured the loan. Iraine and I took quite a risk!

I still maintained my close relationship with Jean, but it became strained with Ben's attitude towards her: why did I have an agent like that? Why didn't I work more, why didn't she know what was going on? Why didn't she put me up for this or that or something else. I didn't concentrate on work, all my energy was given to him. My relationship with Jean was undermined and the saddest time was parting from her. No-one was a better friend, but I couldn't bear to hear the criticism any more. It made me feel split in half. I just didn't recognize Ben's possessiveness. He wanted to be the most important person in my life.

After a silly fight I'd had with Jean about a magazine article, Ben told me not to worry, he'd found a marvellous new agent for me. By this time, I'd lost my own judgement and somehow it seemed he always knew best. I was wrong, and instead of putting it right with Jean and admitting my mistake, I let Ben influence me to find someone else. He wanted me to work with people he knew. These days he knows and deals with the very same people he used to grumble about.

The new agent was handling one of Ben's tours and I played in it. It wasn't ideal, but I needed to make a living. The agent negotiated a salary of £300 a week. Ben said this was too much. However, instead of us sorting this out, he paid me the agreed salary but his office held back £100. I should have let the agent know and perhaps he knew anyway, but I couldn't face fighting over it.

Ben and I were always in a crisis, which led to endless fights. But perhaps the worst thing was the feeling that I was losing my sense of identity.

I stayed that way until I appeared in a show called *Kennedy's Children*. I went for a meeting with the director, Clive Donner, after Deborah Norton had recommended me. She was in the show herself and was exceptionally good in it. Clive Donner had doubts and asked me to read a second time.

Ben asked me one evening if I really wanted to play the part. I said yes, I did, very much. 'In that case,' he replied, 'don't go back and read a second time.' He understood the politics of directing and producing much better than I did. 'Just tell them you'd like to play it and leave it at that.' He was right: I got the part and by working independently of him, I got back some of my confidence.

The play was a huge critical success. The little pub where it was staged was packed with a celebrity audience every night – writers, directors and stars – every evening they were there. Dustin Hoffman saw the show at least twice. Ben was there every night to take me home. I'm still not sure if he ever saw it. It was different from the kind of theatre he was producing.

At another point, Ben and I split up again and he moved out, telling me he had his own apartment in Bayswater. He'd invite me for tea on Saturdays and I'd wonder why it was always so immaculate. I found out later he was staying just along the road with his secretary and her mother. He was hardly ever at his Bayswater flat, if at all. He hated being alone. After that separation, he came back and we talked about our future, and having a child together. Still we kept on fighting and still we couldn't pay the bills.

After four years we separated for the last time. It took me a long time to recover. Neither of us had wanted to hurt each other, but I had been hurt. It was my own doing. Why had I allowed Ben to control my life? I don't know why. It didn't start out that way. It had begun full of love and optimism. A little while after we parted he came to see me. He was tense and pale and told me he'd met someone else and was going to marry her. I respected him for coming and letting me know before I could hear it any other way. From the way he described her she sounded like an ambitious socialite and in anger I said I didn't think it would last for more than seven months. I couldn't see Ben playing a supporting role. When he left I was terribly upset. I had wanted to break from Ben, but I was devastated and found it hard to cope with my feelings. He'd always assured me he'd be there for me. I knew now I was going to lose him. I couldn't stop crying.

Before Ben's visit, I'd been spending time with a very attractive, caring man I'd known for some years. His name was Kenneth. When I told him about Ben getting married he said it was clear that I was still involved with Ben emotionally. Because of Ben's news, I was irritable and strained. With Ben there was always a crisis which I mistook for excitement. I had become hooked on

Ben's way of life or I would have valued Ken properly. He was a genuinely exciting man, passionate and caring, gentle and fun – a special person all round.

I was just getting over my addiction to Ben, because that was what it had been, and forming a close relationship with Ken in the summer of 1978, when my world was turned upside down by a phone call. It was the phone call I'd been waiting for all my life, and it would take many years before anything would ever be the same again. It was the call from Miss Gautry, telling me my mother had been found, and very soon I would speak with her, for the first time in thirty-odd years.

CHAPTER TEN

Kathleen Lloyd's daughter, Jennifer, gave me a lift back from Hemel Hempstead, and during the ride my heart was thumping. After all these years my mother was still alive – it was true! What's more, she had been in Georgia, several thousand miles away, ever since she'd left England. If only I'd known this, the years of not belonging and not knowing where I came from could have been avoided. It was difficult for me to believe I'd actually spoken to my own mother. Jennifer was as excited as me, but I got a jealous pain in my chest every time she talked about my new-found family with such ease. Until that night I hadn't even been aware they existed, and here was someone younger than me, and not even *related*, who regarded my mother as her aunt.

I couldn't sleep at all. Then at three in the morning the phone rang. A friendly voice introduced herself as my sister, Virginia, a strange name to me. She said how delighted her mother was that I'd been found and asked me a lot of questions about Guy and Sunny. When could I come to America so I could meet all my family? I told her I had commitments and couldn't go immediately. I also needed time to get some money together. She said that was no problem, she would send me a ticket. I still couldn't give her an answer. I was very nervous. I had been without a family for so long that I didn't know how I would be with one.

Suddenly, on Virginia's three-way line from Alabama, came my older sister, Joy. It was extraordinary to hear her voice. I hadn't known she was alive either. The last time I'd seen her I was about five and here she was living in the Deep South a few hours away from my mother. Joy was calm and collected compared to Ginny – as she was referred to – and myself.

I said I would try to get there within the month by which time it would be my daughter's school holidays. It was important to keep Nicola's routine steady, and the stability also helped me. My sisters were surprised and pleased that I had a daughter, and Joy started to tell me about her own children, Terry, a girl in her early twenties, and a son of eighteen called Bill. Ginny interrupted to say she also had a son called Rob. With all of these new voices and names pouring over my sleepy head, it seemed like a very strange fairy story.

We talked on for ages. Ginny said the cost didn't matter, that her husband always made long overseas calls because he was in the music business. I kept asking them about our mother, and they came back with warm but non-committal answers.

'Oh, it's impossible to describe Ivy. You'll just have to meet her for yourself.' For the next two weeks I spoke so often with Ginny I felt as if she was my best friend. It's too bad that ten years on, we've never talked that much again.

I wanted to protect my child from the extreme feelings I felt were bound to be all around us, so I decided to go first on my own, with her following two weeks later. I don't know what prompted me to do this, but I'm glad I did. I was about to walk into an emotional minefield.

A one-way ticket to America arrived. Ginny said she would arrange the return ticket later. Months later I found out the ticket hadn't come from Ginny at all, but from Joy. On a very hot August afternoon I landed in Atlanta, Georgia. It was like no place I'd ever been in before. The slow southern drawl was light years away from any other American accent I'd heard before. It was blazingly hot when I stepped on to the tarmac. In the terminal four people were waving and shouting at me. There was Guy, who had been in Aspen for more than a year with his fiancée, a smallish, pretty blonde girl who turned out to be Nancy. Next to her was a slim, blonde woman with her hair tied back, softly spoken with a pretty face, who came forward and greeted me.

'Hi, I'm your sister Virginia! I'm so glad you're here!' At the end of this line, unmistakably, was my elder sister Joy. How I recognized her I will never know, but I did instantaneously. Dark hair and dark eyes, she was a grown up version of the little girl I'd known years ago in the war. They rushed forward and greeted me as if we'd been together all of our lives. Ginny exclaimed to Joy how much like my mother I was.

Ginny's husband, Alex, a large friendly man, was making a business call when I arrived, and he greeted me with a wave. We drove back to their house and had tea together. It was a very large home they had just built, and the interiors were not yet finished. After an hour or two Alex made his apologies and left for a meeting. By now I was really anxious to meet my mother, but Ginny said she'd arranged a treat, dinner at the best restaurant in Atlanta, then a good night's rest for me before leaving for my mother's hometown of Warner Robins in the morning.

Ginny gave me a large room with dark green shutters and a big double bed, decorated very simply and comfortably. It was about midnight local time, but much later for me, and Ginny came in to say good night. We chatted for a short while, until Joy came in the room. Ginny said it was late for me now, and took my older sister away to discuss plans for the next day.

I was woken by Ginny at eight the next morning. She leaned over me gently and said she'd arranged an appointment at the beauty shop, an American term for the hairdressers. She invited me to have any treatment I liked, she would pay. I could feel her disappointment when I said no thank you, but I just wanted to get to Warner Robins as soon as possible.

Ginny left with Joy for the hairdressers and told me to make myself comfortable and help myself to tea or toast. For the life of me, in this very large house, I couldn't find either a kettle or a teapot! I opened the fridge, but it was empty. That seemed unusual because I believed Alex was a gourmet. The house was as quiet as a mouse, with one large room after another all in an unfinished state. I had no idea where Guy or Nancy were sleeping, and I finally got myself a glass of water, some funny toast biscuits, and opened the shutters in my room to let in the morning sun. In front of the window stood a lovely little tree with purply flowers on it. I had the strangest feeling as if I were suspended in time.

The phone rang and I sprang up to find it in the empty house, without success. The ringing finally ceased, its source still a mystery, and I went back to my terrace and sat down quietly again, hoping Joy and Ginny would hurry back. No chance of that. Another hour went by and I decided to wander around the garden. I still hadn't seen a living soul other than Ginny and Joy that morning. The garden was enclosed, which gave me the feeling of being cut off from the rest of the world, so I went back inside and went on another tour of the house!

This time I found some glorious bathrooms-to-be. As I was debating whether it was safe enough to have a shower I heard the sound of soft footsteps nearby. It scared me a little and I stood behind the door. The figure moved into the corridor and I saw that it was Nancy. Thank God for humans at last! I told her that Ginny and Joy had gone off to the beauty shop.

'Oh, dear,' she groaned. 'That means another two hour's wait.' She said on each of the three days they'd been at Ginny's house, Ginny had arranged a treat for Joy and they'd disappeared for most of the day. Apparently Ginny had taken Joy on a shopping spree. She said she wanted to make sure Joy looked smart when she met her family. I thought this was odd, as Joy was quite well off in her own right. Why would she need a new wardrobe to meet a family she already knew?

Nancy miraculously found a way to produce some coffee, and Guy and I sat down and talked. We were going to finally meet our mother after not knowing she even existed! It was great to talk with Guy again. Of course, we'd been in touch since April, but before that there had been a five year gap. He'd had some awful times since, coming to America and having to wash dishes and take other menial jobs to keep going. But he seemed in good shape now. He said he was 'on his way up', living in Aspen and publishing a real estate magazine with a partner. This was the calmest and most together I'd ever seen my brother. I told him my life was less hectic than it used to be, and talked to him about how it felt being a mother myself.

Guy was now as anxious as I was to get going. He said he'd waited for my plane because he didn't want to go to Warner Robins without me. But he appeared less excited than I was about meeting his mother. He couldn't really remember her because he was so young when he'd last seen her.

'I've never had a mother, so I don't know how I feel,' he said. The phone rang again, but we still couldn't find where to answer it.

Ginny and Joy returned, professionally made up and with their hair washed and styled. Joy's was short and chic, and Ginny's hair was done over to one side, with a sparkly comb in it. She didn't like it, and immediately pulled it down and started to brush it out. I wondered why she'd gone to such trouble in the first place.

'Oh, I wanted you and Joy to feel good, and you didn't seem to want your appointments so I took the extra treatments.'

I wanted badly to leave for Warner Robins, and when somebody suggested lunch I showed my impatience. By now both Joy and Ginny had answered the mysterious phone, and each time it was from Warner Robins asking what was holding us up. We got into Ginny's large car with Guy, Nancy and myself in the back, Joy and Ginny in the front. At last we were off!

It would take two hours, three at the most, they told me, to drive to Warner Robins, a medium-sized town south of Atlanta. I settled down, full of anticipation. Guy lit up a cigarette. Ginny looked into the rear-view mirror.

'I hope that's not dope I smell!' she exclaimed. 'I won't allow it in my car!'

We continued on our way, my brother and I plying Joy and Ginny with questions about the family. It was a happy, jolly atmosphere, full of excitement and each question we asked made my curiosity deepen. 'See for yourself,' Ginny would say. Guy and I were both apprehensive. What would we call her? We couldn't possibly call her 'mother', or anything like that, we said, after all this time. We agreed we would both call her Ivy.

Ginny pulled into a road house for lunch. By now I was really fed up with all the stopping and starting, but it was difficult to say how I felt because Ginny was either nervous herself or busy trying to take care of us. She seemed to have no conception of time. Joy must have had thoughts of her own, but she was fairly quiet and what they were I couldn't tell. Nancy was a ray of sunshine in the group, as she was the only one outside the emotional circle. With lunch finally over, we set off on the last leg of our trip, which by now was beginning to seem like *Around the World in Eighty Days*. Despite our feelings running high, we were calm and loving. It's the only time it's happened since I've known my family.

The lovely scenery passed by, but I hardly noticed it. We pulled off the highway and on to a wide boulevard and Joy announced our arrival in Warner Robins. I wondered on what gracious street, and in which of the big wide-set houses my mother would live. Ginny saw me looking and turned around.

'Are you surprised?' she asked. 'Your mother lives quite well, you know.' It hadn't occurred to me to think otherwise. Having left England for America, leaving everything behind, I thought it must have been worth it. We went along a road of smaller houses, but still large by English standards, and pulled into a driveway.

The car door was yanked open by a tall, slim, pretty girl who, to my surprise, didn't look very happy to see us. 'How can you do this to mother!' she shouted. 'She's been beside herself with worry. She thought you'd changed your minds and weren't coming after all. How *can* you be this late!' Ginny didn't say a word, just walked straight by her into the house.

I went into a room with two large sofas at right angles to each other along a wooden wall. There seemed to be a crowd of people in the room, and in the corner sat a smallish woman. A pale-haired young woman sat beside her, with her arm round her shoulders. I stood there for a moment, not knowing what to do. The smallish woman got up and came slowly to me.

'Hullo, Shirley, dear. Do you remember me?'

'Yes, Mummy, I do,' I replied, and to my intense embarrassment, went straight into the corner and burst into tears. I stood there for some minutes trying to compose myself, and then my

240

mother came over with my brother and held me and we were all crying together. We stood in a circle, embracing each other.

'I kept asking the girls which one I should hug first,' my mother said. 'I couldn't decide, so I'm hugging you both.' I realized our semicircle now included Jackie, the girl who'd been holding my mother on the sofa, who I hadn't met properly yet, and Becky, the girl who met us at the car, two of my mother's daughters by her second husband. Joy was there too and we all had our arms round each other. Through a space under my brother's arm I saw a big tall man on the sofa sobbing his heart out. I wasn't sure who he was, but I didn't want him to feel left out, so I asked him would he like to join us.

'Oh, no m'am, no,' he said. 'I'm just so happy to see you all like this. I've just loved Mizz Collins for years.'

Finally we broke away and the introductions began. Becky was my younger sister, Jackie was in the middle and Ginny was the oldest. Jackie took Guy and myself round the whole room. I met her husband Maston, a tall, handsome sports teacher, and his older brother, who was still crying on the sofa. Becky's very handsome husband, Sonny, aged about thirty with long blond hair and a red beard, was dressed in a hippy style. He broke the tension when he suddenly picked me up and twirled me around, saying 'Give me a hug, girl, give me a hug! Look what a gorgeous sister I've gained!' Suddenly there were several children in the room. There was little Maston and Joshua, Jackie's children, aged about five or six, and then Rachel and Clint, Becky's children who were four and six respectively. Ginny was now sitting on the edge of the low coffee table talking intensely to Ivy.

'I promised you your babies, Momma. Here they are! Now you've got your perfect children back again. Now you have everything you want!' My brother and I sat either side of our mother on the sofa, both of us holding her hand.

The strangest thing I noticed was that my hands, which never perspired, were wringing wet. We talked and laughed and cried together, all at once. My mother said she was going to explain the circumstances about why she'd done what she had, and if we could forgive her well and good, and if we didn't, well, she would just have to accept that, and we would never see each other again. She seemed so sad and vulnerable. I found it unbearable and I think my brother did too. The rest of the room faded into a haze.

Two hours had gone by and it seemed like only a few minutes.

Suddenly we looked around and we couldn't find Ginny any-where. More than anyone else it had seemed she had wanted us all to be together: she had master-minded the whole reunion with me, on the phone long distance doing nothing but making plans for the last two weeks. Joy whispered to me that she may have gone to the Holiday Inn, or perhaps had driven back to Atlanta. 'Hopefully we'll see her in the morning,' I said.

If I hadn't been so carried away with my own feelings, I would have been amazed at Guy's reaction. From a man who'd said he hadn't thought about having a mother, and wouldn't know how to behave if he had one, he was now like a three-year-old, crying most of the time, and holding her close whenever he could. In the week we were all together my brother never left her side once. I think Nancy may have felt rather left out with all the emotional drama. When my daughter joined us she thought it was funny that her six-foot-four uncle was always in a cuddle with his tiny mother.

It was getting late by now and Jackie said we'd better get back to her house, as that's where we were staying, not at my mother's. I was surprised at this.

'Oh, you'll like it better at Jackie's,' my mother said. 'The bathrooms are much more suitable there. We've really only got a bath and a half here.' The house looked very cosy and more than comfortable to me, but they'd already made the arrangements.

My mother told us her husband Bill was in the hospital having an appendectomy. 'Maybe that's where Ginny's gone, to see him,' she said. 'He sends you his love, and says he can't wait to see y'all.' During all this time one sister or another would pick up my hands or touch my hair gently.

'Look, Mamma, look! She's just like you. Her hands are even the same shape!' I had always wanted to belong, so I loved hearing this. Guy and Sunny had resembled each other, and I had often been told that I was the odd one out.

We left my mother's house and went to Jackie's and Maston's spacious home, surrounded by high trees in its own grounds. It certainly seemed more luxurious than a sports instructor would have been able to afford in England. Inside, it was equally pretty and nicely decorated. There were two guest bedrooms made up, one with its own bathroom and one without. Before I had a chance to take the one that I thought was for me, with the feminine cover on the bed, and the bathroom, Nancy had moved Guy and herself into the room. Oh, well, I thought, it doesn't matter. It would give them a chance for some much needed privacy. All the attention heaped on Guy had to be a shock for Nancy. She had come from a large family herself, and when she'd met my brother he'd been entirely on his own. Suddenly he had this new huge family, all hugging and kissing him and wanting to be near him.

'You see, Nancy,' Jackie said, 'we've never had a brother before. You're used to it. We're not. And we can't get enough of him.'

The next afternoon we all sat in Jackie's sitting room. I was very glad she had air-conditioning. It would have been too hot for me otherwise. My mother said if she told her story now it would be all she could manage, and that she and Bill had already cried so much over Sunny. She wanted to hear my story about Sunny's illness, but felt she'd be stronger when Bill was there. Could I possibly wait until he came out of hospital? I was glad she suggested this. I just wanted to hear what she had to say. Through the window I could see the trees standing motionless in the heavy heat. My mother asked everyone to keep quiet, and the children were sent outside to play. Before she began I realized with a start that my American sisters knew the story off by heart, the story that I'd been trying to unravel for at least thirty years.

'Well, darlings,' she began, 'you know there was a war on, and there were bombs falling every night. London was a very dangerous place. Your dad wasn't around and I was on my own with the two of you. Sunny and Joy were old enough to be evacuated, but you were too small, so I thought I'd get you looked after in the day nursery. That way I could go to work during the day to make money for the three of us. When I got there I found the nursery had been transferred for safety to Godalming in Surrey. One of the nurses there gave me the matron's address. "Write to her, Ivy," she said, "because I'm sure she will find a place for your two youngest children."

'The matron wrote back to me, "Come and visit us and bring your children with you. You were very good when you worked in the nursery and we'll do what we can to help you." I had to find somewhere for both of you because I had to work and I had no-one to take care of you. Your older sisters had already been evacuated.'

My mother then talked about the train ride to Godalming and suddenly it was as if I was there. I could remember being three and in my seat with her and my brother, who was really more of a toddler.

'We arrived at Sax Mundham, a big stately home that had been given as a nursery for the children of the East End to keep them safe.' I could picture the matron greeting her and I thought I remembered her saying:

'Yes, Mrs Broomfield, I will take your children, but you will have to leave them here. We no longer have any day facilities.'

My mother said she had asked straight away if she could work in the nursery herself, so that she could be with both of us. She got the job, but apparently left after several weeks because matron got cross with her for picking up Ernie whenever he cried. As she said this strange memories flashed through my mind – of being very small, standing and looking up at my mother and watching her go. 'Please don't cry, Shirley Pops,' she had said, turning round. 'You'll only make it worse for me. *You* must look after your brother now.'

My mother paused to take a sip of water and wipe her eyes. I held my breath, afraid to hear what came next. She said she'd got on the train after leaving us and hadn't been able to stop crying. All of her four children were now safe, but gone. She felt empty and lost. She came back to London and found work, and tried to pick up the pieces of her life. Legally, she was still married to my dad, but he was off somewhere with Gypsy. The war was still raging away when the Allied servicemen arrived in England in force. It was then she said that she'd met the second love of her life, a Canadian soldier called Johnny. They fell in love and when he was posted abroad he said he was going to try and forget about her – after all, he had a wife and daughter of his own. A few weeks after Johnny left she'd met an American named Bill, who'd been marvellous to her and had consoled her. She had given up any hope of Johnny coming back when she got a letter from him, saying he was badly wounded, and in hospital, and that's why he hadn't written. He said he still felt the same, he couldn't get her out of his mind, and would get divorced and take care of her children as well. My mother and Bill had already grown close, and he wouldn't allow her to write anything but a cold letter back, informing Johnny that she was pregnant by Bill. This was actually true. My mother was always sad that she couldn't tell Johnny the truth about how much she felt for him.

Both Johnny and Bill knew about her children. In fact, I think Johnny was the man who had come to Edgeworth when I was small. Bill said he wanted us, too, but didn't have the necessary influence or money to fight the authorities to get us. It seemed extraordinary to find out that we had been wanted after all, but through error and fear, nothing was done about it. Meanwhile, my younger sisters in America had always been afraid their mother would go back to England, to her 'perfect children', as Ivy called us. But my mother was terrified to come back. With her overlapping marriages, she might never be allowed to return to America. There was the risk of losing her second family as she had her first. And so Guy, Sunny and myself never knew if our mother was alive or dead, let alone that we had another family on the other side of the Atlantic.

By the time my mother had finished her story I was very sad, as was everyone else. It seemed there had been such dreams lost. Not only had my mother wanted us, but so had the two people who had loved her. What a pity we couldn't have known that just once! To know I was wanted would have meant everything in the world to me when I was growing up.

So that was how we first came to be parted, I thought. From there on we would never be a family again. I would go first to the children's home in Edgeworth, hundreds of miles away, to be followed later by my brother when he was old enough.

The sun began to set outside and my new-found family sat quietly in the room. Then my sisters began to sing songs I'd learned as a tiny girl in the East End of London. I couldn't believe it. Here we were in the Deep South, singing Cockney rhyming songs and wartime ballads. One of them was a song my dad had sung for me in the pub when I'd first arrived back in London, and when he first told me how much I reminded him of my mother.

*

245

Are you lonesome tonight?
Will you miss me tonight?
Are you sorry we drifted apart?
On a clear summer's day
Does your memory stray?
Oh, my dear, will you miss me tonight?

EPILOGUE

At long last I've unravelled the mystery of my birth and now perhaps I can see like everyone else. In the decade since, my journey has continued. I found that finding my family has had an extraordinary effect on me but strangely not the one I expected.

My career is very healthy. In the mid 1980s I made *My Beautiful Laundrette* and I've made several good films since. The happiest one and the best (except for *My Beautiful Laundrette*) is yet to be released. It's called *Hear My Song* and it's catapulted me into playing the adult woman of the young girls I used to play – warm, fiery and hopefully beautiful?

Ah! If only life was as uncomplicated as film – a beginning, a middle and an end. According to my mother, I now have a different birthday, a different name and possibly a different father but that is for the sequel of this book.

Many times I've dragged my feet both mentally and physically on finishing this story and without the support of my publishers, Bantam Press, I wouldn't have had the courage to conclude this particular story. I owe them a great deal for letting me hold a mirror up to myself. As I come to the conclusion, I now know why. I was afraid it would be the end. But life's not like that. It doesn't stand still. So in my follow-up story I will again share with you the joys, the pain and the complete surprises of what it's been like for me to finally unravel my personal mystery.

INDEX